The Sport of Life and Death:
The Mesoamerican Ballgame

The Sport of Life and Death:

The Mesoamerican Ballgame

Edited by
E. MICHAEL WHITTINGTON

With essays by
DOUGLAS E. BRADLEY
JANE STEVENSON DAY
TED J. J. LEYENAAR
MARY MILLER
EDUARDO MATOS
MOCTEZUMA
LAURA FILLOY NADAL
JOHN F. SCOTT
ERIC TALADOIRE
MICHAEL TARKANIAN and
DOROTHY HOSLER
MARÍA TERESA URIARTE
E. MICHAEL WHITTINGTON

With 323 illustrations,
171 in color

Thames & Hudson

To Francis and Lilly Robicsek

This book was published in conjunction with the exhibition
The Sport of Life and Death: The Mesoamerican Ballgame,
organized by the Mint Museum of Art

Mint Museum of Art
Charlotte, North Carolina
September 22, 2001–January 6, 2002

New Orleans Museum of Art
New Orleans, Louisiana
February 16, 2002–April 28, 2002

Joslyn Art Museum
Omaha, Nebraska
June 8, 2002–September 1, 2002

The Newark Museum
Newark, New Jersey
October 1–December 29, 2002

This book and the exhibition it accompanied were sponsored by:

NATIONAL ENDOWMENT FOR THE
HUMANITIES
The National Endowment for the Humanities: expanding our
understanding of the world

NATIONAL
ENDOWMENT
FOR THE ARTS
The National Endowment for the Arts

The Rockefeller Foundation

The Mint Museum of Art is supported by the Annual Fund Drive of the Arts
& Science Council–Charlotte/Mecklenburg, Inc.; the North Carolina Arts
Council, a state agency; the City of Charlotte; and its members.

Edited by Myra Engelhardt.
Contributions by Eduardo Matos Moctezuma and Laura Filloy Nadal were
translated from the Spanish by María Velasco and Debra Nagao, respectively.

© 2001 The Mint Museum of Art, 2730 Randolph Road, Charlotte,
North Carolina 28207

First published in the United States of America in hardcover in 2001 by
Thames & Hudson Inc., 500 Fifth Avenue, New York, New York 10110

Library of Congress Catalog Card Number 2001087252
ISBN 0-500-05108-9

Half-title: Hacha of a player wearing a dolphin helmet, cat. 73.
Frontispiece: Drawing by Christoph Weiditz (1528) showing central Mexican
ballplayers performing at the court of Charles V.
Page 5: *(left)* Model of a ballcourt, cat. 30; *(right)* human-head *hacha*, cat. 75.
For illustrations shown on pages 6–7, 10–11, and 14–15, see p. 283.

Printed and bound in Singapore by CS Graphics

LIST OF LENDERS

American Museum of Natural History, New York

Art Institute of Chicago, Illinois

Art Museum, Princeton University, New Jersey

Bowers Museum of Cultural Art, Santa Ana, California

Chrysler Museum of Art, Norfolk, Virginia

Cleveland Museum of Art, Ohio

Denver Art Museum, Colorado

Denver Museum of Nature and Science, Colorado

Field Museum of Natural History, Chicago, Illinois

Hudson Museum, University of Maine, Orono, Maine

Jay I. Kislak Foundation, Inc., Miami Lakes, Florida

Los Angeles County Museum of Art, California

Metropolitan Museum of Art, New York

Mint Museum of Art, Charlotte, North Carolina

M.M. DeYoung Memorial Museum, Fine Arts Museums
of San Francisco, California

Museo de Antropología, Universidad Veracruzana, Xalapa,
Mexico

Museo del Templo Mayor, Mexico City, Mexico

Museo Nacional de Antropología, Mexico City, Mexico

National Museum of the American Indian, Smithsonian
Institution, Washington, D.C.

New Orleans Museum of Art, Louisiana

North Carolina Museum of Art, Raleigh, North Carolina

Peabody Museum of Archaeology and Ethnology, Harvard
University, Cambridge, Massachusetts

Philadelphia Museum of Art, Pennsylvania

Private Collection

St. Louis Art Museum, Missouri

San Antonio Museum of Art, Texas

Snite Museum of Art, University of Notre Dame, Indiana

Worcester Art Museum, Massachusetts

Yale University Art Gallery, New Haven, Connecticut

NOTE TO THE READER
The following abbreviations are used in this catalogue:
INAH Instituto Nacional de Antropología y Historia, Mexico
MAUV Museo de Antropología, Universidad Veracruzana, Xalapa, Mexico
MNA Museo Nacional de Antropología, Mexico City, Mexico

CONTENTS

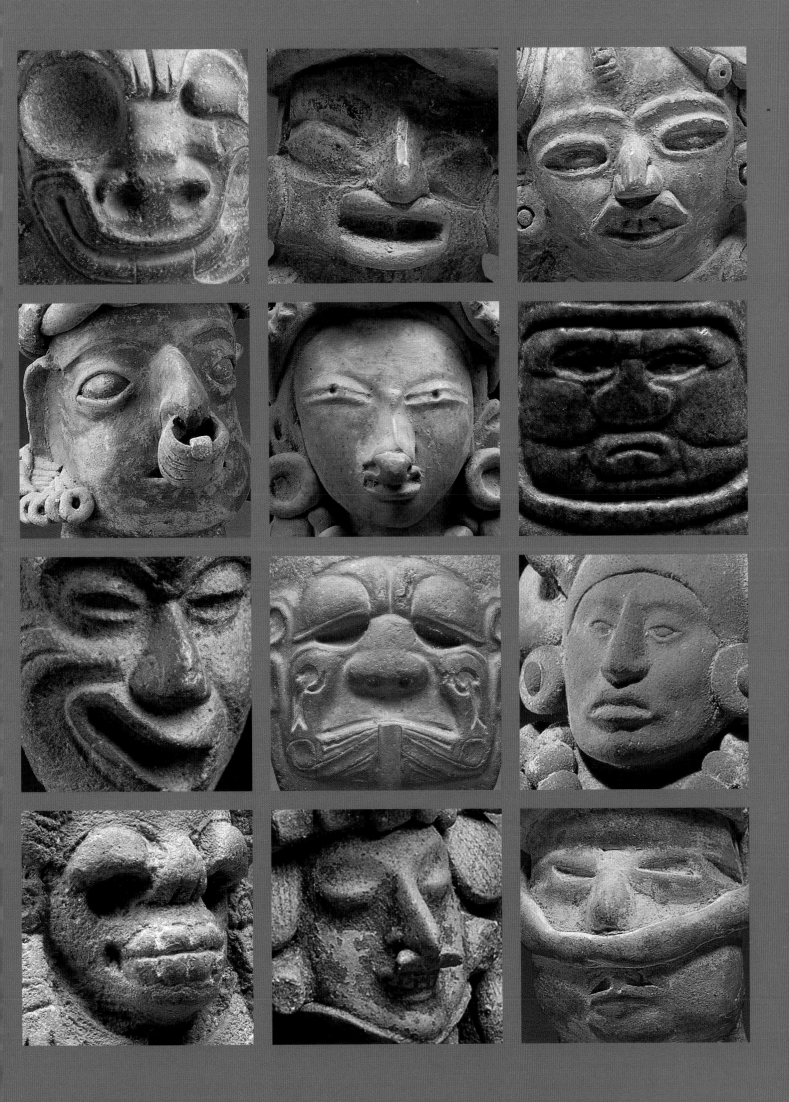

FOREWORD

The presentation of *The Sport of Life and Death: The Mesoamerican Ballgame* is a series of "firsts" for the Mint Museum of Art. Although the museum is acknowledged to possess one of the nation's great collections of Ancient American art, this is the first national traveling exhibition organized by the museum in this exciting field. The ballgames of ancient Mexico, Guatemala, Belize, and Honduras have long fascinated scholars and the general public alike. Visitors to the region today marvel at the ruins of magnificent stone ballcourts where teams of athletes once competed before kings. Yet, surprisingly, this is the first traveling exhibition on this fundamental topic to be organized in the United States. The trio of prestigious national foundations that have supported this exhibition—the National Endowment for the Humanities, the National Endowment for the Arts, and the Rockefeller Foundation—speaks volumes about the efforts of the Mint staff and their many outstanding collaborators.

For this exhibition, objects have been assembled from public and private collections in the United States, as well as from public collections in Mexico. The range and beauty of the art works in the exhibition is breathtaking. From the tiny jade carvings by the Olmec depicting their ballplayer kings, to the ring-shaped stone goals that once stood in Aztec ballcourts, *The Sport of Life and Death* illuminates some of the greatest triumphs and tragedies in early Mesoamerican history. The Mint is fortunate to have established relationships with the Museo Nacional de Antropología, the Museo del Templo Mayor, and the Museo de Antropología, Universidad de Veracruzana—three of Mexico's most distinguished cultural institutions. Many of these exceptional works of art have not previously been exhibited outside Mexico, and we are honored by the spirit of generosity with which they were loaned.

I commend curator E. Michael Whittington for undertaking the monumental responsibility of organizing this project. He began this effort shortly after joining the museum staff six years ago. His first task was to assemble an internationally recognized panel of advisors. This catalogue, with interdisciplinary essays contributed by scholars from the United States, Europe, and Mexico, is the fruit of those labors. At the Mint Museum of Art we use our Ancient American collections to further the understanding of our shared humanity. This fascinating exhibition, with its examination of the lives and experiences of cultures long past and how they parallel phenomena in our modern societies, is a superb example of this philosophy in practice. I'll never sing 'Take Me Out to the Ballgame' in quite the same way again.

MARY LOU BABB
TRUSTEE CHAIR
MINT MUSEUM OF ART

In the sweet-sounding Nahuatl language of ancient Central Mexico, the ballgame was called *tlaxtli* or *tlachtli*. But it was more than a sport as we conceive it today. For over two millennia, the Mesoamerican game had profound symbolism and ritual. It was a cosmic ceremony; a true rite of life and death. Playing the ballgame symbolized duality— an encounter between opposites—night and day, masculine and feminine, and the sun against the stars and moon. The sacred book of the Quiché Maya, the *Popol Vuh*, describes an encounter between demigods who descended into the Underworld to play ball with the Lords of Death. To this ancient ritual sport, which sometimes ended with the decapitation of the players, scholars have attributed diverse symbolic, religious, and even political, connotations.

Splendidly illustrated in the exhibition, *The Sport of Life and Death: The Mesoamerican Ballgame*, there are different ways to see, senses to experience, and forms to understand the cosmology that is integral to the pre-Columbian game. The Consejo Nacional para la Cultura y las Artes (National Council for Culture and Art), through the Instituto Nacional de Antropología e Historia (National Institute of Anthropology and History), has contributed with works of art that evoke the splendor and mystery of the ancient rubber ballgame common to the vast region of Mesoamerica. Thanks to the fortunate invitation of the Mint Museum of Art, the occasion of this exhibition brings together the efforts of institutions, universities, and scholars in the United Sates, Mexico, and Europe.

In the modern countries where the rubber ballgame was once played—Mexico, Guatemala, Honduras, and even the United States—more than 1,500 ballcourts have been discovered. These courts were sacred spaces in the ceremonial centers of pre-Columbian cities. There was even a ballcourt in the heart of the great Aztec capital Tenochtitlan, present-day Mexico City. Presiding over the ceremonial aspects of the game was the Aztec deity Xochipilli, god of the ballgame. The ballgame continues to be played in the western state of Sinaloa; called *ulama*, it is played with the hips, and the players still dress in the old manner using deerskin loincloths and cotton belts.

I am grateful to those who have made it possible to bring together once more the amazing elements of the ancient Mesoamerican ballgame—a sport of great civilizations, a duel between the heavenly bodies, and a struggle between humanity and the gods. The coincidence of the ritual of life and death at the beginning of this new century is propitious for the re-encounter between our sister nations and for reflecting on the origin and vision of our ancestors and the cosmos. I applaud this exhibition celebrating one of the most original civilizations of humankind.

SARI BERMÚDEZ
PRESIDENTA
CONSEJO NACIONAL PARA LA CULTURA Y LAS ARTES

◀CONACULTA · INAH ❀

ACKNOWLEDGMENTS

Exhibitions are created for a variety of reasons not altogether apparent to the casual visitor. All too often, the contemporary exhibition is a combination of a happening and a shopping experience rolled into one. But, if one asks curators why we undertake the maddeningly complex tasks of organizing exhibitions, we will often respond that it began with a simple question. Thus the entire exhibit process can be seen as an attempt to address and answer basic queries. Such is the case with *The Sport of Life and Death: The Mesoamerican Ballgame*, which started as a thin file folder containing a couple of photocopied articles and images of yokes and *hachas* assembled while a student. At that time authorities agreed that the playing of games with a rubber ball was one of Mesoamerica's defining cultural markers. But was there one game or a variety; what did the games mean to those ancient societies, and what, if any, were the modern implications of this ancient activity? These were just a few of the fundamental questions I filed away in anticipation of one day investigating. That opportunity came when I joined the staff of the Mint Museum of Art and presented a ballgame exhibition proposal to Charles Mo, Vice-President of Collections and Exhibitions. I am grateful for his initial enthusiasm and unwavering support of this project.

One of the great benefits of this exhibition has been the establishment of new collegial and institutional relationships. I thank the committee of advisors who helped shaped the exhibition's concepts and refine its goals. They are Jane S. Day, Gillett G. Griffin, Ted J. J. Leyenaar, Mary Miller, Laura Filloy Nadal, John F. Scott, and Eric Taladoire. Joining this distinguished group were additional scholars whose essays have contributed immeasurably to the success of this catalogue. I am most grateful to Dorothy Hosler, Eduardo Matos Moctezuma, Michael Tarkanian, and María Teresa Uriarte for their insights and generosity. My sincere gratitude

to the National Endowment for the Humanities (NEH), the National Endowment for the Arts, and the Rockefeller Foundation for their generous support of this catalogue and its accompanying exhibition. A special note of thanks is due the NEH's Nancy E. Rogers, John Meredith, and, especially, Sara Ridley. That agency's rigorous application process, combined with its staff's generosity in assisting grant seekers, deserves to be a model for project development and funding.

The Sport of Life and Death would not have been possible without the generous assistance of institutions and colleagues in the United States and Mexico who made their collections available for research and loan: American Museum of Natural History, Charles Stanish; Art Institute of Chicago, Richard Townsend; Art Museum Princeton University, Maureen McCormick and Matthew Robb; Bowers Museum of Cultural History, Armand Labbé; Cleveland Museum of Art, Susan Bergh; Denver Art Museum, Margaret Young-Sanchéz; Denver Museum of Nature and Science, Ryntha Johnson; Hudson Museum, University of Maine, Orono, Stephen Whittington; Jay I. Kislak Foundation, Arthur Dunkelman; Los Angeles County Museum of Art, Virginia Fields; Metropolitan Museum of Art, Julie Jones; M. M. DeYoung Memorial Museum, Kathleen Berrin; Museo del Templo Mayor, Leonardo Lopez Luján and Laura del Olmo Frese; National Museum of the American Indian, Smithsonian Institution, Mary Jane Lenz; New Orleans Museum of Art, John Bullard and Paul Tarver; North Carolina Museum of Art, Mary Ellen Soles; Peabody Museum of Archaeology and Ethnology, Harvard University, Genevieve Fisher and William Fash; Philadelphia Museum of Art, Michael Taylor; St. Louis Art Museum, Diane Mallow; San Antonio Museum of Art, Marion Oettinger; Snite Museum of Art, Douglas Bradley; Worcester Art Museum, James Welu; and Yale University Art Museum, Susan Matheson. I am most grateful to Barbara and

Justin Kerr for their friendship, advice, and cheerful handling of last minute requests for photographs. Everyone should have a friend like Meagan O'Neil, a superb scholar and a barrel of laughs. In Mexico, I am indebted to Bertha Cea, Senior Cultural Officer with the United States Embassy. I wish to acknowledge Jaime Nualart, Coordinador de Asuntos Internacionales, CONACULTA; Carlos Córdova, Director de Exposiciónes Internacionales (INAH); and Paola Albert, Exposiciónes Internacionales (INAH) for their assistance in negotiating loans and permits. I am most thankful to Dr. Felipe Solís, Director of the Museo Nacional de Antropología; Dr. Eduardo Matos Moctezuma, Director of the Templo Mayor Museum; and Dr. Rubén Morante, Director of the Museo de Antropología, Universidad Veracruzana, Xalapa for their generosity in lending works from their collections. I am most appreciative to Michel Zabé for his excellent photographs and Karen Anderson Zabé for her hospitality while I was in Mexico City. I thank Marta Turok for her knowledge and advice and Tatiana Falcón for her assistance with the many details of photography and permits.

The staff, trustees, and volunteers of the Mint Museum of Art deserve the credit for bringing this exhibition to fruition. Special recognition is extended to the museum administration staff: Michael Smith, Deputy Director, for his sound fiscal and contractual oversight; Hannah Pickering and Lois Schneider for their expert care in the vitally important tracking of exhibit expenses, and Jan Campos for her encouragement and good humor. Technical support and much-needed banter were provided in equal measure by John West. My heartfelt thanks to Sally Baker, Development Officer; Harry Creemers, Vice-President for Development; Phil Busher, Public Relations Director; Carolyn Mints, Director of Community Relations; Cheryl Palmer, Vice-President for Education; Mark Leach, Director of the Mint Museum of Craft and Design; and Sara Wolf, Museum Librarian and Liaison to the Latin American Community, for their tireless efforts to make this exhibition a success. I extend my appreciation and admiration to the museum's collections and exhibitions division for their talent and hard work; especially to Martha Tonisson Mayberry, Registrar; John Thornbury, Collection and Exhibition Assistant; Kurt Warnke, Head of Design and Installation; Emily Blanchard and Craig Harmon, Graphic Designers; William Lipscomb and Leah Blackburn, Preparators; and Mitch Francis, Cabinet Maker. I am especially indebted to Katherine Stocker, Collection and Exhibition Assistant, for her superb handling of thousands of tedious details combined with her amazing insights on how always to perform a task more efficiently. I thank my fellow curators Mary Douglas, Barbara Perry, and Kari Delapp for patiently listening to my ideas even though they have heard them all before.

My thanks to Trustee Chair, Mary Lou Babb, for guiding our institution during the interim period between Presidents. My deep appreciation to Molly Lawrence for her superb drawings and Myra Engelhardt for her careful editing of this complex manuscript. I am most grateful to the staff of Thames and Hudson. I thank Luchi Aveylera and Werner Fields for their translation assistance. A heartfelt note of thanks to Alexsandra McClain—the world's best museum intern—and my admiration to the museum docents, the unsung heroes of our profession. Finally, no project in this field could be undertaken without the recognition of Dr. and Mrs. Francis Robicsek, the donors whose vision and generosity created the Mint's Ancient American collections.

E. MICHAEL WHITTINGTON
CURATOR OF PRE-COLUMBIAN AND AFRICAN ART
MINT MUSEUM OF ART

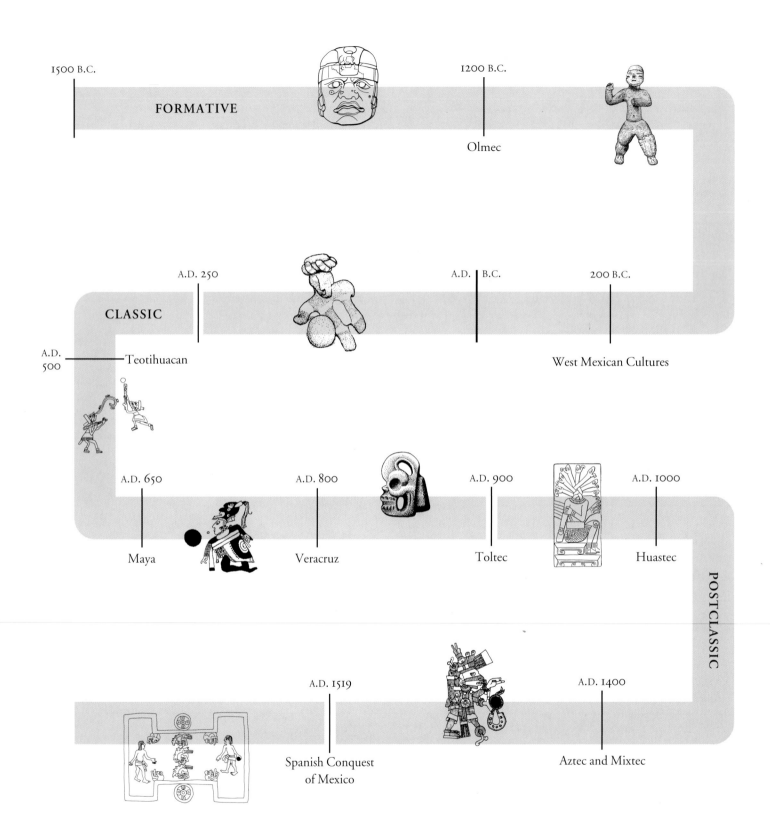

1500 B.C.

FORMATIVE

1200 B.C.

Olmec

A.D. 250

CLASSIC

A.D.
500

Teotihuacan

A.D. | B.C.

200 B.C.

West Mexican Cultures

A.D. 650

A.D. 800

A.D. 900

A.D. 1000

Maya

Veracruz

Toltec

Huastec

POSTCLASSIC

A.D. 1519

A.D. 1400

Spanish Conquest
of Mexico

Aztec and Mixtec

Timeline of Mesoamerican
cultures.

E. MICHAEL WHITTINGTON

INTRODUCTION

This is the account, here it is:
Now it still ripples, now it still murmurs,
ripples, it still sighs, still hums, and it is empty
under the sky.
Here follow the first words, the first eloquence:
There is not yet one person, one animal, bird,
fish, crab,
tree, rock, hollow, canyon, meadow, forest.
Only the sky alone is there; the face of the earth
is not clear.
Only the sea alone is pooled under all the sky;
there is nothing whatever gathered together.
It is at rest; not a single thing stirs.
It is held back, kept at rest under the sky.[1]

So opens the *Popol Vuh*, the Maya story of creation. Beginning in a time of profound quiet and stillness, the gods made the earth and all its creatures, they planted the first maize, and, finally, they created humanity. The actions of the gods were models for human behavior. Not coincidentally, the gods were terrific ballplayers. The *Popol Vuh* establishes the absolute preeminence of the ballgame in ancient Maya mythology and life, and provides the framework for much of our interpretation of this activity. The actors in this drama inhabit a region we now call Mesoamerica—the modern countries of Mexico, Guatemala, Belize, Honduras, and El Salvador. The story's protagonists, the Hero Twins Hunahpu and Xbalanque, are ballplayers without peers, talents they inherited from their deity fathers.

The modern *Popol Vuh* was transcribed in the mid-16th century from an ancient hieroglyphic text using the Roman alphabet. In the early 18th century, a Spanish friar copied this document and added a Spanish translation. This is the copy that survives in Chicago's Newberry Library, with its parallel versions in Quiché Maya and Spanish. The *Popol Vuh* is divided into three parts: the story of creation; the exploits of the Hero Twins and their forebears; and a dynastic history of the Quiché Maya nobility.

For the Maya gods, creation was a process of some trial and error. Humanity was unsuccessfully fashioned first from mud, then maize, and finally wood, before our own present forms were created. The Hero Twins, Hunahpu (Hunter) and Xbalanque (Jaguar Deer) are then introduced. As the reader quickly realizes, they are not mere mortals. Among their initial exploits was the defeat of the proud and boastful Seven Macaw. With his jeweled teeth and eyes, Seven Macaw challenged the radiance of the sun itself; one of Seven Macaw's sons Zipacna—crocodile—was a collaborator is this presumptuous act. The Hero Twins removed Seven Macaw's teeth and eyes with their blowguns, and put maize in their place. Thus were Seven Macaw and his crocodile scion forever defeated. These, and other plot elements of the *Popol Vuh*, are commonly illustrated in the many ballgame-related artworks of southern Mesoamerica.

Then, in flashback, the story switches to the Hero Twins' forefathers—Hun Hunahpu (One Hunter) and his brother, Vucub Hunahpu (Seven Hunter). The clamor created by these enthusiastic ballplayers as they bounced the ball around the court greatly disturbed the Lords of the Underworld. The Lords trick the brothers into coming to the Underworld of Xibalba to play the ballgame. The brothers lose the game and are sacrificed by the Xibalba Lords, their bodies buried in the ballcourt. As a final humiliation, the head of Hun Hunahpu is displayed in a calabash tree. A young goddess, Xquic, visits the tree to see the unusual display. The head of Hun Hunahpu spits in her hand, impregnating her with the Hero Twins,

Hunahpu and Xbalanque. Forced to leave Xibalba when her pregnancy is discovered she ascends to the surface of the earth where she gives birth to the Hero Twins.

When the Hero Twins come of age, they discover their ballplaying gifts, becoming even better players than their father and uncle. The Underworld Lords now summon the Hero Twins to Xibalba for a ballgame and a series of tests. Not only do the Twins win the game, but they outwit the Xibalba Lords at every trap set for them. Ultimately, the Hero Twins retrieve the bodies of their father and uncle from the ballcourt and place them in the sky to become the sun and the moon. So, for the ancient Maya and other Mesoamerican cultures, this story of creation and the activities of the gods and humanity become inseparable from the ballgame.

Making this mythology possible was the marvelous natural material we call rubber. An indigenous Mesoamerican species, rubber was unknown in the Old World: when the Spanish first caught sight of bouncing balls, they thought them surely possessed. The great chronicler Fray Bernardino de Sahagún commented that the balls were "bouncing, noisy, and noise-making."[2] The games and their players made such an impression on the Spanish that among the New World riches Cortés took back with him to Europe was a team of ballplayers. These players thrilled the court of Charles V with their athletic prowess;

a spectacle recorded by court artist Christoph Weiditz (frontispiece).

Rubber ballgames were played throughout Mesoamerica, from at least around 1200 B.C., as some of the essays here discuss, until the time of the Spanish Conquest in the 16th century (figs. 1 and 2). They reached great heights of spectacle and elaboration in Mexico, Guatemala, Belize, and Honduras, but they were also played on a much simpler scale as far north as Arizona, by the Hohokam peoples.[3] Rubber ballgames also extended eastward into the islands of the Caribbean, including Hispaniola (Haiti and the Dominican Republic) and Puerto Rico. There, the Taino played ballgames resembling those of Mesoamerica, in specially constructed courts and with players outfitted in a variety of elaborate costumes.[4]

Here, we seek to provide an overview of the Mesoamerican games and the environmental and cultural framework that created them. The essay by Laura Filloy Nadal explores the natural history of rubber and its rich cultural legacy. The work of Michael Tarkanian and Dorothy Hosler demonstrates that ancient techniques of processing this material have continued uninterrupted to the present day. Several authors have concentrated on interpreting the numerous works of art that commemorate the ancient games and their players. Douglas Bradley examines some of the very first ballplayers: ceramic figurines depicting the players as both kings and commoners.

1 Map showing regions in Mesoamerica, the Caribbean, and the Southwestern United States where rubber ballgames were played.

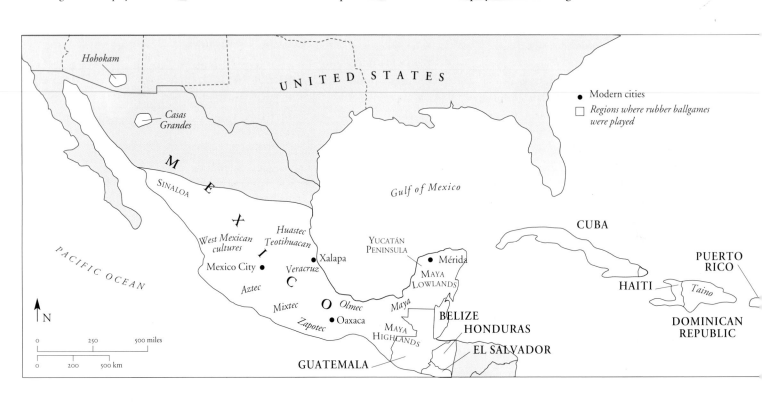

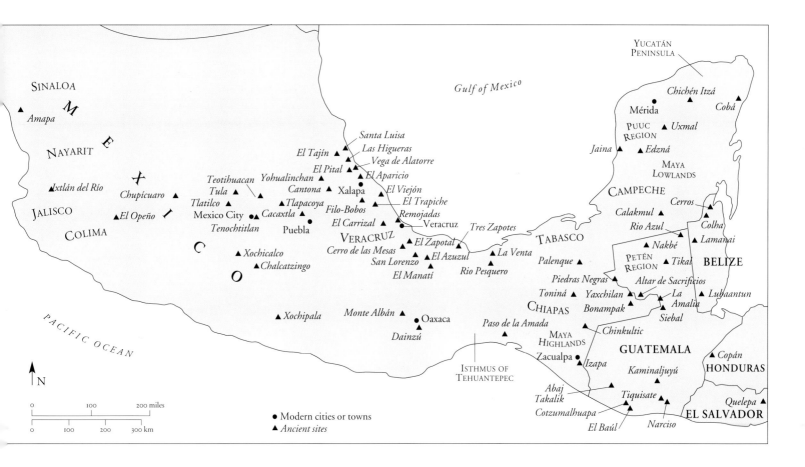

The artistic and architectural zenith of the
Mesoamerican ballgame was reached on Mexico's
Veracruz coast during the Late Classic Period.
John Scott's survey of the stone equipment used
in the games provides a context for this artistry.

That the ancient Mesoamerican ballgame was
richly layered with symbolism is readily apparent.
Several authors have focused on interpreting
what the ballgame actually meant to ancient
people by analyzing these symbols. María Teresa
Uriarte looks at a variety of diverse symbols in
the codices (painted manuscripts) and ballcourt
sculptural reliefs. For Mary Miller, each time the
ancient Maya played the ballgame, they enacted
the exploits of their greatest ballplayers, the Hero
Twins themselves. Jane Day carries this concept
even farther, suggesting that the ballcourts were
great theaters where mythic pageants were
regularly staged.

Among the many tangible reminders of the
ancient games are the actual surviving courts
where the athletes competed. Eric Taladoire's
architectural survey of where, when, and why
these courts were constructed has profound
implications for Mesoamerican cultural history
in general. The Great Ballcourt of Tenochtitlan—
the Aztec capital city—is the subject of Eduardo
Matos Moctezuma's essay. Now almost
completely covered by Mexico City's Metropolitan
Cathedral, recent excavations have uncovered
ritual offerings buried in the ballcourt itself.

Finally, two essays point to the survival
and illustrate the legacy of this ancient sport.
Ted Leyenaar documents the rubber ballgames
played in the Western Mexican state of Sinaloa.
Called *ulama,* these contemporary games are
the closest parallels to many of the games
depicted in ancient works of art. The concluding
essay establishes parallels between the exotic
world of ancient Mesoamerica and our own.
This author's hope is to spark recognition that
the modern phenomena we cherish as uniquely
our own are ancient and universal.

Note on Dates and Terminology

Scholars have organized Mesoamerican cultural
history into a chronology beginning with the
Formative Period (*c.* 1500 B.C.–A.D. 100), Classic
(*c.* A.D. 250–900), and Postclassic Periods
(A.D. 1000–1519). It should be noted that these
divisions define broad social and economic
trends and thus their beginning and end dates
should not be taken strictly. Scholars disagree
over chronology; this disagreement is reflected
in the diversity of opinions in this volume.

The term Aztec, referring to the Nahuatl-
speaking inhabitants of the Valley of Mexico, is
used in preference to the more specialized Mexica.

LAURA FILLOY NADAL

1 RUBBER AND RUBBER BALLS IN MESOAMERICA

Long before the arrival of the Spaniards, the peoples of the Americas exploited a great diversity of exuded matter from various plants that grew in the tropical regions of the continent. In most cases, these plant secretions were used in their natural, unaltered state. Among them were *tzictli* (*Achras sapota*), a gummy resin used mainly in the production of images of deities; *copal* (*Bursera* spp.), an aromatic resin that was burned during ceremonies; and the gum of the *nopal*, or prickly pear cactus (*Opuntia* spp.), a powerful binding agent employed in mural painting.

Other plant secretions had to be treated before they could be utilized. This was the case with rubber, or *hule*, a natural polymer known throughout a vast territory extending from the Southwestern United States to the Gran Chaco in Argentina.[1] Archaeological evidence indicates that rubber was already in use in Mesoamerica by the Early Formative Period (1600 B.C.).[2] Many centuries later, by the time of the first encounters with Europeans, rubber had become a widely exploited raw material. It was produced in huge quantities in tropical zones, from where it was exported to all corners of Mesoamerica and even beyond its frontiers.

Mesoamerican people used rubber for many, varied purposes. Its exceptional properties made it the perfect substance for attaching stone implements to wooden handles, as well as for making tips for drumsticks to play the *teponaztli* (horizontal wooden drum), protective gear to shield against arrows, and footwear for the nobility. And rubber's medicinal properties led to a variety of applications, including curing ear and lip wounds, tongue and throat diseases, and providing relief from headaches and different kinds of abdominal pains.

A large proportion of rubber production was consumed in magical and religious activities. For example, one common ritual practice was spattering bark paper with rubber melted over a fire. This act recreated the way raindrops were sent to the earth by the Tlaloques (tiny supernatural beings who aided the Rain God). Rubber was also used in the form of black paint to decorate the body and insignia of deity images, priests, and those who impersonated gods (fig. 4). In other cases, rubber was the basic material for making *ulteteo* (rubber gods), small anthropomorphic figurines that played a central role in festivals dedicated to water deities.[3]

3 A pottery tripod bowl containing offerings of copal and rubber, from the Sacred Cenote at Chichén Itzá, Yucatán, Mexico. Late Postclassic Period, Maya, A.D. 1350–1539; dia. 6.5 in (16.5 cm); Peabody Museum of Archaeology and Ethnology (cat. 2).

4 Nappatecuhtli, one of the Nahua rain gods. His insignia, costume, and staff are shown spattered with rubber—marked as asterisks. Redrawn from Sahagún, *Primeros Memoriales*, fol. 265r.

As depicted in the codices (painted manuscripts), rubber offering balls tend to appear in the hands of gods and officiating priests, inside temples, on altars, in braziers, on top of reservoirs and whirlpools, and even above the glyph for offering. A long feather is frequently shown inserted into the core of an offering ball (fig. 5).[4]

Balls manufactured for the ritual ballgame were indispensable for this ritual activity. The game had strong religious connotations and was practiced by various Mesoamerican societies.[5] Game balls, like balls for offerings, were solid, extremely compact, and consequently very heavy. They had very regular surfaces and were distinguished by their dynamic bounce (fig. 6).

A Material with Amazing Qualities

Sixteenth-century chroniclers and missionaries were clearly extremely curious about rubber, a material of exceptional qualities which was unknown in the Old World up to that point. What particularly attracted their attention was the elasticity and lively movement of the balls used in the American game. At that time balls used by Europeans were made of wood, leather, or cloth and thus had considerably less bounce.

It seems that it was Christopher Columbus who was the first to take notice of the unique qualities of these strange artifacts. During his second trip to the American continent (1493–96), the Genoan navigator witnessed a ballgame in Hispaniola (modern Haiti and the Dominican Republic) and was so impressed by the experience that when he returned to Seville he took back with him a rubber ball.[6] Years later, Fray Bartolomé de las Casas was also a spectator at a game, as he described in his celebrated

5 A scene from the *Codex Borgia* depicting a deity holding a rubber offering ball. Another ball is being burnt on a brazier inside a temple. (Redrawn from plate 14.)

6 An illustration from Durán's *Historia de las Indias de Nueva España y Islas de Tierra Firme* shows players competing on an I-shaped ballcourt. The figure on the right holds a rubber ball.

If we examine pre-Columbian iconographic representations and historical documents from the 16th century, however, it is clear that the main use of rubber was to manufacture balls, both as offerings and for the ritual ballgame. The former, called *ultelolotli* in the Nahuatl language, were smaller than those used in the game and were slightly irregular in shape. Priests and worshippers offered them to supernatural beings as venerated gifts. In general, such balls were burned in braziers and bonfires in front of images of deities, although they were also buried inside pyramids and shrines, or were cast into lakes, cenotes (natural sink-holes), and springs.

Memoriales. There, he details the characteristics of the ball, putting special emphasis on its magnificent bounce when it hit the floor.[7] A similar passage is found in the work of Fray Diego Durán. The Dominican friar writes that

> they call the material of this ball *hule* (rubber) … jumping and bouncing are its qualities, upward and downward, to and from. It can exhaust the pursuer running after it before he can catch up with it.[8]

The fascination with the game and its agile balls went beyond mere eye-witness accounts. In 1528, Hernán Cortés himself took a group of indigenous players to Europe for the express purpose of conducting a public demonstration in the court of Charles V. Fortunately, Christoph Weiditz, one of the amazed spectators, has left us a description of this memorable moment, accompanied by a lively drawing showing two players in the heat of the game.

In time, simple curiosity about these rubber balls became a scientific interest in the properties of the plant from which they were made. The first detailed description of the *ulquahuitl* (rubber tree) was written between 1571 and 1576 by Francisco Hernández, the celebrated proto-physician of Philip II. In his monumental *Historia Natural de la Nueva España*, Hernández not only specified the distinctive features of *ulquahuitl* and some of its curative properties, but he also included a fairly accurate drawing of the plant (fig. 7). Rubber was also described in the *Rerum Medicarum Novae Hispaniae Thesaurus*, a study of medicinal plants published in 1651 by the Italian physician Nardo Antonio Recchi.[9]

With the arrival of the Age of Enlightenment in the 18th century, studies of the various American rubber plants multiplied, and as a consequence Europeans began to exploit this material. Charles-Marie de La Condamine, the French explorer and scientist, was one of the key figures in this development. In 1735, he was sent to the New World by Louis XV of France and the Academy of Sciences of Paris. During his trip, La Condamine became aware of the extraordinary qualities of latex, and he enthusiastically recommended its exploitation. Later, in 1775, Europe put rubber to its first commercial use: as India rubber, or the eraser.[10]

Another significant step in the history of research on rubber took place in the capital of New Spain (Mexico City) on June 2, 1794. On that day, on the occasion of the inauguration

7 A rubber tree illustrated in the late 16th-century *Historia Natural de Nueva España* by Francisco Hernández. It was identified by its Nahuatl name *ulquahuitl* or *holquahuitl*.

of the Royal Botanical Garden of Mexico, Professor Vicente Cervantes scientifically christened the *ulquahuitl* as *Castilla elastica*. He gave it the generic name *Castilla* in recognition of the eminent explorer and botanist Juan del Castillo, and he chose the specific epithet *elastica* to indicate the principal physical property of the rubber obtained from the latex of the tree.[11]

By this time, rubber was being used in large quantities in Mexico City. According to Jesuit Francisco Javier Clavijero, it was employed, among other things, as a sealant to waterproof surfaces. As he noted in his *Historia Antigua de México*:

> the elastic resin that Mexicans call *olin* or *oli*, … comes from the *olquahuitl*, which is a tree of considerable height; … the *ule* (rubber) [which] flows from the wounded trunk is white … the ancient Mexicans made from it their balls, which bounce higher than those (blown by) the wind, although they are much heavier. Today in addition to this use, it is employed in place of wax to make capes, boots, and hats impermeable to water.[12]

Rubber was not used on a global, industrial scale, however, until after 1839, the year when the process of vulcanization was discovered by Charles Goodyear. This treatment consists of

Castilla elastica
Other species
Parthenium argentatum Gray
Parthenium incanum

UNITED STATES

M E X I C O

PACIFIC OCEAN

Gulf of Mexico

CUBA

HAITI

BELIZE
HONDURAS
EL SALVADOR
GUATEMALA

DOMINICAN
REPUBLIC

N

0   250   500 miles
0   200   500 km

8 Map showing the distribution of rubber-producing plants in the United States, Mexico, and the northern half of Central America.

adding a certain amount of sulfur to the latex, which both improves the elasticity of the rubber and increases its resistance to temperature changes. Importantly, vulcanization also means that the rubber maintains its shape indefinitely.[13]

Rubber Plants

There are more than 12,500 species of plants that produce a milky liquid known as latex. Of these, only 2,000 produce latex that contains rubber particles—a natural hydrocarbon of high molecular weight. The best-known species are those belonging to the American botanical families *Apocynaceae* (*Hancornia* spp.), *Artocarpaceae* (*Castilla elastica, C. ulei, C. markamiana, C. panamensis*), *Asclepiadaceae* (*Asclepias subulata, A. erosa*), *Compositae* (*Parthenium argentatum, P. incanum*), and *Euphorbiaceae* (*Hevea brasiliensis, H. guianensis, Manihot glaziovii, M. dichotoma, Sapium thompsonii, Micrandra minor*).[14]

Rubber species take many different forms, ranging from large trees with lush foliage, to vines, bushes, and grasses. The vast majority grow in intertropical regions (to 45° latitude). They proliferate mainly in hot, humid zones below an altitude of 2,300 ft (700 m) above sea level and where there are fertile soils that are not compacted. Other characteristics of rubber species include a tolerance of high temperatures (never falling below 64° F / 18° C) and high levels of rainfall (from 80 in to 160 in (2,000 to 4,000 mm) annually).[15]

In Mexico, rubber-producing trees are found growing in the wild along the coastal plains and

in the southern region of the country. One of the most abundant species is *Castilla elastica*, which grows in the modern states of Sinaloa, Nayarit, Colima, Jalisco, Michoacán, Guerrero, Chiapas, Tamaulipas, Veracruz, Tabasco, Campeche, Yucatán, and Quintana Roo. This same species also extends south of the Mexican border, reaching all of Central America and the northern part of South America (fig. 8).[16]

Castilla elastica has a wide variety of common names in Mexico, many of them in indigenous languages. For example, it is known as *palo de hule* ("rubber stick") on the Pacific Coast. To the Tarascans of Michoacán it is *taracuata*; to the Chontals of Tabasco, *lacu*; to the Chinantecs of Oaxaca, *tiniang, niasé*, or *mo-tiná*; and to the Zapotecs also of Oaxaca, *yagalatzi*. On the coastal band of the Gulf of Mexico, the Huastecs of Veracruz and Tamaulipas call it *pem*; the Nahuas of Puebla and Veracruz, *oliquahuitl*; the Totonacs of Veracruz, *tsacal*; and the Yucatecs of Yucatan and the Lacandons of Chiapas, *k'ik*.[17]

Castilla elastica is a species that grows easily, at times reaching heights of over 80 ft (25 m). It is a leafy tree, with perennial leaves measuring 8 to 18 in (20 to 45 cm) in length and 4 to 8 in (10 to 20 cm) in width. Its bark is grayish brown, with a smooth, or slightly cracked surface and abundant outgrowths of corky tissue. Its trunk is rather narrow and the first branches sprout at a great height from the ground, a characteristic that facilitates the extraction of latex.[18] *Castilla elastica* has specialized cells in the form of channels distributed throughout the trunk, branches, and roots, especially close to the surface. The metabolic product of these channels is the liquid known as latex. When the bark is scored, the channels are opened and the latex flows freely. In general, the latex drips without interruption for two to five hours, until it coagulates when the internal pressure of the cells equals that of the atmosphere.[19]

Rubber plants also grow beyond the Tropic of Cancer, though they are not tall, leafy trees, but rather small bushes, many of them belonging to the genus *Parthenium*. These plants are native to the arid zones of northern Mexico (Chihuahua, Nuevo León, Coahuila, Durango, Zacatecas, San Luis Potosí, Querétaro, and Hidalgo) and of the Southwest United States (Texas, New Mexico, and Arizona).[20] They are found at altitudes of between 1,970 and 6,560 ft (600 and 2,000 m) above sea level, in zones of low precipitation (8–16 in (200–400 mm) annually) and extreme temperatures, ranging from -5° to 86° F (-15° to 30° C), and tend to grow most successfully in areas of gentle slopes, at the foot of hills, and in areas of calcareous rock.[21] The two most common species are *P. argentatum* Gray and *P. incanum*. The former is commonly known as *guayule* (in the states of northern Mexico), *afinador* ("tuner" in Zacatecas), and *hierba de hule* ("rubber grass"; Durango), while the latter is known as *guayule hembra* ("female *guayule*"; San Luis Potosí), *hierba blanca* ("white grass"; Querétaro) and *Mariola* (Querétaro and Hidalgo).[22]

Parthenium argentatum Gray, or *guayule*, is a small bush, no larger than 24 in (60 cm) in height. Its roots extend rapidly, and its leaves are covered with silvery white hairs, from which it gets its name.[23] Unlike *Castilla elastica*, the *guayule* does not have laticiferous channels; instead, the latex is secreted by cells that are distributed throughout the tissue of the plant. To extract the latex, it is therefore necessary to pull up the bush completely, wash and grind its roots, then separate the rubber particles from the plant tissue by filtration and flotation.[24]

Latex Extraction and Rubber Preparation

Latex is a viscous, whitish suspension. When exposed to air it becomes even thicker and changes color, taking on increasingly yellowish, grayish, or blackish tones. In general, the composition of the suspension is highly complex—it contains particles of rubber, water, resin, esteric oils, waxes, carbohydrates, mucilages, tannins, sugars, acids, and salts. The percentage of these components varies from one plant species to another, affecting the quality of the rubber.[25]

Chemically, rubber is a polymer composed of a large number of chains of carbon and hydrogen atoms, the general formula of which is $(C_5H_8)_n$ or *cis* polyisoprene. While in the plant, the rubber particles take the form of small globular shapes dispersed in the latex. Because these globules have a negative electrical charge, they are mutually repelled in Brownian movement (a natural continuous motion of particles in a solution), which insures the stability of the suspension.[26] When the latex is extracted from the plant and comes into direct contact with the air, with a substance with an acid pH, or with the enzymes of certain bacteria, the rubber particles rapidly group and the latex begins to coagulate. In the case of *Castilla elastica*, the latex coagulates as a consequence either of these natural agents or intentional procedures such as smoking, heating, or adding certain plant juices (see Tarkanian and Hosler).[27]

Whatever the causes of coagulation, at the end of the process the latex has separated into solid and liquid parts. Filaments are formed which move toward the surface, interconnecting in the process. In this way, when the watery part of the latex is removed, soft strips of rubber are obtained; these are resistant and can be stretched, immediately returning to their original dimensions (a property known as elastic deformation). While they are still fresh, slight pressure on the strips is sufficient to form compact lumps of rubber, a quality essential for making balls for offerings and for the ballgame.[28]

9 On rubber plantations workers score the bark of the trees diagonally to start the flow of the latex.

Juan de Torquemada, another method was for a person to collect the latex directly in his hands and then rub it over his body; when it dried, it could be pulled off the skin in strips.[30]

Once collected, the latex is boiled with the juice or roots of certain plants found in the same regions as the rubber species. Most important are *Operculina rhodocalix* (*machacuana* or *San Miguelito*), *Calonyction aculeatum* (*guamol*, *cuaja leche* or "milk curdler," *flor de luna* or "moon flower"), *Ipomoea alba*, *I. bona-nox*, or *I. violacea* (*machacuana*).[31] Boiling separates the rubber from the other components of the latex, and the addition of juice and roots accelerates the coagulation process, while at the same time increasing the plasticity and elasticity of the rubber. Recent studies suggest that sulfonic acids present in plants of the *Ipomoea* genus would produce a certain degree of vulcanization of the material.[32] At the end of this process, long, grayish-colored elastic threads are obtained, which then gradually turn black. The rubber is now ready for use.

Archaeological Remains of Pre-Columbian Rubber

The wealth of iconographic and written evidence on the widespread use of rubber in Mesoamerica contrasts with the limited number of archaeological artifacts that have survived. Only around a hundred pre-Columbian objects made of this raw material are recorded. The majority are preserved in public museums, including the Museo Nacional de Antropología and the Museo del Templo Mayor in Mexico City; the Southwest Museum in Los Angeles, California; the Princeton University Museum of Art in Princeton, New Jersey; the Peabody Museum of Harvard University in Cambridge, Massachusetts; the British Museum in London; and the Musée de Nîmes in the south of France.[33]

Because of the great vulnerability of rubber to all agents of deterioration it is no exaggeration to say that the discovery of such artifacts is one of the most unusual events in Mesoamerican archaeology. From the very moment they are produced, objects made from rubber undergo rapid structural transformations affecting their color, shape, size, and weight. In general, these processes are accelerated when artifacts are deposited in an archaeological context, leading to their total destruction. However, it should be noted that the type and speed of such changes vary according to the physical and chemical characteristics of each archaeological object,

10 A modern *Hevea brasiliensis* plantation in El Palmar, Veracruz, Mexico. The trees are fitted with receptacles to collect the latex.

Today, we have no archaeological or historical evidence for the precise pre-Hispanic techniques used for latex extraction, rubber preparation, and the manufacture of balls. However, we do know some of the details of traditional procedures practiced during the Colonial period, the 19th century, and even today, which surely have their roots in ancient Mexico. In general, historical and ethnographic sources agree that latex has to be obtained from mature trees. The most common technique today is to cut into the bark with shallow diagonal incisions to open up a channel (fig. 9). In this way, latex wells up to the surface and flows to the base of the trunk, where it is collected in a receptacle, or in a small hollow dug in the ground (fig. 10),[29] in which case the rubber inevitably becomes dirty, taking on a blackish tone, and has a penetrating odor. According to the 17th-century chronicler Fray

the particular nature of the matrix in which it is buried, and the agents of deterioration present.

Rubber, like other organic materials, is characterized by its chemical instability, due to the presence of double bonds in its molecular structure which tend to break very easily. Breakage of the bonds may be caused by a variety of agents of deterioration, including oxygen, ozone, light, heat, copper, manganese and other metals, strong acids and alkalis, oils, fats, organic solvents, fungi, and bacteria.[34] Rubber can only be preserved in environments in which these agents of deterioration are absent, or at least kept to a minimum.

It is interesting to note that *all* known Mesoamerican rubber artifacts come from contexts that have been flooded by relatively still freshwater. The unique preservation of these artifacts can be explained by several factors: clean bodies of water in constant renewal; temperatures consistently below 68º F (20º C); low levels of oxygen; the absence of light; and water and sediments with a neutral pH and a low concentration of metals.[35] These conditions are present at the Sacred Cenote at Chichén Itzá, a Maya site in the northern peninsula of Yucatán; the spring of El Manatí, an Olmec site in southern Veracruz; and in the flooded offerings discovered in Tenochtitlan, the Aztec capital that today lies buried beneath Mexico City.

Significantly, the majority of rubber objects recovered to date in the locations mentioned—three sites belonging to very different times, places, and cultures—are balls. However, they do not share the same physical characteristics of shape, nor do they seem to have fulfilled the same function in antiquity. In the case of the 10 objects found in 1988 and 1990 by the El Manatí Project, all are approximately ovoid in shape and range between around 3 and 6 in (8 and 15 cm) in diameter (fig. 11).[36] More recently, Ponciano Ortíz and María del Carmen Rodríguez, the excavators of El Manatí, discovered two more balls, which are spherical and larger, measuring 10 in (25 cm) in diameter.[37] Little can be said with certainty as to their function. If they were used in the ballgame, we would be looking at the earliest evidence of this practice. The balls have been dated to around 1600 B.C.; the oldest ballcourt known so far was built between 1400 and 1250 B.C.[38] However, the suggestion that these balls might have been tossed into the spring as an offering to water deities is credible.[39]

In comparison with the El Manatí balls, those recovered from the waters of the Sacred Cenote

11 A rubber ball recovered from the site of El Manatí in Veracruz, Mexico. The waterlogged condition of the site has preserved many fragile rubber and wooden artifacts. Formative Period, Olmec; 3.4 × 10.6 in (8.6 × 27 cm); Museo Nacional de Antropología, Mexico City (cat. 1).

at Chichén Itzá are much smaller (around 1.6 in (4 cm) in diameter) and their surfaces are considerably more irregular. Unfortunately, we do not know the exact number of Maya balls salvaged by Edward H. Thompson between 1911 and 1922, and by Román Piña Chán between 1967 and 1968.

Publications and existing technical reports indicate that some of them were found inside ceramic vessels (fig. 12) and that there were other rubber objects in the Cenote: anthropomorphic figurines, copal balls covered with melted rubber, projectile points with remains of rubber ties, and other amorphous fragments.[39] These artifacts had been tossed into the water as offerings and, based on associated ceramic materials, probably can be dated to the Classic and Postclassic periods.

12 Made in the form of a deer, this ceramic vessel was filled with a mixture of rubber and copal incense. It was recovered from the Sacred Cenote at the site of Chichén Itzá, Yucatán, Mexico. It had been tossed into the Cenote as an offering. Late Postclassic Period, Maya, A.D. 1350–1539; 4.3 × 6.5 in (11 × 16.5 cm); Peabody Museum of Archaeology and Ethnology, Harvard University (cat. 4).

13 An Aztec rubber ball recovered from Offering S in the House of Eagles in Tenochtitlan (Mexico City). Note the straight-sided wide groove with a rounded bottom, which was for the insertion of a feather.

14 A detail from the *Codex Mendoza*, an Aztec manuscript created shortly after the Spanish Conquest which lists the tribute from the province of Tochtepec. Twice a year, this province shipped 16,000 rubber balls to the Aztec capital Tenochtitlan.

Archaeologists have excavated rubber artifacts from the ancient city of Tenochtitlan on at least five separate occasions. The earliest discovery dates to 1936–37, when Eduardo Noguera explored the stone offering box found in what was formerly the Plaza of the Volador. Among the materials found was a rubber ball, but its size is

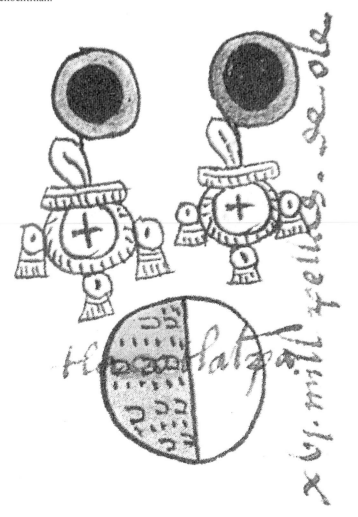

not reported.[41] In the late 1960s, Jordi Gussinyer excavated a structure (Building L) in what is now the Pino Suárez Metro station. In the interior of this circular-plan building he found a stone box containing, among other offerings, a small rubber vessel.[42] The discovery of a dozen rubber objects, among them two balls, at several points on Line 2 of the Metro dates to the same time.[43]

Other artifacts of considerable interest were found in two different contexts in the Ceremonial Precinct of the Aztec capital. The first is the main ballcourt, a building explored by Eduardo Matos Moctezuma and his colleagues during work on the foundations of the Metropolitan Cathedral (1991–97).[44] Associated with the end zones of the ballcourt were a pair of offerings consisting of miniature objects symbolically related to the ballgame.[45] Significant among these are two votive representations of balls for the game, measuring some 2.75 in (7 cm) in diameter, with porous, rigid, crackled surfaces (see fig. 103). In addition, one side of each ball is flattened from resting on the flat interior surface of their respective offering boxes for centuries.

The second context was the so-called House of Eagles. In this building, excavated between 1991 and 1997, Leonardo López Luján found 10 complete balls and 2 incomplete ones in Offerings S, U, and X.[46] Although their shape has changed with the passage of time, it is clear they were originally spherical, with diameters ranging between 2.4 and 3.3 in (6 and 8.5 cm). One characteristic feature of these balls is the presence of a wide groove with straight walls and a curved bottom (fig. 13). This groove must have served to hold the quill of a feather, just as depicted in numerous native codices (see fig. 5). It seems clear from all the evidence, therefore, that this group of balls was an offering.

In recent years, rubber balls from the House of Eagles have been the subject of several specialized chemical analyses, including FTIR (Fourier Transformed Infrared Spectroscopy), NMR (Nuclear Magnetic Resonance), and GC/MS (Gas Chromatography/Mass Spectroscopy).[47] Results indicate that 95 per cent of the raw material used in the production of these objects was pure, natural rubber (*cis* polyisoprene, whose botanical origin was probably *Castilla elastica*) and that, in general terms, it was in good condition. The origin of this polymer could be found in the tropical coastal regions of Mesoamerica, where the majority of rubber species grow.

In connection with this, it is interesting to note that the *Codex Mendoza* records that the province of Tochtepec (in the modern state of Oaxaca) sent Tenochtitlan a total of 16,000 rubber balls as twice-yearly tribute (fig. 14).[48] We cannot, however, exclude the possibility that this material could have been acquired via trade. According to Fray Bernardino de Sahagún, rubber was commonly sold at the great market of Tlatelolco, the twin-city of Tenochtitlan.[49]

The Manufacture of Rubber Balls

Sixteenth-century sources describe in simple terms the traditional techniques for making rubber balls. According to Fray Juan de Torquemada, Gonzalo Fernández de Oviedo, and Peter Martyr d'Anghiera, it was a straightforward process of forming a lump of rubber by hand, then modeling it gradually into a compact ball.[50] For example, Martyr d'Anghiera tells us: "they heated the juice [latex], which becomes harder as it is heated and a lump is made, and rubbing it, [each person] shapes the ball as he pleases."[51] Oddly, these historical descriptions differ from modern ethnographic records. In fact, the technique employed today by the Lacandon Maya of Chiapas, the Tarahumaras of Chihuahua, and the Mestizos of Sinaloa is completely different from 16th-century reports.[52] The modern procedure consists of concentrically rolling hot strips of rubber, like threads on a spherical skein of yarn. To avoid the formation of air pockets during the manufacturing process, each layer is carefully smoothed with the fingers, or the object is beaten firmly on a flat stone or perforated with a thorn. In this way, the action is repeated again and again until a solid, compact mass of the desired size is formed.

Such discrepancies in our information and the fact that the Maya glyph for rubber in the *Codex Dresden* is a spiral (fig. 15), raises some doubts as to the veracity of the historical texts.[53] In order to establish whether these suspicions were correct, seven Aztec archaeological balls—ballgame and offering balls—and two modern ethnographic balls—one from Sinaloa and another from Oaxaca—were analyzed by Helical Computed Tomography (Helical CT).[54] This technique allowed the interior of the balls to be examined in detail and as a result several thin layers of rubber arranged in a spiral were clearly distinguishable. Between the different layers, particles of powder were detected that perhaps had been deposited on the strips of rubber in the course of the rolling process (figs. 16–18).

The Specific Functions and Multiple Meanings of Ballgame Balls

Size is one of the main determinations of function of the rubber balls. From pre-Columbian times until today, there is a clear correlation between the diameter of balls and the type of game in which they are used. Iconographic depictions of the ballgame from the Classic Period (A.D. 300–900), for example, show hip strokes in association with large balls; strokes with a wooden bat with a medium-sized ball; and strokes with a hand device or glove, with a small ball.[55] By the Postclassic Period (A.D. 900–1519), the most common styles of the game are played with the hip, forearm, foot, or a bat (fig. 19).[56]

Unfortunately, written accounts from the 16th century only rarely mention the dimensions of balls, and they never mention a relationship

15 A deity sitting on top of a ballcourt, from the *Codex Dresden*, a Postclassic Maya manuscript. Inside the court is a spiral ball, the Maya glyph for "rubber."

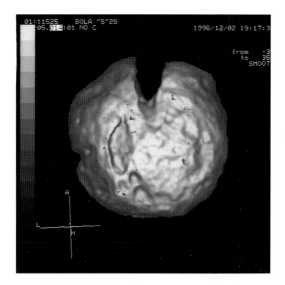

16 Computerized model of an Aztec rubber offering ball (Offering S in the House of Eagles; fig. 13). Note the groove for the insertion of a feather.

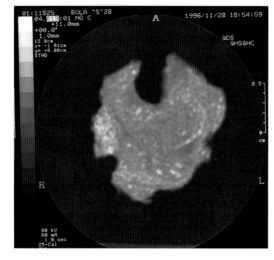

17 Helical Computed Tomography of an Aztec offering ball (Offering S in the House of the Eagles). The ancient rolling technique can be appreciated thanks to this technique.

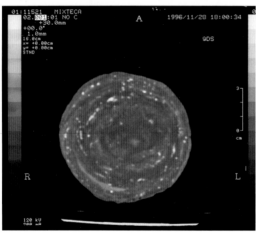

18 Helical Computed Tomography of a modern game ball from Oaxaca. The rolling technique is clearly visible.

or hip game, is fairly large, although it never exceeds 8 in (20 cm) in diameter, nor 9 lb (4 kg) in weight. Logically, the size of the ball used in the forearm variant of the game is smaller: it weighs between 16 and 18 oz (450 and 500 g). And the so-called Mixtec style uses very small balls, between 3 and 5 in (8 and 12 cm) in diameter, and between 6 and 10 oz (170 and 280 g) in weight.[58]

As for the religious symbolism of the balls for the game, there are some basic connections that should briefly be mentioned. The most obvious is with movement. In the Nahuatl language, there is a surprising resemblance between the terms "rubber" (*olli*) and "movement" (*ollin*). This similarity is probably due to the fact that in the pre-Hispanic period these words may well have been used as synonyms, given the conceptual proximity between the lively bounce of the ball and the movements of mundane and divine beings.[59] A second link may be made with the notion of vitality. On the one hand, in our 16th-century sources liquid rubber sprinkled on paper offerings is compared with drops of rain and the tears of the Tlaloques.[60] On the other, both the Aztecs and the Maya equated the latex that flowed from the inside of the tree with blood and semen, fluids indispensable for the functioning of the universe. To the Yucatec Maya, the word *k'ik* simultaneously means "rubber" and "blood." Similarly, in the *Popol Vuh*, the ball for the game is called *quic*, a Quiché Maya term that also means "blood."[61]

A third symbolic connection is with astral bodies, in particular the Sun and Venus, and also links the preceding two points with the spherical shape of the ball. For example, in many Classic Period Maya iconographic representations, balls of large dimensions have inscriptions in their interior. The inscriptions are associated consistently with God N or God L. Both deities represent the Sun at the moment it descends into the Underworld, where it will die, only to be reborn later. In other contemporary images, sacrificed descendants that symbolize the demise of the Sun are seen within balls. Consequently, the game can be seen as alluding to astral death as the beginning of cosmic preservation and transformation.[62]

Other authors also have pointed to the existence of the ball/human head/soul/ear of corn/seed symbolic complex. This interpretation is based on representations showing balls with a superimposed skull on their interior and of players sacrificed by decapitation, a ritual act which ended many of the games.

between the size of these objects and the type of game played. The most explicit document on this subject is perhaps the *Relación de Texcoco*, written by Juan Bautista Pomar. Even so, this source is limited to informing us that the balls were "very round," of the size of "a medium-sized human head" and that they weighed "four pounds" (fig. 20).[57] Ethnographic records are much more precise. For example, the ball used for the *ulama*,

From this perspective, the headless body represents the ballcourt with its four corners, while the head represents the ball, with a life of its own.[63] In summary, the people of Mesoamerica symbolically linked rubber balls with movement, vitality, fertility, celestial bodies, and rebirth.

Conclusions

The study of rubber and rubber balls provides us with an opportunity to investigate diverse aspects of botany, forestry, technology, ritual practice, and the cosmology of ancient and contemporary Mesoamerican societies. The use of rubber has a long history. Although it is uncertain when this raw material was exploited for the first time, archaeological evidence indicates that it was already known some 3,500 years ago. Furthermore, chemical analysis confirms that some surviving artifacts were made of natural rubber (*cis* polyisoprene) of high purity. According to many specialists, this polymer was obtained from the latex of *Castilla elastica*, the most common rubber species in ancient Mesoamerica.[64]

Other research has revealed that juice of plants of the genus *Ipomoea* was added during the heating of the rubber to improve its physical properties and that strips of rubber were rolled to produce balls for offerings and for use in the game. Balls made for the game, which had a profound religious significance, varied in size depending on the type of game being played.

One important point to stress again is the major conservation problems confronting rubber artifacts when they are found in archaeological contexts. And, as if this were not enough, the rate of deterioration of the few examples that have come down to us increases from the moment they are recovered by archaeologists. Light and oxygen are the greatest enemies of rubber, causing irreversible damage. Therefore, museum curators must be aware of the rarity and vulnerability of these materials, and we must increase our efforts to preserve these wondrous objects for future generations.

19 *(above left)* An *ulama* player using his hip to hit the ball, illustrated in the *Codex Mendoza*.

20 *(above)* This detail from the *Codex Magliabechiano* shows an *ulama* player in the end zone of an I-shaped ballcourt. Human skull markers further define this zone. He is about to serve the rubber ball to his opponents.

DOUGLAS E. BRADLEY

2 GENDER, POWER, AND FERTILITY IN THE OLMEC RITUAL BALLGAME

Among the earliest works of art from Mexico are ceramic figurines of Olmec rulers dressed as ritual ballplayers. The Olmec are regarded as the mother culture of Mesoamerica and established the cultural template followed until the arrival of the Spanish.[1] Olmec heritage included the symbolic basis for later hieroglyphic writing systems, personal blood sacrifice by rulers to feed a pantheon of gods worshipped by later cultures until the Conquest, human sacrifice to meet similar ends, the burial/temple pyramid, the layout of ceremonial centers according to astronomical sightlines, and the ritual ballgame, among much else. Olmec rulers played a game in which a rubber ball was volleyed back and forth between two teams by hitting it with the hip, the thigh, or a padded belt worn around the waist (fig. 22). The padded belts and arm and leg bands depicted on these early figurines are the first expressions of similar or identical equipment worn by ballplayers of later Mesoamerican cultures.[2] So ancient and so important was the ritual ballgame that, by 1500 B.C., an Olmec ruler's costume was complete only if it included ritual ballgame equipment in addition to rulership regalia and religious symbols of fertility.

Olmec civilization originated in the swampy Gulf Coast lowlands of the present-day Mexican states of Veracruz and Tabasco, but spread its cultural outposts and trade networks throughout Mesoamerica. The ritual ballgame was one of the most important Olmec cultural exports. As its name implies, the ritual ballgame was both a religious and an athletic event. Although the ritual ballgame is referred to in the singular, at least two different types of games were played at the dawn of Mesoamerican civilization, and many others developed in the ensuing 3,500

years. In addition to ruler ballplayer figurines, non-royal females were also depicted as ballplayers (fig. 23). Oddly, there are no Olmec non-royal male ballplayer figurines—all male ballplayer figurines depict rulers. The royal male and non-royal female types of Olmec ballplayer figurines wore two different types of protective equipment, but both were united by the religious

21 The corn (maize) kernel on the forehead and the sprouting corn dots on this stone *yuguito* or kneepad emphasize the connection between the ballgame and fertility. Early–Middle Formative Period, Olmec, 1500–300 B.C.; Pacific Slope of Mexico/Guatemala; *basalt*; h. 6 in (15.2 cm); Snite Museum of Art, University of Notre Dame (cat. 12).

22 This figurine depicts an Olmec masked ruler ballplayer wearing a helmet and padded waist protector. Middle Formative Period, Olmec, 1100–300 B.C.; Mexico, Veracruz/Tabasco; *serpentine*; h. 3.3 in (8.3 cm); Snite Museum of Art, University of Notre Dame (cat. 10).

24 Drawing of a figurine fragment showing the loincloth, padded belt, and mirror pendant—the typical accessories worn by Olmec ruler ballplayers. San Lorenzo, Veracruz, Mexico; *pottery*; h. 4 in (10.2 cm); Snite Museum of Art, University of Notre Dame. 89.8.

symbolism of fertility. Their equipment and fertility symbolism contributed to the creation of a ballgame legacy inherited by other cultures that has lasted to this day. The precise origin of the ritual ballgame is lost in antiquity, but the presence of female ballplayers suggests that it began as a game played by ordinary people and evolved into a religious ceremony controlled by rulers. Logic suggests that non-royal males must also have been ballplayers, and their lack of representation as figurines creates an enduring puzzle in Mesoamerican art.

Olmec male ballplayer figurines are found in two regions separated by at least 350 miles (560 km). They originate in the earliest known Olmec site of San Lorenzo in Veracruz, and they are also found in Tlapacoya and Tlatilco —two Olmec trading outposts in the Valley of Mexico. The figurines are composed of individual small

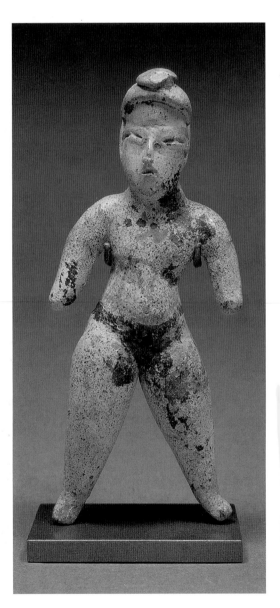

23 A non-royal female ballplayer is depicted in this pottery figurine. Her painted buttocks belt, with its rectangular panel covering the groin, drew the buttocks together to lessen the sting of the ball's impact. Early Formative Period, Olmec, Pilli-type, 1500–1300 B.C.; Central Mexico, Tlapacoya; *pottery*; h. 5.1 in (13 cm); Snite Museum of Art, University of Notre Dame (cat. 18).

25 (*opposite*) Ruler ballplayer wearing a bichrome mask, a large padded waist protector, a mirror pendant, and a corn fertility headdress. Early Formative Period, Olmec, Pilli-type, 1500–1300 B.C.; Central Mexico, Tlapacoya; *pottery*; h. 8.3 in (21 cm); Snite Museum of Art, University of Notre Dame (cat. 8).

elements of clay that are joined together and then fired, slipped, and painted. Earthquakes, burrowing animals, and new construction projects often break such figurines, and their surfaces are almost always damaged by exposure to the frequent rise and fall of groundwater, or by chemical reactions with the soil or other substances with which they have been buried.

In the Gulf Coast region of Veracruz and Tabasco acidic soils and high groundwater levels have destroyed the majority of perishable Olmec material culture, such as wooden sculpture. Even the durable slip surface layer fired onto most of the region's ceramic figurines and vessels is frequently eroded. Figurines and ceramics from trade outposts in the central highlands of Mexico, especially from the Valley of Mexico and the modern states of Mexico, Morelos, and Puebla, are better preserved.

San Lorenzo and Tlapacoya Figurines

When Michael Coe and Richard Diehl excavated San Lorenzo, they discovered eroded fragments of ruler ballplayer figurines in three of the earliest phases, dated from about 1500 to 1100 B.C.[3] Each ballplayer fragment takes the form of a tripod that stands on two legs and a rear support. These players are costumed in a three-part loincloth and padded waistband and wear a mirror pendant (fig. 24). The head of each one has been deliberately removed, and some heads have been recovered separately. On most, a mask covers the lower part of the face and raised circular dots or short projections adorn their headdresses.[4]

During her excavations at Tlapacoya, Christine Niederberger Betton discovered a type of figurine she named "Pilli," which belonged only to the period 1500–1300 B.C. Males make up 76 per cent of the Pilli-type figurines, and a large number of those are ballplayers that also stand on tripods.[5] This type of ballplayer wears a large padded belt or waistband, elbow- and kneepads, wrist and ankle bands, a mask, and a mirror pendant hanging over the belt (fig. 25). An elaborate headdress covered with circular dots, sometimes inside a U- or V-shape, completes the costume of these figurines. Tlapacoya Pilli ballplayers are broken at the neck or in the middle of the body. They have been recovered from general archaeological contexts such as trash heaps, but not in burials or ritual deposits. Ballplayer figurines excavated at Tlatilco by earlier archaeologists have similar characteristics to those from Tlapacoya.[6]

All Olmec ruler ballplayer figurines are defined by costume elements that are important religious and political power symbols as well as by their unique tripod stance. The U-shaped arrangement with a dot in the middle, a raised circular dot, or a raised U- or V-shape are all corn (maize) kernel symbols.[7] Life and fertility were controlled by Olmec male rulers, and these concepts were depicted on Olmec ritual ballgame sculpture by a variety of corn plant symbols, especially the kernel. Although corn and fertility symbolism are found on other images of Olmec rulers, it is clear that the ballgame was a religious activity that pleased the gods and promoted new life and agricultural fertility. From its earliest appearance in Olmec art, the religious iconography of fertility was intimately connected to the ritual ballgame.

The Tlapacoya ruler ballplayer figurine (fig. 25) wears a vertically divided red and cream mask that covers only the lower part of his face and represents a deity expressing the Mesoamerican principle of duality.[8] Such a mask (known as buccal) allows the wearer to assume the identity and power of the being depicted, while preserving his own identity. If the being is a deity or a deceased ruler, this is an important union of political and religious power and a dramatic claim on the right to rule.

Mirrors like the one represented on the Tlapacoya ballplayer have been shown to be symbolic connections to the power of the Sun God and links to the spirit world in Mesoamerican art, beginning with the Olmec.[9] The person who combines a deity or ancestor mask with a mirror claims the right to rule not only by inheritance but also by a right that is divine and endorsed by the gods.

26 Bloodletting perforator
with ballplayer figure;
Formative Period, Tlatilco
Culture, 1300–1000 B.C.;
Mexico, Guerrero,
Xochipala; *stone, white
pigment*; h. 8.5 in (21.7 cm);
The Art Museum,
Princeton University
(cat. 27).

Rulership and the Ballgame

Rulership came with responsibilities, however. Olmec rulers offered their own blood as a sacrifice to feed and nourish the gods. Olmec bloodletters and perforators are the earliest surviving Mesoamerican implements used to cut and pierce the skin to draw sacrificial blood (fig. 26). Archaeologists have discovered bloodletting implements lying across the groin of a buried Olmec ruler, which was probably a reference to the practice of drawing blood from the most fertile organ, the penis.[10] The act of bloodletting was not illustrated in Olmec art, but it was a common theme of the Classic Period Maya (A.D. 250–900), a culture heavily influenced by the legacy of Olmec civilization. The symbolism and context of Olmec bloodletting offer a prototype for Maya blood sacrifice and beliefs. Among the Maya, offering blood was probably a symbolic reenactment of the sacrifices the gods made when they gave their own lives to create the world.[11] As a result, blood sacrifice is both a symbol of death and a source of life throughout Mesoamerican history.

Corn symbolism, emphasizing the gift of life and fertility to the Olmec ruler and his people, was balanced by the symbolic death the ruler endured when he perforated his penis and offered blood to feed the gods. Corn and sacrifice created a duality typical of the Olmec world view in particular and of Mesoamerica in general: living beings create sacrificial death, and sacrificial death creates life.[12] The Olmec ruler's ritual ballgame equipment and the game itself are symbols of that duality. The structure of the ritual ballgame was a duality metaphor for all human existence, not simply winning and losing, but living and dying as well. There is no evidence for Olmec human sacrifice upon the outcome of a ritual ballgame, but the emphasis on fertility dictates a life/death cycle of events, both real and mythical. The power of the duality of the ritual ballgame mirrored the power of the ruler himself: it was the ability to create life from death. Death always won,

sacrifice was always made, and life was always renewed.

Close scrutiny of Olmec monumental male stone figures and small-scale male ceramic figurines has revealed important similarities between costume elements and playing equipment worn by ruler ballplayers. There is a one-to-one correspondence between the San Lorenzo ruler ballplayer figurines and San Lorenzo Monument 34 (fig. 27). This life-size basalt sculpture depicts a kneeling ruler in his role as a ballplayer wearing a Sun God mirror pendant, a padded waist protector, a loincloth, armbands, and kneepads.[13] Comparisons have also revealed that the forms and symbolic structures of other Olmec monumental stone ruler ballplayers from Veracruz and Tabasco are identical to the Tlapacoya Pilli ballplayer figurines.[14] For example, San Lorenzo Tenochtitlan Monument 1, a life-size stone ruler ballplayer kneeling on the abdomen of a subjugated figure, has the same type of padded belt and leg and ankle bands as a Tlapacoya Pilli-type ruler ballplayer figurine.[15] In addition, the padded belt on the front of Monument 1 has vertical bands identical to those found on other Tlapacoya ruler ballplayers.[16] It is clear that Olmec fertility, rulership, and ballgame symbolism on the monumental stone figures from the Gulf Coast carries the same meaning on the ceramic figurines from Tlapacoya and Tlatilco.

Thus a narrow set of Olmec ritual ballgame religious beliefs connects the three sites of San Lorenzo, Tlapacoya, and Tlatilco: the ruler who communicates directly with the gods and who controls fertility must be a ritual ballplayer in order to do so. In contrast to this is the almost universal Olmec cultural and economic presence documented by other types of ceramic figurines, vessels, portable stone sculptures, cave paintings, and stone reliefs found in the archaeological records of sites ranging from Central Mexico to Costa Rica. This suggests there was a conservative ritual ballgame religious movement limited to San Lorenzo Olmec believers that was responsible for the development and spread of the symbolism of corn fertility, rulership, and the ritual ballgame. The religious beliefs associated with ballplayer figurines appear to have been just one particular form of devotion among others at San Lorenzo, even though ballgame equipment was an essential part of a ruler's costume throughout the Olmec world.

Female Ballplayers

Other Pilli-type ballplayer figurines from the site of Tlapacoya depict females with strong secondary sex characteristics. They have breasts that hang outside the outlines of hourglass-shaped torsos, and painted red nipples applied after firing to further distinguish them from males.[17] There is absolutely no consistency between the female and male ballplayers, however. Female ballplayers appear to be ordinary people—they wear no recognizable political regalia and they have only minimal corn fertility symbols in their hairdos or headdresses.

Encircling the waist of the Tlapacoya female ballplayers is equipment consisting of a black-painted belt with a rectangular panel that covers the groin (see fig. 23). From the belt, a black strap hangs down the front of the left thigh. One red-striped panel hangs from the loincloth and covers the side of the upper left thigh and another protrudes above the loincloth and covers the lower right side of the torso. This configuration of belt, pendant strap, and panels arranged diagonally across the body is distinctive, and is proof that women dressed as ballplayers. It shows that they played a variety of the game in which the ball could be deflected with the waist, hip, or thigh. The black belt with the pendant strap is a buttocks belt used to draw the buttocks together to make them a more effective hitting implement and to reduce the sting of the ball's impact. The pendant strap may have cushioned the impact of the ball or softened the player's fall in the ballcourt, or it may have had a symbolic function that is not yet understood.[18]

Either red panel may have provided protection against abrasion from the ballcourt surface, depending upon the angle of the ballplayer's dive to hit and return the ball with a shot from her opposite hip. Equipment used to protect the body from abrasion is almost always located on the side of the body opposite the one used to hit the ball. A protected dive or playing stance allows the mass of the body to be shifted across the player's center of gravity more accurately and the force of the impact to be increased. Broad hips and a low center of gravity located in the pelvis give a woman a natural advantage over a man in the ballgame because she can get under the ball and hit it more solidly and easily. To lower a male's center of gravity from his sternum to his waist, he must wear a reasonably heavy padded belt or other equipment around his hips, as ballplayers of later cultures did.

A lack of examples, poor paint preservation, and the simplicity of the protective equipment have obscured the identification of most Olmec female ballplayers, however. No more than one in four Tlapacoya Pilli figurines are female, and the evidence suggests that female ballplayer figurines are a small fraction of that number.[19] Since the painted protective equipment was applied after firing, it is not permanent. Pilli female figurines and fragments are usually found in burials and domestic contexts that include trash deposits.[20] They commonly have black manganese deposits fixed upon their surfaces by aerobic bacteria. For this to occur, the figurines must have been located in an underground chamber with at least a temporary oxygen supply, such as a tomb or a cavity. These bacteria do not survive in a context deprived of oxygen, such as on a figurine surrounded by dirt.[21]

The Sexual Dichotomy in Ballplayer Figurines

From the beginning of Olmec civilization around 1500 B.C., ballplayer figurines from the Valley of Mexico were marked by a sexual dichotomy. The Olmec were the first Mesoamerican culture to make ballplayer figurines, and the religious symbolism of corn unites all of them. Differences

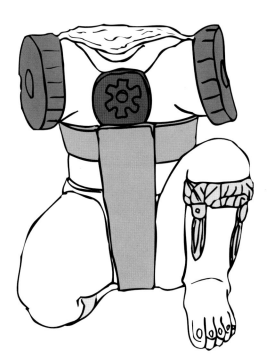

27 This drawing of San Lorenzo Monument 34, shows a kneeling Olmec ruler ballplayer. Note the mirror pectoral, the waist belt, and kneepads. San Lorenzo Tenochtitlan, Veracruz, Mexico; *stone*, h. 31.1 in (79 cm).

in equipment must reflect differences in the way the ritual ballgame was played, however, and may shed light on differences in its religious meaning. All male ballplayer figurines are rulers, all stand on tripods, all wear masks and Sun God mirrors, all wear headdresses and/or costumes with corn fertility symbolism, and all have padded belts of greater or lesser thickness (fig. 28). San Lorenzo ruler ballplayer figurines do not have elbow- or kneepads, wrist or ankle bands, but San Lorenzo Monument 34 does, and so do the ballplayer figurines from Tlapacoya and Tlatilco. All female

28 Ruler ballplayer with extended arms; Early Formative Period, Olmec, Pilli-type, 1500–1300 B.C.; Central Mexico, Tlatilco; *pottery*; h. 6.8 in (17.1 cm); Snite Museum of Art, University of Notre Dame (cat. 9).

ballplayer figurines stand on two legs, none wear any discernible political regalia, most have sculpted corn dot hairdos or headdresses, and all wear the buttocks belt and protective pads. Some have the pendant strap hanging down one thigh.

All male ballgame equipment is sculpted by applying strips of clay to the figurines before firing. This suggests the figurines are dedicated to a single use, or a narrow set of related uses, and perform important religious fertility and political functions. To do this, it was absolutely necessary that they be able to stand erect as tripods. The ballgame equipment on female figurines is painted on after firing. It appears that female figurines were made for a variety of purposes and may not have been depicted as ballplayers until the need arose, perhaps well after they were acquired. This suggests that the religious fertility function indicated by the corn symbols sculpted onto female figurines is broader than the narrow, optional religious fertility function the figurines have as painted ballplayers. The appearance of this dichotomy between sculpted/painted equipment at the very beginning of Olmec art argues an ancient role for the ballgame in Olmec society. Specialized ballgame equipment on figurines of both sexes suggests the ballgame was a basic religious and social activity, but not an exclusively royal one.

Pilli-type male ballplayer figurines are found headless or broken across the middle and discarded in general refuse or trash heaps. Nowhere else in Mesoamerican art are images of rulers so abundant or so casually disposed of after use. The few female ballplayer figurines that have been identified have manganese deposits on their bodies, indicating they were placed in underground chambers or tombs. Nowhere else in Formative Mesoamerican art are female images so rare.

The most conservative interpretation would be that both types of Olmec ballplayer figurines belong to the same ballgame religious belief system, but that each has a separate function within it. The large numbers of surviving Pilli-type male ballplayer figurines covered in corn imagery argue for a function related to agricultural fertility.[22] Perhaps Olmec rulers played a game in which the forces of drought and death were symbolically defeated in order to deliver life and plenty to their subjects. Or perhaps the figurines were charged with religious fertility and broken and discarded when their charges were exhausted, like used batteries. It is important to remember that some Olmec portable and monumental stone sculpture was cut or broken to remove heirloom fragments or to decommission the stone for other uses.[23] This is especially true of the Olmec colossal stone heads and monumental stone figures depicting male rulers, and it may have been done to kill the image and release the spirit or power of the individual.[24] With the potentially dangerous spirit gone, a large hunk of raw material such as a colossal head or altar could be safely quarried for different purposes.

If female ballplayer figurines were interred with the dead, they may have played the ritual ballgame for the deceased in the afterlife, defeated the gods of death, and allowed the deceased to assume a higher position in the spirit world. Or perhaps only female ballplayers were allowed to have female ballplayer figurines buried with them. A female ballplayer figurine may have been cached in a chamber for a ritual purpose related to its fertility symbolism and its femininity. The corn fertility symbolism in the hairdo possibly expanded upon the ballgame duality metaphor and renewed life from death.

Among many others, two enduring questions remain. Why are only rulers and females depicted as ritual ballplayer figurines? What does the lack of non-ruler male ballplayer figurines say about the functions of the rulers and females? Research strategies that attempt to answer these questions will shed much light on Olmec rulership and religion, as well as on the ritual ballgame. After 1300 B.C., both male and female Olmec Pilli-type ballplayer figurines disappear from the archaeological record in the Valley of Mexico.[25] Ballplayer figurines depicting males continued to be made and used in Olmec sites in Veracruz and Tabasco. The simple buttocks belt and pendant strap worn by Olmec female ballplayer figurines are identical to those worn by male and female ballplayer figurines of the Tlatilco Culture that emerged in the Valley of Mexico after 1300 B.C. (fig. 29). But Tlatilco Culture ballplayers carry a new fertility symbol—the triangular handprint of the earliest non-Olmec deity, the goddess known as the Displayed Deity.[26] Her handprints mimic the shapes of kernels of corn, and they are sculpted and painted on both the fronts and backs of the heads of Tlatilco Culture figurines in exact parallel to the way corn fertility symbols are used on Olmec figurines. In addition, Displayed Deity handprints/corn kernels are painted and incised on the bodies of figurines dedicated to her. There are no obvious Tlatilco Culture male ruler figurines, and females vastly outnumber males. Most of the few males are ballplayers, as are some of the females.

Olmec religious tradition bonded fertility and the ritual ballgame, and Olmec equipment established the playing style, but the Tlatilco Culture ballgame religion is dedicated to a new goddess of fertility. This is the legacy of the Olmec ritual ballgame—a celebration of the duality of life (fertility) and death that reinforced the religious, social, and political structures of succeeding cultures in the Mesoamerican world for the next 3,500 years.

29 Standing humpback Old God ballplayer; Early Formative Period, Tlatilco Culture, 1300–1000 B.C.; Puebla, Mexico; *pottery*; h. 6.8 in (17.2 cm); Snite Museum of Art, University of Notre Dame (cat. 19). This figurine wears a buttocks belt commonly seen on male ballplayers.

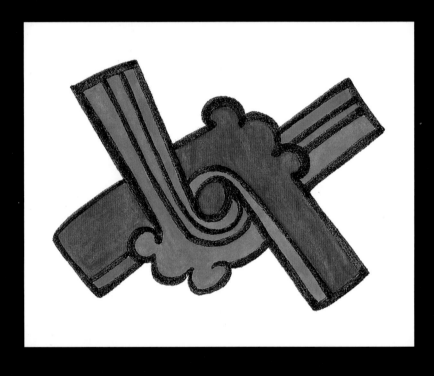

MARÍA TERESA URIARTE

3 UNITY IN DUALITY:
THE PRACTICE AND SYMBOLS
OF THE MESOAMERICAN BALLGAME

The survival of the Mesoamerican ballgame through the centuries and despite so violent a transformation as the Spanish Conquest undoubtedly demonstrates the deep significance of this pre-Hispanic activity. For the ancient Americans who played the game, its meaning was multi-layered. It was not only an amusing pastime but also a way to sublimate social violence through sacrifice. Furthermore, it was a means of settling territorial disputes and thus functioned as an allegory for warfare. Among the ballgame's deepest meanings were connections with rites of fertility and a replication of astronomical cycles, with references also to

altered states of consciousness. The ballgame can thus be seen as a metaphor for life and death.

In Mesoamerica a game has been played with a rubber ball since the Olmec era. The earliest known archaeological site from which actual ballgame paraphernalia has been recovered is El Manatí, on Mexico's Gulf Coast. A series of objects related to the game has been unearthed there, both in archaeological excavations and as chance finds by local farmers. These include a stone yoke (see Scott) and serpentine-form scepters, the latter pointing to an already well-developed ideological relationship between the game, power, and serpents. The discovery of

30 The symbol for the day *Ollin*, from the *Codex Borgia*. *Ollin* means "movement," and must be related to the Nahuatl word for rubber, *olli* (or *ulli*), referring to the remarkable characteristics of the material.

31 Ballplayer relief, Dainzú, Oaxaca, Mexico; Late Formative Period, Zapotec, 400 B.C.–A.D. 150. The ballplayers display postures related to ballgame, and are wearing feline masks.

33 *(opposite, above)* Mural fragment with ballplayers with bats; Early Classic Period, Veracruz, Las Higueras; A.D. 300–500; Mexico, Gulf Coast; *plaster, paint*; 22.8 × 38 in (58 × 96.6 cm); Museo de Antropología, Universidad Veracruzana (cat. 93).

32 Mural fragment; Mexico, Teotihuacan, Tepantitla Palace; Middle Classic Period, *c.* A.D. 400–500. The players are using bats and wearing skirts and capes.

wooden anthropomorphic sculptures and rubber balls was remarkable for Mexican archaeology, since these are the only rubber balls of a size consistent with use in the ballgame found in an archaeological context. Secondary burials of children and of a skull suggest possible relations with later cults such as those of decapitation and child sacrifice.[1]

Other Mesoamerican sites dating to the Formative (1500–100 B.C.) where evidence for the ballgame has been found include El Opeño in Michoacán, and the slightly later site of Dainzú, Oaxaca (fig. 31). Iconography at these sites includes feline masks, possibly relating to a deity, at Dainzú, and the playing of a ballgame using bats, or handstones, at El Opeño (see Day). In Mexico, the game has been played with a bat for centuries. This version of the game is also portrayed on mural paintings at the Tepantitla Palace compound at Teotihuacan, an Early/Middle Classic Period (*c.* A.D. 400–500) site in Central Mexico (fig. 32). The murals here appear to depict "teams" using bats to keep the rubber ball in play. One player is carrying a ball tied with a bow and is wearing a skirt and cape.

At the site of Las Higueras in Central Veracruz

(fig. 33), there are two different sets of supposed players with bats. Interestingly, in the modern-day state of Michoacán, some groups still play a version of the game using bats and a burning ball, supposedly an allegory related to the daily journey of the sun across the sky (fig. 34). And at El Carrizal, Veracruz, a Late Formative site, yokes bearing the effigy of a toad or the earth monster have been found (see Scott).[2] Thus, at an early stage, a system of symbols relating to the ballgame had begun to take shape, which was enriched with the passing of the centuries.

The Ballgame and Astronomy
There has been much speculation about the links between the ballgame and astronomy. The *Codex Borgia*, a Central Mexican manuscript painted around A.D. 1500, is one of the richest sources for this symbolic relationship.[3] The clearest astronomical connection is with Venus. Throughout the *Codex Borgia* symbols of Venus are associated with the game. Other objects also show this relationship, such as the crenulated forms of Teotihuacan ceramics from both Central Mexico and southern Mesoamerica. In both the *Codex Borgia* and the Tepantitla

34 *(below)* Modern ballplayers in Michoacán, Mexico, using sticks or bats. At the beginning of the game, the ball is set on fire and is supposedly an allegory of the sun. The game is played at night, making the effect of the fire ball very dramatic.

Palace murals, the bodies of some ballplayers are painted with red stripes. Such body decoration (fig. 35) adorned the victims sacrificed in honor of Tlahuizcalpantecuhtli—the god of Venus, or the morning star. Xolotl was this deity's counterpart —Venus as the evening star. As the companion or alter ego of the deity Quetzalcoatl, Xolotl wears a cut conch pectoral. Mary Miller and Karl Taube state that the word "xolotl" in the Nahuatl language often refers to concepts of twins and deformity. Xolotl also serves as the patron of the day *Ollin*, meaning "movement" and related to the word for "rubber" in Nahuatl.[4]

For the Aztecs, Xolotl was the patron deity of the ballgame. A beautiful song recorded in the 16th century by the Spanish chronicler Fray Bernardino de Sahagún affirms this relationship:

> He plays with the ball
> Old Xolotl plays with the ball
> In the magical ballcourt
> Xolotl plays with the ball
> Man of the land made of jade
> See him.[5]

The overlapping Aztec gods Xochipilli-Macuilxochitl were also among the deities related to the ballgame, dancing, and chanting.[6] Other deities who enjoyed a special relationship with the game include Quetzalcoatl, Tlazolteotl, and Cinteotl (the young Maize God).[7]

The pre-Hispanic world view was shaped by the belief in a persistent struggle among the gods and humanity's desire to maintain a cosmic order. This is perhaps best exemplified by the sun's daily triumph in its struggle against the gods of the

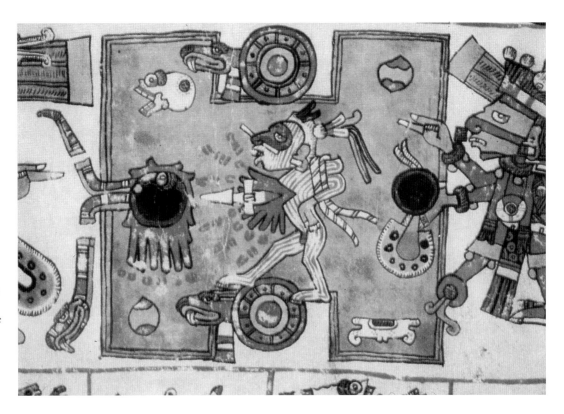

35 A scene from the Central Mexican *Codex Borgia* (plate 21). The bodies of sacrificial victims of the cult dedicated to Tlahuizcalpantecuhtli were painted with red stripes. Tlahuizcalpantecuhtli is the version of Venus-Quetzalcoatl as a Morning Star.

Underworld. The delicate balance of the cosmic order could only be maintained through the sacrifice of human beings. Ultimately, the triumph of light over darkness is only possible through human sacrifice. Another cosmic aspect is also linked to human offerings and the agricultural cycle: different moments in the solar year—solstices and equinoxes—and their relationship with the rainy and dry seasons and the rebirth of plants. It is probable that both war and the ballgame were practiced during the dry season in order to favor the rains.[8]

The ballgame was one means by which human offerings of blood and death were accomplished. From the pre-Hispanic perspective, the taking of life was necessary in order to perpetuate life. The ballgame offered the defeated contender in war and conquest the opportunity of being sacrificed with honor. Such actions replicated the deeds of the Hero Twins who defeated death in the Quiché Maya epic the *Popol Vuh*. As the sun defeats the night with each dawn, the player's sacrifice and offering of blood on the ballcourt enable the plants to germinate anew and assure the sustenance of his people. Thus was the ballgame related to the universe through sacrifice, decapitation, and mutilation. This can be seen most dramatically in the relief carvings from the sites of El Tajín, El Baúl, Vega de Alatorre, and Izapa. At Chichén Itzá, reliefs show a victorious player holding in his hand the head of his defeated opponent, who is kneeling in

front of him (fig. 36). Seven serpents bud from the neck of the kneeling player. Surrounding the scene is a plant, possibly a species of *Datura*—a genus known for its psychotropic properties. The ball between the players takes the form of a skull. Life and Death; a plant growing thanks to men's sacrifice and blood. But there is also a connection with the universe, through the equinoxes and the rainy season. Significantly, above Chichén Itzá's great ballcourt, in the Temple of the Jaguars, there are mural paintings related to war, sacrifice, and the sun.

The pre-Hispanic codices associate the sacrificed players with the rains, vegetation, and fertility, as well as the sun's victory over darkness.[9] But the ballgame also fulfilled a social function: the enemy defeated in war maintained his honor because he was allowed to die in the game. This deep meaning is reflected in the *teotlachtli* (ballcourt) of Mexico-Tenochtitlan: the gods become human and play; there is the sense of a game made sacred, or a divinity that plays as humans do. Throughout history, humanity has always conceived of the divine in human terms. The passions and fears of Greek gods, for example, reflect those of mere mortals. In pre-Columbian Mesoamerica, humans believed the gods' behavior mirrored their own. The epic account in the *Popol Vuh*, in which the inhabitants of Xibalba (the Underworld) were defeated in a ballgame, demonstrates this. Among many rites and rituals in ancient

American societies, the ballgame was one way of participating in this transcendental task.

The Primordial Concept

The ballgame symbolizes a struggle between opponents and opposites. Representations of plants, trees, and skeletal figures relate to fertility and the maintenance of cosmic order through sacrifice. There are other consistently depicted motifs that accompany representations of the game or the objects related to its practice, which at first sight may seem unconnected to it: snakes, crocodiles, toads, turtles, snails, mollusks, butterflies, jaguars, and certain plants such as water lilies (*Nymphaea*) and *Daturae* (toloache). Most of these are commonly depicted in the codices as well as on ballgame objects. What was the connection that linked these subjects?

Some of these motifs are associated with the ballgame itself, in particular with its ceremonies. Scenes of heart extraction and dismemberment are frequent themes in the ballcourt reliefs (figs. 36 and 37) and the numerous ballgame-related portable objects, such as *hachas*, *palmas*, and ceramic vessels. And in such scenes, for instance in the reliefs at Chichén Itzá and El Tajín, blood turns into snakes or plants.

Butterflies appear frequently in Mesoamerican art from the Formative to the Postclassic periods and from the Central Mexican site of Teotihuacan to the Gulf Coast and the Maya region. At Teotihuacan they are associated with the ballgame and are depicted on a number of ceramic objects as well as in the murals decorating the Tepantitla Palace (fig. 38). The so-called Tlalocan mural in this palace compound portrays numerous figures playing different forms of the ballgame, some accompanied by butterflies. The butterfly symbolizes transformation, because from a ground-dwelling larva it turns into an aerial being.

In pre-Hispanic art everything had meaning: decoration in and of itself was not an objective for ancient artists. Therefore, the symbols constantly associated with representations of the ballgame must have contained a common

36 Ballcourt relief at Chichén Itzá, Yucatán, Mexico; Late Classic/Early Postclassic Periods, Maya, A.D. 800–1200. The victorious contender holds the head of his opponent in his hand. A plant, possibly a datura, surrounds the scene.

denominator. Finding the link in this ideological substratum enhances our understanding of the deep meaning of the game for ancient Mesoamericans, its wide geographic dissemination, and its survival into modern times.

Duality

One of the most frequently discussed aspects of the game is the union of opposites on the court. The encounter between players epitomized unification through opposition. The court was the symbolic access to the Underworld and at the same time the channel for the sun's rebirth every day.[10] The cosmos and the depths of the earth existed as a dual concept. The primordial concept of fusion through the struggle between opponents is central to understanding the Mesoamerican world.

The common thread linking toads, turtles, and crocodiles is that all three live both on land and in water. Water is also part of the jaguar's natural habitat: jaguars are excellent swimmers, and turtles and fish form part of their diet. The enigma thus begins to become clearer once we have established the link between the symbols associated with the game.

Representations of water lilies are linked with many concepts in Mesoamerican cultures. Their most obvious association is with water; they frequently appear in the mouth of Tlaloc, the Central Mexican Rain God. They are also related to the entrance to the Underworld, the Maya symbol for which is still water. At Teotihuacan, countless vases and murals depict the open flower or its buds. Let us therefore look for its most obvious relation to all the other symbols. The water lily is a flower. Flowers usually grow on land, but not water lilies— they have a dual nature, like butterflies, toads, crocodiles, and turtles. This union of opposites is inherent to all the symbols mentioned. Less apparent perhaps is the duality of mollusks; however, although they are aquatic, they do not swim but rather move along the seabed. They act as terrestrial beings, so they too are dual.

All these symbols appear in relation to the ballgame. They are the most frequently represented themes on markers, ballcourts, yokes, *palmas*, ceramic vases, and jewelry. The profundity of the dual concept is confirmed by many allegorical figures. One is the union of the jaws of a toad or a jaguar as access to the

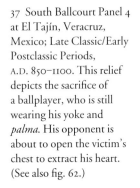

37 South Ballcourt Panel 4 at El Tajín, Veracruz, Mexico; Late Classic/Early Postclassic Periods, A.D. 850–1100. This relief depicts the sacrifice of a ballplayer, who is still wearing his yoke and *palma*. His opponent is about to open the victim's chest to extract his heart. (See also fig. 62.)

Underworld. Another is water, or rather the earth–water link—which again forms access to the world of the dead.

One additional fact is highly significant: the rhizomes of water lilies are hallucinogenic.[11] This little-known peculiarity of the plant leads us to another duality: the taking of consciousness-altering substances to enter a different reality. The use of psychotropic substances is a very common practice, linked with a perception of a nature that interacts. The desire to enter a different reality is a common one in humans, regardless of the time or place to which they belong. Through initiation rites humans seek to perceive a different world, and time passing in a different way, and to experience reality totally and comprehensively. Comprehensively, in that the perception of a different reality—such as in dreams or psychotropic hallucinations—is experienced in conjunction with the sensory awareness of a normal state of consciousness.

Research on biochemical alterations in the brain caused by consciousness-altering substances or practices enables us to appreciate the changes in an individual's perception. Such perceptual changes are a result of mystical experiences that make it possible to reach a different state of mind. Among the most frequent methods to achieve this are the reiteration of syllables (such as Hindu mantras); monotonous repetition of music—whether accompanied by dances or not—as practiced by the Sufis of the Middle East; bloodletting or prolonged fasting, as among the Christian mystics of the Middle Ages; meditation; and the ingestion of plants, mushrooms, or substances derived from animals, such as toads of the *Bufo* genus, which alter brain chemistry. All these practices create a feeling of perceiving the world in a different, more intense, way, similar to dreams and, perhaps, to death.[12] This is probably why most initiation rites speak of voyages to the world of the dead.

Consciousness-altering practices therefore create a unity in duality; that is, different worlds unite in a single reality through the mystical experience. This may be why the water lily was for the Maya, and perhaps also for the people of Teotihuacan, the symbol of access to that different reality, induced by its psychotropic effects, and, at the same time, the symbol of the still water of access to the Underworld. The water lily opens its petals at dawn and closes them at sunset, which reinforces its symbolic content. Furthermore, its rhizomes

38 Mural fragment from Tepantitla Palace, Teotihuacan, Mexico; Middle Classic Period, A.D. 400–500. A butterfly is shown surrounded by ballplayers.

39 Mural fragment from Tepantitla Palace, Teotihuacan, Mexico; Middle Classic Period, A.D. 400–500. Water lilies are a symbol of the Underworld, transformation, and renovation. These flowers close their petals at sunset, and reopen them at dawn. Their rhizomes are hallucinogenic. Tlaloc, the rain god, is often depicted with a water lily in his mouth.

and on the steps at Yaxchilan. In short, their presence cannot be fortuitous. Perhaps their role in the *Popol Vuh*—a rope holds the head of Hunahpu—allows us to get closer to their symbolic content. The head identifies, expresses, perceives, supports; the head is crowned and in our own times leaders of governments are called "heads of state." Hunahpu, the twin creator, loses his head and recovers it. The myth refers to the head in more than just the physical sense—undoubtedly the Quiché story also alludes to the head with a deeper meaning. Moreover, the rope suggests continuity. In this myth what is lost and what is recovered is also Hunahpu's father's head, which is displayed in a tree. The head then spits into the hand of a princess of the Underworld, fertilizing her, and she gives birth to the prodigious dual beings, Xbalanque and Hunahpu, the brothers who, by playing the ballgame, defeat death.

There is one more consideration we can examine in relation to the head. Human beings are identified by the head. We perceive the world through our senses, widely regarded as situated

40 Ballcourt relief, Chichén Itzá, Yucatán, Mexico; Late Classic/Early Postclassic Periods, Maya, A.D. 800–1200. This scene of human sacrifice is surrounded by vegetation, possibly a species of the genus *Datura*.

are a violent emetic, which associates them with purification.

In the Tepantitla Palace murals we see depictions of Tlaloc with a water lily in his mouth (fig. 39), and very possibly, a hallucinogenic morning glory (*Turbina corymbosa*) grows in the middle of the scene. A datura is probably represented in the relief from the Great Ballcourt at Chichén Itzá (fig. 40).[13]

According to van Bussel, the ballcourt is an allegory for access to the Underworld.[14] He bases his proposal on various sources of evidence. These include the fact that in the Quiché language the word *hom* means "tomb" as well as "ballcourt." Representations of steps on numerous works of art also suggest that the Hero Twins of the *Popol Vuh* descended steps to reach the Underworld. Furthermore, the ballgame implies the possibility of resurrection. The Hero Twins defeat the Lords of Death. The moral of the story is that life triumphs over death and the cosmic order is maintained. The sun and the stars may descend into the Underworld, but they return from it once more.

Ballgame scenes often contain ropes or lassos. We can find them in the ballcourt markers from Copán (fig. 41), Cotzumalhuapa, and Teotihuacan. They also appear on panels of the southern court of El Tajín, on Altar 8 at Tikal,

in the head. For the Aztecs, one aspect of the soul, the *tonalli*, is located in the head. Thus, to acquire an enemy's head is to capture his power. Maybe that is why the victorious ballplayer holds his enemy's head in his hand.

Van Bussel analyzes the relationship between the Maya words for "blood" and "rubber" (*k'ik*) and semen (*k'ik'ei*), and concludes that the ballgame may be an allegory of life through dynastic succession.[15] Also, the serpent-shaped batons found at El Manatí may be insignias of power, like the spurts of blood coming from the decapitated body in the reliefs from Chichén Itzá (figs. 36 and 40). The snake that substitutes for blood, associated with the fertility of the earth, also becomes an allegory of power.

There is one last symbol I would like to analyze, that of *ollin*, which shares the same origin as the word "rubber" in Nahuatl, *olli* or *ulli*. Ollin—the movement of the rubber ball; this could be the movement that arises in the unity of opposites on the court, the movement of the stars, the movement of the ball in the court of men, and also the ball in the *teotlachtli*, where gods play as humans, in the center of access to human and divine realities.

The harmonious duality, the balance that humans seek and find in nature and all its manifestations, is only a reflection of the very duality of our inner being, and of the search for the unified being. The ultimate absolute that unifies opposing forces. The symbol *ollin* (see fig. 30) is the clearest graphic manifestation of the pre-Hispanic world, equivalent to the Chinese symbol of yin and yang that unifies opposites. The concept of two opposing directions meeting in one underlies ancient Mesoamerican culture and is evidenced in one of its most important manifestations: the sacred ballgame.

41 Ballcourt marker from Copán, Honduras; Late Classic Period, Maya, A.D. 700–900. Ropes or lassos are often found in scenes related to the ballgame.

JOHN F. SCOTT

4 DRESSED TO KILL: STONE REGALIA OF THE MESOAMERICAN BALLGAME

Representations of ballplayers created by native Mesoamerican artists before the Spanish Conquest show them in far more elaborate costumes than those worn by the Tlaxcaltecan ballplayers depicted by Christoph Weiditz playing in front of a Spanish audience in the 1520s (see frontispiece). These two players wore only rawhide shorts belted over their buttocks and leather gloves, apparently on both hands.[1] Late pre-Columbian native depictions of ballplayers show men in elaborate headdresses and costumes, standing or seated in ballcourts, but typically not actively engaged in play. For this reason we believe they are involved in pre- or post-game ceremonies, sometimes featuring the ball and sacrificial victims. The players clearly could not have worn all their regalia during the active game, although what they did wear could very probably have been incorporated into their costumes. They may have paraded out in their full regalia before the game, removed most of it prior to play, and put it back on again at the conclusion, when the result determined which players were to be sacrificed. Since the winning players may have participated in the sacrifice, they were therefore "dressed to kill."

Ancient Mesoamerican stone objects commonly called *yuguitos*, yokes, *hachas*, and *palmas* are now regarded as elements of ballgame regalia. From the 19th century on, these objects have been analyzed by scholars to determine their functions, which have been obscured by traditional names inspired by their imagined purpose or descriptive of their shapes. The following analysis examines the shapes within their temporal context to assist in understanding their original purposes, and how those purposes and shapes evolved through time.[2]

Yuguitos

Yuguitos are the earliest documented stone ballgame objects in this group. They take their common name from the Spanish diminutive of yoke (*yugo+ito*). These "little yokes" have been excavated in chamber tombs at El Opeño (fig. 43), a site in the west central Mexican state of Michoacán dated to the Early Formative, *c.* 1500 B.C. In the same tomb as one plain *yuguito* was a group of ceramic figurines depicting ballplayers (see Day, fig. 65).[3] The association between *yuguitos* and the ballgame, long suspected, is therefore likely. These stone *yuguitos* probably served as protectors, perhaps to hit the ball with the fist, as in a later Tarascan game played in the region.[4] Unfortunately the equipment represented on the small ceramic figurines does not specifically render such *yuguitos*. Three of the

42 The front of this *palma* depicts a coyote-masked man standing on top of a temple platform. Carved in low relief on its reverse side is a complex scene of animal-masked participants in a scene of human sacrifice, with dismembered limbs being grabbed by a bat diving from the sky. Early Postclassic Period, Veracruz; *c.* A.D. 900–1200; Mexico, Gulf Coast; *stone*; Cleveland Museum of Art (cat. 130).

43 This plain *yuguito* may have been worn on the hand. Early Formative Period, *c.* 1500 B.C.; Mexico, Michoacán, El Opeño; *stone*; 3.25 × 4.25 in (8 × 11 cm); MNA.

44 From the same site as the first Jalisco tombs excavated undisturbed, these half-yokes reveal a variant of hip protectors from those known in the core area of Mesoamerica and suggest the use of cords to attach them. Early Protoclassic Period, *c.* 100 B.C.–A.D. 100; Mexico, Jalisco, Tabachines; *stone*, one with a horizontal groove, 8.75 × 3.75 in (22.5 × 9.5 cm), and the other with two holes at the ends, 7.5 × 4.3 in (19 × 11 in); Museo Regional de Guadalajara.

45 *Yuguito* with twisted human face; Formative Period, Olmec, 900–600 B.C.; Mexico, Veracruz; *granite*, 5.1 × 5.1 in (13 × 13 cm); The Art Museum, Princeton University (cat. 13).

figurines carry heavily ribbed T-shaped objects in their left hands, perhaps ball deflectors, and they also wear heavy padding on their lower left legs from the knee down. One other possibility is that *yuguitos* may have been ritual equivalents of knee protectors. Might the *yuguito* have secured the bottom of leg padding on the lower shin? Use of stone protectors with cord ties can be inferred for two later half-yokes associated with the Tabachines style of Jalisco state during the Protoclassic (100 B.C.–A.D. 300): one has a horizontal groove into which a cord could fit, the other has two large holes at each end.[5] Both forms suggest that a cord was used to attach the objects, in these cases around the waist (fig. 44).

Yuguitos are widespread in northern Mesoamerica—one has been excavated in Tlatilco[6] and others are attributed to Tlapacoya, both in Central Mexico, and others to Guerrero state and the Olmec area. Several of these are carved with grotesque faces, often interpreted as facial deformities caused by being hit by the hard rubber ball (fig. 45), a fate common to modern hockey players. The orientation of these images suggests that the stones would have been viewed with the curved portion uppermost and the face forward, thereby supporting the theory that they were fist protectors.

Yokes

Yokes are U-shaped stone objects. Contrary to what their popular name may suggest, yokes could never have been used around the necks of large domesticated draft animals, since these did not exist in pre-Hispanic Mesoamerica. One early hypothesis suggested they were placed around the necks of sacrificial victims.[7] It was only in the mid-20th century that the theory that

46 The stone of this plain yoke is fine and dense, not native to the alluvial Gulf Coastal plain where it was discovered by farmers. Formative Period, Olmec, *c.* 900 B.C.; Mexico, Veracruz, El Manatí; *greenstone*, 14.5 × 13 × 3.75 in (37 × 33 × 9.5 cm); INAH, Veracruz City.

these objects were really ballgame belts gained widespread scholarly acceptance.[8]

The earliest documented standard-size yoke was recently recovered at the site of El Manatí in Mexico's Gulf Coast state of Veracruz. Reportedly, it was placed above two adults buried seated facing each other.[9] Unfortunately this was an accidental find made by farmers, not archaeologists, so the yoke's context remains hearsay. The surface of the dark, greenish-black stone is smooth and undecorated (fig. 46). It has slightly spreading open ends and is not symmetrical, one side being slightly shorter and more open than the other, and the radius of curvature of the two halves is not equal. The top and outside are more polished than the interior and bottom, a practice which continues with Classic Period yokes. Its reported association with a serpentine human figurine suggests it may date from the late Early to Middle Formative Period (*c.* 900 B.C.), when use of jade-like greenstone was common. However, the excavators of the site have documented that the ballgame was played during the Early Formative (1500–900 B.C.) since rubber balls recovered from that level are of the size used in the ballgame of both ethnohistoric as well as modern times.[10] Wooden sculptures nearby also date to about 1200–900 B.C. The excavators suggest that a pair of 2-ft (0.6-m) wooden staffs recovered at El Manatí might have been used as ballgame bats.[11] The El Manatí yoke is similar in its general

parallel-sided, U-shaped configuration to one at Princeton University (fig. 47) said to have come from Río Pesquero, Veracruz,[12] a site associated with fine jade full-face masks. The yoke was crafted of a finely grained greenstone, and was much more smoothly and regularly carved than the yoke from El Manatí. Like Inca stonework, its subtly undulating surface makes it seem organic, although it lacks any recognizable representation.

Other than these protective belts, we are ignorant of the full panoply of elements worn by ballplayers during the Middle Formative Period in the Central Mexican highlands. Figurines of the Early Formative Period, however, wear a thick

47 Ballgame yoke; Middle Formative Period, Olmec, *c.* 600 B.C.; Mexico, Veracruz, Río Pesquero. *greenstone*, 4.5 × 13 × 15.6 in (11.5 × 33 × 39.5 cm); The Art Museum, Princeton University (cat. 14).

48 The Tepatlaxco Stela depicts a bearded player being dressed by his attendant. Stylistic details reflect the Veracruz variant of the Izapan style found along the Peripheral Coastal lowlands of Mesoamerica, from the Gulf Coast across the Isthmus of Tehuantepec to the southern Maya region. Early Protoclassic Period, *c.* 100 B.C.–A.D. 100; Mexico, Veracruz, Tepatlaxco; *stone*; 72.5 × 16.5 (184 × 42 cm); MNA.

play in such elaborate regalia, although they may have worn it before or after the ballgame, or perhaps during ceremonies related to it. This does not mean that all equipment is purely ceremonial. The ballplayers from Early Formative El Opeño wear elaborate hand and shin protectors, but only one wears a rolled belt and loincloth of the type worn by players of historical times.[13]

The strongest evidence for the use of torso protectors comes from the Protoclassic in central Veracruz. The Tepatlaxco Stela (fig. 48) represents a ballplayer being dressed by his "squire," who has wrapped many layers around the player's torso.[14] This is the type of torso protector Maya players later wore (see fig. 56). The additional straps visible on the Tepatlaxco player's short skirt may be the leather hip protector worn in historical times and documented in the state of Sinaloa.[15]

The Tepatlaxco player also wears a padded protector on his right knee, straps under his left knee, and some wide strips wrapped around his hands like those worn by the Dainzú (Oaxaca) players illustrated on reliefs of the same period.[16] The Dainzú players are often represented holding a small ball in their wrapped hands while actively engaged in play wearing grill-fronted helmets. Significantly, in the *Popol Vuh* from the southern Maya area, the equipment worn by the Hero Twins when playing the ballgame included gloves and a mask.[17]

The earliest documented examples of relief-decorated stone yokes come from the site of El Carrizal in the Remojadas area of central Veracruz. At that site, Bertha Cuevas de Álvarez discovered two related burials of human bones,

belt, shin protectors under each knee, as well as many other clearly ceremonial elements, including a small buccal mask—the type covering just the mouth (see also Bradley, this volume). It is doubtful whether athletes could

49 The subtle high relief around the top and exterior side of this yoke represents the standard toad image. The other yoke found with this one has unique hyperboloid curves superimposed on the design, perhaps suggesting the meeting of two worlds, under and upper. Toad yoke; Early Protoclassic Period, Remojadas, *c.* 100 B.C.–A.D. 100; Mexico, El Carrizal, Veracruz; *greenstone*; 16.25 × 13.75 × 4.5 in (41 × 35 × 11.5 cm); MAUV.

each accompanied by ritually broken stone yokes carved with high-relief crouching toads wrapped around the exterior.[18] Both yokes depict earth monsters in the form of a batrachian, the name given to the family of frogs and toads (fig. 49). Characteristic of true toads are the enlarged parotid glands extending back from the eyes over the front legs.[19] In the giant toad of Mexico (*Bufo marinus*), these contain hallucinogenic toxins. This creature played the role of an earth goddess in Mesoamerica,[20] called Tlaltecuhtli, a male name, by the Aztecs,[21] possibly to represent its dual nature. Its protruding rear crouching legs on the open ends of the yoke could have been functional: cords wrapped around them would have completed the circle around the wearer's waist and better secured the yoke. In addition, the yokes have an inward curve at their open ends which hugs the curve of the wearer's waist and they might not have required further fastening because of the resulting tight fit. How the yoke could have been worn can be seen on a ceramic figurine from Veracruz, now in the collection of the San Antonio Museum of Art (fig. 50).

Auguste Génin reported acquiring a yoke on a ranch at El Carrizal, Veracruz, which may be one now in the Musée de l'Homme in Paris.[22] Its high-relief imagery, while similar in style to that of the two yokes mentioned above, has a rounded nose representing the jaguar, the avatar of the night sun in Maya iconography. On its open rear ends, the Génin yoke has low-relief profile faces wearing bird-head helmet masks facing each other; these men are probably an early version of the Hero Twins of the later *Popol Vuh,* who played the ballgame against the Lords of the Underworld.[23] The exterior sides of the yoke are incised not just with interlocking scrolls but also with profiles of these same Hero Twins holding up handstone rings (fig. 51).[24] These may be the rings referred to in the *Popol Vuh* as part of the Hero Twins' ballgame equipment, although by the Postclassic Period such rings could also have been portable markers or goals.[25] Simpler and smaller cylindrical handstones with looped ends accompanied the yokes in the burials at El Carrizal.[26] The exact function of such handstones remains uncertain. Perhaps they served as counterweights, or were used in a version of the game that allowed the players to use handstones actually to strike the ball.

50 This player with earth monster mask is wearing a carved yoke terminating in animal heads. Late Classic Period, A.D. 700–900; Mexico, Gulf Coast, Veracruz; *pottery,* 5 × 10 × 6.8 in (12.7 × 25.4 × 17.2 cm); San Antonio Museum of Art (cat. 53).

51 If this yoke dates to the same period as the excavated area at El Carrizal, it has the earliest low relief designs, which are typically placed on plain areas such as the jaguar's belly. Later examples exhibit scrolled interlaces on all surfaces except the bottom. Jaguar yoke with low relief incisions; Remojadas, 100 B.C.–A.D. 300; Mexico, Veracruz, El Carrizal; *stone,* 15.75 × 15 × 5 in (40 × 38 × 12.5 cm); Musée de l'Homme, Paris.

During the Protoclassic and Early Classic periods in the Huastec region of northern Veracruz, eastern San Luis Potosí, and southern Tamaulipas, artists fashioned solid ceramic figurines representing ballplayers (fig. 52).

A careful study of all these Huastec figurines should be undertaken to determine the use of ballgame equipment. For example, some of their yokes are carved with the images of crouching animals like actual stone yokes, and are closed by a large disk over their open ends.[27] Such disks have not survived and thus must have been made of perishable material. Also perishable were the knee protectors and the thick quilted pads many Huastec ballplayer figurines also wear over the backs of their hands.[28]

An Early Classic yoke was excavated at the central Veracruz site of El Viejón. From the

excavation photograph, the sides of the yoke seem very straight and the angles sharp, in contrast to the organic roundness and inward curvature of the Protoclassic yokes.[29] Yokes of this style have very parallel sides, which would have made them more difficult to wear than the yokes from the Protoclassic because they would not fit so snugly around the waist.[30] From this it is possible to conclude that by the Early Classic, the yokes became non-functional in the ballgame itself but continued to be worn in ceremonies.[31]

Several yokes from the Middle Classic Period have a motif of sunken footprints encircling their perimeters. Given the context of such footprints on contemporaneous murals from Teotihuacan, such as those in the Tetitla Palace showing a net jaguar approaching a temple, footprints represent a journey. In a ballgame context, they perhaps mark the journey into the Underworld taken by the Hero Twins. A polished blackstone yoke found in the Central Mexican state of Tlaxcala, dated around A.D. 700, has alternating footprints pecked into both its polished surfaces.[32] Four encircle the top and five encircle its outer sides, nine in total—the number of levels of the Underworld in Mesoamerican myth. In both rows a noticeable gap has been left just behind the final footprint. Yokes are not ordinarily found in the Central Mexican highlands, where a bat was used to hit the ball in the Classic Period; the Tlaxcala yoke represents the Gulf Coast version of the ballgame, in which the ball was struck with the hip.

A similar, dark graystone yoke of the same period from El Zapotal, south-central Veracruz, has three encircling footprints—all of the right foot—in a matte finish pecked into its highly polished exterior (fig. 53). This reveals a misunderstanding of Central Mexican iconography derived from Teotihuacan influence at the height of its political and cultural dominion during the Middle Classic Period (A.D. 400–700).

A closed yoke now in the Musée d'Ethnographie, Geneva, has two deeply sunken footprints on the outer sides surrounded by dots. Although originally published as from El Baúl on the southern Pacific slope of Guatemala,[33] it has recently been reattributed to Veracruz.[34] The flat end closing the yoke creates a shape that would have been difficult to put on. Three fragments of such closed yokes were excavated in Late Classic contexts at Tres Zapotes in south-central Veracruz.[35] An additional fragment then thought to come from a closed yoke[36] may have been from an open one because of its similarity to an open yoke from the site of El Trapiche in central Veracruz (fig. 54). Both yokes have an extreme inward curvature, a raised interior rim, and a delicacy of profile which seem inspired by the thin closed yokes. García Payón recovered the El Trapiche yoke from what he considered to be either Middle[37] or Late Formative period levels.[38] Having located and examined it in the Museo de Antropología in Xalapa, I no longer consider it to be Formative.[39]

An excavated whitish yoke from El Zapotal has an incised interior border on its top surface similar to the low-relief borders modeled in three dimensions on the yokes from Tres Zapotes and El Trapiche. Unique to this yoke are the nine vertical plaques incised from the top plane around onto the outer sides. Plaques like these are used to render scales of serpents in Mesoamerican art, and the number nine may again contain a reference to the nine levels of the Underworld and/or the Lords of the Night, the nine deities who alternately rule over different nights. This treatment is very similar to a yoke from the San Antonio Museum of Art, with overlapping scales and inlaid fangs of shell (fig. 55), although this creature has definite avian characteristics as well.

Unlike the perishable torso protectors worn by Maya lowland ballplayers, now visible only on works of art (fig. 56), yokes in the southern Maya area had apparently spread there during the Classic Period as part of the cultural interchange in the peripheral lowlands of Mesoamerica, and

53 This yoke with three footprints pecked around the side was excavated at El Zapotal, Mound 2, Trench 9, with Burial 46. Middle Classic Period, Nopiloa, *c.* A.D. 550–700; Mexico, Veracruz, El Zapotal; *graystone*, 16.5 × 12.75 × 4.25 in (42 × 32.5 × 10.5 cm); MAUV.

54 Perhaps buried in an already abandoned Formative Period site, this plain yoke reflects the shape of contemporary Late Classic closed yokes, which also have a raised molding around their interior edges. Late Classic Period, Remojadas, *c.* A.D. 600–900; Mexico, Veracruz, El Trapiche; *graystone*, 16.5 × 13.75 × 3.25 in (42 × 35 × 8.2 cm); MAUV.

55 This yoke combines characteristics of serpents and birds. Late Classic Period, *c.* A.D. 700–900; Mexico, Gulf Coast, Veracruz; *stone, red pigment, shell*, 16.5 × 14 × 14 in (41.9 × 35.6 × 35.6 cm); San Antonio Museum of Art (cat. 82).

perhaps specifically as a result of the migration of the Pipil. These were Nahua-speakers who had previously occupied southern Veracruz, where they adopted the Gulf Coast style of ballgame. The southern Maya yokes are U-shaped and open ended. On Maya carved yokes, serpent iconography seems dominant. They have a flat top and bottom surface—the bottom being narrower than the top. Generally these yokes have a straight exterior wall beveling inward from top to bottom. The interior wall is vertical and either straight or slightly rounded. A distinctive characteristic common to the majority of yokes from this area is the rounding or beveling of the top edge of the interior wall.[40]

56 Late Classic depictions of Maya ballplayers, such as this standing ballplayer whistle, show thick padding around the waist secured by a belt. Late Classic Period, Maya, A.D. 600–900; Mexico, Campeche, Jaina Island; *pottery*; 6 × 2.8 × 3 in (15.2 × 7 × 7.6 cm); Mint Museum of Art (cat. 103).

On carved yokes—only a third of those surveyed by Shook and Marquis—serpent iconography seems dominant. Some serpents are feathered, suggesting celestial links, rather than the dominant Underworld references of Veracruz yokes. Shook and Marquis document many associated yokes and *hachas*,[41] and also identify a large cache, now dispersed, from the site of Narciso in Guatemala.[42] It contained possibly 52 yokes, linked with the number of years in a Mesoamerican ritual "century," when the ritual and the solar calendars realign. The physical attributes of the Narciso yokes suggest a Veracruz origin since they differ noticeably from other southern Mesoamerican yokes in being heavier, of better quality, and having a higher polish on the top and exterior surfaces, which have convex walls. Likewise, their iconography suggests a Veracruz origin: motifs include a crouching toad, human heads and skulls carved in high relief on the exterior surface, an upraised arm with clenched hand motif, the "long-snout" composite animal head, and severed human legs. All but the first of these motifs are typically found on Late Classic yokes. More usual in Guatemala than Veracruz was the heavy use of red pigment, which apparently covered this cache and was used to paint designs on three otherwise plain yokes.[43]

Beginning in the latter half of the Late Classic and continuing into the Early Postclassic, the iconography of Veracruz yokes became extremely individualized. Nonetheless, they typically retained the overall composition established in the Protoclassic by the crouching toad and jaguar, widespread Underworld symbols in Mesoamerica. The relief carving of yokes closely parallels the monumental reliefs with interlaced scrolls in ballcourts at the dominant north-central Veracruz site of El Tajín, dated by Jürgen Brüggemann to A.D. 800–1150.[44]

At El Tajín, no complete yokes have yet been found, although a few broken fragments have been recovered from fill. But, at the closely related site of Santa Luisa in Gutiérrez Zamora, Veracruz, a complete yoke was recovered from the burial of a young man whose body was placed inside the yoke. This is the closest burial association between owner and object. Yet the sides of this yoke definitely diverge, making it unlikely that it was worn during play.

Nearby were the remains of an older man, considered a companion to the younger man. This individual was buried with a copper tube, evidence of an Early Postclassic date since metal

does not appear in Mesoamerica until then.[45] In the high relief design encircling the yoke, a young male figure replaces the more standard crouching toad, and his hands grasp the necks of two serpents which intertwine in relief on the top and sides of the yoke. This composition relates to reliefs on three El Tajín ballcourts south of the Pyramid of the Niches.[46]

Hachas

Hacha is the Spanish term for axe. These objects were so named because many later examples have thin edges, giving them an axe-head-like appearance. They were worn as appendages to the yoke, inserted into its side by a tenon or overlapping the top by means of a rear notch. Such a relationship is shown on numerous figurines and on a Veracruz yoke-effigy bowl (cat. 60).

The earliest excavated *hacha* is a rounded stone head, unlike the thin forms of later examples. It was found in association with a broken, smooth stone yoke in a burial from El Viejón in central Veracruz and has been dated to A.D. 450–550.[47] The *hacha* depicts an old man's head with closed eyes, clearly a reference to death (fig. 57). Later, scenes of decapitation of a ballplayer appear in the Chichén Itzá ballcourt reliefs. Such stone heads when worn on the player's belt (yoke) allude to previous defeated opponents.[48] The longitudinal crest which curves back across the top of the El Viejón stone head and a lateral flange at the back of the head may refer to the crest of a bird. The *hacha* is notched

at the base to overlap the yoke during ceremonies in which we assume surrogate trophy heads were displayed.

The largest group of yokes and *hachas* found thus far in burial contexts comes from the site of El Zapotal in south-central Veracruz. The site was excavated by Manuel Torres Guzmán and his associates from 1974 to 1976. Unfortunately, the results have not yet been published, so the complete context of the group cannot be given here.[49] An *hacha* from the Mint Museum of Art collection (fig. 58) is very similar in type and material to one from El Zapotal,[50] although the Mint's is more compressed laterally and has some animal features. Both depict anthropomorphic heads with longitudinal crests. At present both *hachas* resemble skulls, but possible original inlays in the eye sockets, and teeth in the mouth, may have given them more life-like appearances. Thus, unlike the earliest *hacha* which was a stone version of a trophy head, these faces are very much alive. These and all *hachas* excavated at El Zapotal are notched in the back.

57 The face of a grimacing old man, his eyes closed in pain—or death—strongly suggests the agony of defeat in the ballgame. The victor would wear this trophy head overlapping the top of the yoke in the rituals preceding and following the game. Rounded head *hacha* with rear notch; Middle Classic Period, Remojadas, A.D. 450–550; Mexico, Veracruz, El Viejón; *blackstone*; 8 × 6 × 5.5 in (20.5 × 15 × 14 cm); MAUV.

58 This *hacha* depicts a head with human and feline characteristics. Middle Classic Period, Veracruz, A.D. 550–650; Mexico, Gulf Coast; *greenstone*; 5.5 × 3.9 × 3.1 in (13 × 9.8 × 7.9 cm); Mint Museum of Art (cat. 69).

60 *(opposite, left)* An anthropomorphic bird's head, this *hacha* from El Zapotal was excavated in Mound 2, Trench 9, Burial 15, along with fig. 59. It has a lateral crest around the top of the head, the upper rear of which is concave. The mask-like features are sharply outlined in segments. Middle Classic Period, Nopiloa, A.D. 550–700; Mexico, Veracruz, El Zapotal; *graystone, traces of red pigment*, 6.75 × 5.5 × 6.25 in (17 × 14 × 16 cm); MAUV.

A pair of burials recovered from Trench 9 of Mound 2 at El Zapotal were each accompanied by a yoke and an *hacha*.[51] The yoke from the higher-status burial of the two has a more abstracted toad, rendered by grooves sunk in the white stone yoke (fig. 59). This carving reveals the fossilization of the original iconography of the Underworld toad that first was documented on yokes during the Protoclassic at El Carrizal, and suggests that yokes were no longer intimately associated with the earth monster. The accompanying *hacha* (fig. 60) shows a divergence from the old concept of a severed trophy head: it represents the head of an anthropomorphic beaked bird (birds were often sacrificed).

The lower-status burial immediately below this one has a coarsely made yoke and *hacha* set.[52] The sides of the plain yoke show a marked splay as they extend back toward the open end, reinforcing the implication that yokes were no longer used in actual play. The only decorations on this yoke are three grooves near, but not precisely at, the center front, suggesting notches incised after manufacture as records of ballgame triumphs. The associated *hacha* represents a rough-surfaced, somewhat compressed human head with a slight scroll curving up on each temple, both features similar to the Mint *hacha* (fig. 58). Its eye sockets may once have been inlaid with shell, but now the empty sockets, along with the bare crown, give a skull-like appearance to the head. Its lateral compression,

like that of the monkey-skull *hacha* from the same site (fig. 61), indicates the tendency toward a thin axe-like form which increases in the latter part of the Late Classic.

A very thin stone *hacha* from Napatecuhtlan in central Veracruz provides an excavated example of *hacha* shape in the latter half of the Late Classic.[53] It was placed beneath a jar containing a secondary burial of a heavily built man.[54] It apparently represents the severed head of a defeated ballplayer whose tongue lolls out of his mouth and has a perforation, possibly to hold a sacred greenstone bead such as those placed in the mouths of the dead. The elaborate headdress of stiff vertical feathers recalls those of ballplayers shown before and after the actual ballgame in the reliefs lining the South Ballcourt at El Tajín. The height of this *hacha* suggests the tall *palma* form which evolved from *hachas*, apparently at the end of the Classic Period.[55]

Thin stone *hachas* spread to the southern Maya area during the Late Classic. Most southern Guatemalan and Salvadoran *hachas* are squared in the lower rear, not notched or tenoned. Since this area is never polished or decorated, it may have once been mounted in a slot.[56] Although human and death heads appear in the iconography of these southern *hachas*, 65 per cent of the representations are of animals or animal headdresses.[57] Three caches of nine *hachas* each, all of different representations and many painted red, have been recovered from

59 The toad image on this yoke, which has very parallel sides, has been reduced to sunken grooves on the sides. Middle Classic Period, Nopiloa, A.D. 550–700; Mexico, Veracruz, El Zapotal; *whitestone*, 6.5 in (42 cm); MAUV. Excavated in Mound 2, Trench 9, Burial 15, with fig. 60.

Escuintla Department, Guatemala. Again the number nine has Underworld associations, specifically with the nine Lords of the Night among the Maya.[58]

Palmas

Palma means palm branch in Spanish, and these stone objects, with their thick triangular bases and splayed tops with radiating ribs, do indeed resemble palm fronds. Although *palmas* have been examined closely in terms of their function and decoration, there has been very little study of the evolution of these forms. Like late yokes, figurative *palmas* also display a wide variety of representations, suggesting they, too, are late in the sequence of ballgame regalia. Their projecting bases would overlap the top of the yoke in the same position as notched *hachas*. Generally taller than *hachas*, *palmas* required stabilization, possibly by the wearer's hands held in front. Such hand positions are occasionally represented in high relief on the *palmas* themselves.[59]

Palmas are also shown frequently in relief scenes of the Terminal Classic and/or Early Postclassic, such as the famous El Tajín South

Ballcourt reliefs showing players with yokes and concave *palmas* in ballcourts, surrounded by mythical beings. One relief represents the face-off, with a large ball between the feet of the two players. The opposite relief represents a ceremony at the end of the game, in which a player is being killed by heart sacrifice (fig. 62). Here the outcome of the game is made explicit: blood sacrifice is necessary to feed the sun and keep the cosmos going, as required by the gods in the Aztec myth of the fifth creation. Another well-known relief cycle of the same period, on the Great Ballcourt at Chichén Itzá, repeats the theme of human blood sacrifice, this time by decapitation of the front man of a seven-member team. In this case the blood sacrifice seems to nourish plant fertility, for the seven spurts of blood from the severed neck of the player turn into cacao plants. All players are dressed in quilted arm padding and knee guards, carry animal-faced handstones, and wear thick yokes with *palma*-like inserts. However, no extant stone *palmas* have a similar design so they may actually represent bats.

A *palma* excavated at the Veracruz site of Santa Luisa represents a naturalistic harpy eagle

61 *(above, right)* The forehead of this monkey-skull *hacha* is compressed into a sharply defined ridge, indicating the more axe-like shape which gives *hachas* their traditional name. *Hacha* iconography in the Late Classic is moving away from human decapitation to more varied subjects, perhaps associated with the individual wearer, such as his spirit totem animal. Monkey-skull thin head *hacha* with rear notch; Late Classic Period, Nopiloa, A.D. 700–900; Mexico, Veracruz, El Zapotal; *stone, orange pigment, shell*; 7.75 × 5 × 3.25 in (20 × 13 × 8 cm); MAUV.

62 Drawing of one of six reliefs placed in the center and at each end of the two walls bordering the South Ballcourt at El Tajín, Veracruz, Mexico; this one is in the northeast corner. Late Classic/Early Postclassic Periods, A.D. 850–1100. Within the sloping profile of a ballcourt one player holds back the arms of the victim to expose his chest to the knife held by a second player. A skeletal god descends from above to receive the offering. To the left, another skeletal god emerges from a large jar to observe the sacrifice. (See also fig. 37.)

with a longitudinal crest of feathers,[60] perhaps making explicit the longitudinal crest depicted in abstract form on early *hachas*. The short proportions of this *palma* reveal the object's similarity to earlier *hachas*. An excavated offering of two *palmas* at Rancho el Paraíso in Banderillas, central Veracruz, demonstrates the range of designs and use of high-relief scenes in the Early Postclassic.[61] One *palma* has an abstract design like a bird's crest, much like those worn by the decapitated figures in low relief on the four stelae from El Aparicio, Veracruz (fig. 63), a site which I have dated to the Early Postclassic.[62] The platform is like a staircase ornamented with simplified versions of the T-shapes found on the staircases of Tajín Chico's outer rim buildings (dated to the Early Postclassic), overlooking the North Ballcourt and religious buildings in lower El Tajín.[63] Motifs from many *palmas* emphasize sacrifice, and the tightly curled scroll patterns may signify blood.[64] A *palma* with similar background scrolls, now in the Cleveland

Museum of Art, depicts a coyote-masked man standing on top of a less clearly defined scrolled platform (see fig. 42). Carved in low relief on its reverse side is a complex scene of animal-masked participants in a human sacrifice, with dismembered limbs being grabbed by a bat diving from the sky.

The distribution of *palmas* is mainly limited to the Gulf Coast region and El Salvador, where the Nahua-speaking Pipil population has been concentrated from the Postclassic to the present.[65] An excavated cache from the site of Quelepa in eastern El Salvador yielded three plain yokes, an *hacha*, and two *palmas* with aquatic motifs: a lizard and a water bird whose spread wings create the flaring back of the *palma*. This cache dates to the upper end of the Classic and the beginning of the Postclassic.[66]

Conclusion
In conclusion, the ballgame appears in the beginning of the Mesoamerican Formative,

as do the still-enigmatic *yuguitos*. Full-size plain yokes appear very early, if we can trust the report of the farmers who discovered the El Manatí yoke, datable perhaps to around 900 B.C. But representational yokes first appear in the Protoclassic in the image of toads and felines, avatars of the Underworld. The subtly inward curving ends of these yokes suggest they could remain on a player even during action.

Beginning in the Early Classic, yokes are more rigid and sharply cut, with their sides perfectly parallel, suggesting that they were no longer worn. Heaviness of yokes is not a good reason to reject their being worn since their weight is distributed very evenly on the wearer's hips. Associated with them are small stone heads notched to overlap one arm of the yoke. The great variety of yokes from El Zapotal, during the earlier half of the Late Classic Period, and their association with head *hachas*, some slightly thinned laterally, imply that almost every player had his own stone yoke and *hacha*, which he probably wore only during ceremonies before and after the actual game.

Hachas are replaced by *palmas* by the Early Postclassic, and the decoration then of both yokes and *palmas* is highly diverse and individualistic. At this time both *palmas* and reliefs associated with ballcourts clearly establish that this regalia is worn during sacrificial ceremonies: players were literally "dressed to kill" or be sacrificed.

Before the end of the Early Postclassic Period (A.D. 1200), these small stone paraphernalia cease to be made, perhaps due to a more secular approach to the game as reported by the Spanish chroniclers who later witnessed it with its attendant gambling.

63 The decapitated player on this monument from El Aparicio is wearing a yoke and *palma*. The *palma* is the fan-shaped type commonly associated with El Tajín and nearby sites. Monument with decapitated ballplayer; Early Postclassic Period, Veracruz; *c.* A.D. 900–1200; Mexico, Gulf Coast, El Aparicio; *stone*; MNA (cat. 133).

JANE STEVENSON DAY

5 PERFORMING ON THE COURT

Games are a means, through make-believe, of coping with the world. [1]

The birthplace of the first team sports played with a rubber ball was not Europe, nor Asia, but the ancient Americas. While the rest of the world was caught up in contests of individual athletic skills such as jousting, footraces, swimming, and wrestling, New World cultures were fielding teams of ballplayers who competed against each other on specially designed stone courts. Beginning possibly around 1500 B.C., these teams were the first to play with a ball made of rubber—as opposed to the wooden or leather spheres used in other parts of the world—and it was the elastic, bouncing nature of solid rubber balls combined with the concept of team play that made the New World games unique.

In the late 15th and early 16th centuries, when the Spanish arrived in the Americas, they witnessed this dramatic game, first on the islands of the Caribbean, then, in 1519, in the great Aztec capital city of Tenochtitlan. Rubber was unknown in Europe and Asia, and the astonished Spanish soldiers thought the bouncing rubber ball must be magic or the work of the devil. From that time on, lively rubber balls began to replace their leaden wood and leather European counterparts.

There was an immense enthusiasm for team competition among the indigenous peoples of the New World, particularly in Mesoamerica, an enthusiasm unrivaled in any other place until recent times. Today team games have become a phenomenal feature of American life and a hallmark of contemporary culture around the world. The modern games of football, basketball, soccer, and volleyball perpetuate traditions established 3,500 years ago in the New World. Teams and heroes, music and rituals, gambling, and rubber balls of various sizes were all part of sports long ago just as they are today.

Putting the Game in Context

The ballgame was first played around 1500 B.C. on the Gulf Coast of Mexico by the Olmec—Mesoamerica's first great civilization. This hot, tropical setting formed the backdrop for the evolution of formalized teams, rubber balls, standardized protective equipment, religious rituals, and ballcourt architecture (see both Bradley and Taladoire). Eventually, these concepts spread throughout Mesoamerica and into the American Southwest and the Caribbean Islands, becoming one of the true hallmarks of pre-Columbian civilization. More than 1,500 ballcourts have been found in Mesoamerica, and many more probably still lie undiscovered beneath the streets and buildings of modern cities in Mexico and Guatemala.[2] Together with the art associated with them, such as ceramic figurines and vessels, stone sculptures, carved monuments, wall murals, and specialized gaming equipment, these ballcourts provide the fundamental evidence for this ceremonial sport.

Between 1500 B.C. and A.D. 1521, with some notable exceptions (a few ballcourts were as large as a football field; others big enough for only two players), courts averaged 120 by 30 ft (36.5 by 9 m). They were shaped like a capital "I" with parallel masonry walls enclosing a long narrow playing alley that connected two end zones (fig. 64). Made of cut stones, originally whitewashed and painted with vivid colors, the courts were impressive, costly structures designed for ritual performances. Stone sculptures of the gods and small temples dedicated to them were frequently incorporated into the walls. On the interior, courts were often decorated with tenoned stone heads, carvings of jaguars, serpents, or raptors; and at some sites, life-sized stone friezes depict post-game rituals of human sacrifice. According to the location where the game was played, the

64 An I-shaped ballcourt at Monte Albán, Oaxaca, Mexico; Classic Period, A.D. 300–900.

65 These figurines excavated in a tomb at El Opeño form the earliest known group representing Mesoamerican ballplayers. Early Formative Period, 1500–900 B.C.; Mexico, Michoacán, El Opeño; *pottery*, 3.25 × 2.5 in (9.3 × 6 cm) average; MNA.

rubber ball itself also varied in size. In Central Mexico, the Aztecs played a game with a ball about the size of a softball. From southern Mesoamerica, in some depictions of the Maya game, it appears to be as large as a beach ball.

Playing the Game

The ritual ballgame was played throughout Mesoamerica for more than three thousand years. Not surprisingly, it varied somewhat in both method of play and in meaning. We know from the early Spanish chronicles (beginning with the Conquest in 1519) that in the Aztec form of the game, for example, only the buttocks and knees could make contact with the ball. Eyewitnesses record that the ball was made of heavy, solid rubber, weighed 6 to 8 lb (3 to 4 kg), and was bounced against the walls of the court and from player to player at a fast pace. Points were scored when a ballplayer either missed a shot at one of the two vertical stone hoops set opposite each other at center court, was unable to return the ball to the opposing team before it bounced twice, or allowed the ball to bounce outside the boundaries of the court.[3]

Although basic elements of the game appear consistent throughout Mesoamerica, the Aztecs probably played only one form of the sport and depictions of games in painted wall murals, and ceramic images of ballplayers dressed for the court, suggest there were other ways of playing. Figurines are particularly illustrative, portraying contestants wearing various combinations of attire and gear, including yokes, *hachas*, knee- and elbow-pads, arm bands, helmets, and heavy gloves. In addition, objects carried by players— bats, sticks, *manoplas* or handstones—imply numerous methods by which the ball may have been manipulated on the courts (for descriptions of this equipment, see Scott).

The Meaning of the Game

The significance of the complex Mesoamerican ballgame has been the focus of research and speculation by many scholars.[4] A basic interpretation is that the ball and its movement in the court symbolize the movement of heavenly bodies in the sky, the game being seen as a battle of the sun against the moon and stars. The universal struggle between the opposing forces of day and night, good and evil, life and death was symbolically enacted by opposing teams on the ballcourt.

Clearly associated with this view of the game is the cult of fertility. Agricultural communities everywhere depend upon earth's bounty for survival; and agricultural productivity, in turn, requires the warmth and light of the sun and the timely occurrence of seasonal rains. Human sacrifice by decapitation is a recurring theme in ballgame imagery. Streams of blood spurting from the neck of a decapitated victim may be seen as watering the earth or as an offering to sustain the sun in its daily battle against the forces of the night.

Although this analysis of the ballgame's significance is somewhat simplistic, it underlies many more complex explanations of the elaborate religious and secular rites associated with the sport and illuminates its broad appeal to diverse audiences. The ballgame and its accompanying ceremonies clearly satisfied the innate needs of pre-Columbian cultures for more than 3,000 years. At its most basic level, ritual activities such as the reenactment of myth and sacrificial offerings were an attempt to impose order on an inexplicable universe and to tame the unruly cosmos for the benefit of humankind.

This essay will focus on two aspects of the game: the concept and continuity of team sports in pre-Hispanic societies and the dramatic, theatrical events that took place on the ballcourts of ancient Mesoamerica.

Playing as a Team

Mesoamerican Pre-Columbian Pop Culture: The Team

> To play alone is a primary move
> of mind,
> but to learn the rules
> For playing with another
> is a partnership of mind and spirit
> An identifying of body and soul to win
> not as one
> but as a team.[5]

Seeing oneself as a member of a group rather than as an independent individual is socially significant within a society. Personal sacrifice for overall good, a shared adherence to a set of common rules, and participation in team ritual serve to bond members of a group into a functioning unit. Historian William McNeill asserts that, beginning very early in the human record, group activities such as dancing, singing, hunting, work teams, military drills, and eventually team games were integrating factors in

human development.[6] The use of music, chanting, and song to inspire work groups; the close cooperation among hunters to increase their success in the chase; and the almost hypnotic impact of extended periods of rhythmic dancing are examples of activities that facilitate physical and emotional unity.

Nowhere was the power of group coherence more evident than in Mesoamerica, where a ritual team sport was credited with the regeneration of life and the maintenance of cosmic order. The playing of the game promoted human bonding and emphasized the qualities of cooperation and obedience to rules as a means to achieve success. This ritual game of chance, with its focus on the concept of a team rather than on an individual, both reflected and influenced the societies in which it developed and surely contributed to the unique culture and worldview of pre-Columbian Mesoamerica.

To date, the first documented evidence for this association of teams and games can be found in a group of eight ceramic figurines recovered in an archaeological context from a tomb at the site of El Opeño in the modern Mexican state of Michoacán.[7] Results of radiocarbon dating places these figurines at around 1500 B.C., Mesoamerica's Early Formative Period. They were found as a group and represent a ballgame scene (fig. 65). Five of the figures are male; they stand as if ready to hit a ball with the rectangular *manoplas* or heavy mitts in their hands and wear padding around the knee and lower leg. The other three figures are females, who recline or sit as if watching the game. Aside from protective padding on the males, all eight are nude except for a helmet-like head covering. The figures are clearly intended as a *scene*. Numbers of other figurines dressed as ballplayers are known from contemporaneous Formative Period sites in Tlapacoya and Tlatilco in the Valley of Mexico and Xochipala in the western state of Guerrero (figs. 66 and 67). The figures wear a variety of ballgame padding and carry gaming equipment. Like the El Opeño figurines, these may originally have

66 Many single figurines, such as this one and fig. 67, may originally have been part of group scenes. Standing ballplayer figurine; Formative Period, Xochipala, 1200–900 B.C.; Mexico, Guerrero; *pottery*; 6.4 × 3.4 × 2 in (16.3 × 8.5 × 5 cm); The Art Museum, Princeton University (cat. 22).

67 Standing ballplayer figurine; Formative Period, Xochipala, 1000–800 B.C.; Western Mexico, Guerrero; *pottery*; 4.75 × 2 × 1 in (11.1 × 5.1 × 2.3 cm); Denver Art Museum (cat. 25).

a horizontal baton or bat with both hands. It is obvious that some myth or story is reflected in this dramatic scene. Even more tantalizing is the possibility that the *Popol Vuh*, the Maya creation myth concerning the Hero Twins who play a ballgame against the Lords of the Underworld (here represented by the jaguars), may well have originated with the Olmec.

At the Middle Formative Olmec site of La Venta (900–400 B.C.) the tradition of dramatic grouping of figures continues. A group of figurines, known as Offering Number 4, were recovered in a cache at the site.[9] They were arranged in a scene consisting of 16 male figurines made of stone grouped in front of six miniature incised jade columns, or stelas. One figure stands alone, facing the other 15, with his back to the stelas. Unfortunately, the significance of the grouping is lost to us.

Ceramic groups or teams are also found in West Mexican shaft tombs, dating from the slightly later Late Formative and Protoclassic periods (400 B.C.–A.D. 300). These figures wear various types of diagnostic protective gear and depict ballgame activities.[10] Most obvious and best known are the miniature models of actual ballcourts (fig. 68), all but one complete with players, balls, and spectators. The exception depicts two men fighting in the middle of the playing field, suggesting activities other than ballgames may have taken place on the courts

68 A lively ballgame is taking place in center court in this model. Textiles are stacked along the edge of the court, suggesting these were the prizes for the enthusiastic wagering of the spectators. Model of a ballcourt; Late Formative Period, Ixtlán del Río, 300 B.C.–A.D. 200; Western Mexico, Nayarit; *pottery*, 5.5 × 8 × 13 in (14 × 20.3 × 33 cm); Los Angeles County Museum of Art (cat. 30).

been part of mortuary ballgame scenes, but any evidence for contextual association is lost.

More very early evidence supporting the use of sculpture to compose dramatic scenes comes from San Lorenzo in Veracruz, the first great Olmec site (1500–900 B.C.). This site specifically, and Olmec culture generally, exerted strong influence on succeeding cultures, thus data from excavations there are particularly significant. Ann Cyphers has recently concluded from her work at the site, that many, if not all, of the immense stone sculptures found at San Lorenzo and outliers were once positioned in scenes on the terraces of public buildings where they could be viewed by the populace from afar.[8] These scenes, in Cypher's opinion, depicted an assortment of religious myths and served to validate the ruling elite. The large stone monuments may even have been rearranged periodically in order to illustrate different stories.

One set of figures from the El Azuzul Acropolis, in the San Lorenzo area, is particularly interesting: a pair of identical male stone figures, almost life size, were discovered there in association with two stone jaguar sculptures. The two seated young men are dressed alike in matching yokes, headdresses, and loincloths. They lean forward facing the jaguars and grasp

(fig. 69). All the models were found in the modern Mexican state of Nayarit and portray (except as noted above) teams at play. Team members are depicted fallen to the ground in the act of returning the ball or standing expectantly at either end of the court, waiting for the ball to come their way. Spectators seated on the walls along the playing alley are equally part of the action; they lean forward to watch the game or talk and gesture excitedly to their neighbors.

In addition to these models we also find evidence of the ballgame in miniature ceramic groupings from burials in the West Mexican state of Colima. One such group is modeled fully in the round and the tiny figures wear heavy ballgame yokes with either a false phallus or an animal-head *hacha* attached at the front (fig. 70). Some of the West Mexican figures blow conch-shell trumpets, while others dance or perform acrobatics. It is difficult to document whether all these figurines were really ballplayers; more likely, some were performers participating in ballgame rituals. There is little doubt that entertainment formed part of the colorful events at a ballgame, so such groups wearing ballgame yokes may actually be related to the other activities of a team. Another set of figures, also dressed as ballplayers, appear at first glance to be warriors (fig. 71). They carry weapons and are posed in aggressive stances, but the spears and clubs in their hands may instead be bats and paddles used in playing the ballgame. In fact, the roles of warrior and ballplayer may often have been identical, with participants for either drawn from the same groups or teams of young men.[11]

Closely related to the Colima groups are miniature figurines from tombs at the Middle Formative site of Chupícuaro in Michoacán. Hundreds of solid ceramic male and female figurines were recovered at that site during a hurried salvage operation before the construction of a dam. Like their Colima counterparts, certain groups of the figurines are very stylized, wearing ballgame yokes, arm bands, and leg guards;

70 *(above)* Ballplayer figurine group; Late Formative Period, Colima, 200 B.C.–A.D. 300; Mexico, West Coast; *pottery*; 1.5 × 1 × 0.3 in (3.8 × 2.5 × 0.6 cm) average; San Antonio Museum of Art (cat. 48).

69 In this model of a ballcourt spectators watch a wrestling match taking place in the center of the ballcourt. The figure observing the action may be a referee. Late Formative/Early Classic Periods, 200 B.C.–A.D. 300; Mexico, Nayarit, Ixtlán del Río; *pottery*; 6.5 × 14.5 × 11 in (16.5 × 36.8 × 27.9 cm); Worcester Art Museum, Massachusetts.

71 Figurines of ballplayers or warriors with bats or weapons. Late Formative Period, 300 B.C.–A.D. 300; Mexico, Colima; *pottery*; h. 6 in (15.2 cm) average. Private collection.

many hold balls, play musical instruments or wear phallic yokes.

It is easy to imagine that these various groups of early Western Mexican figurines were once arranged in scenes depicting rituals or festive

72 Female ballplayer figurine; Late Classic Period, Huastec, A.D. 800–1000; Mexico, Gulf Coast; *pottery*; 8 × 3.5 × 1.5 in (20.3 × 8.9 × 3.8 cm); Denver Art Museum (cat. 54).

events associated with the ballgame. In each of the groups described above, the ballgame-related figures fall into sets that visually appear to have been made by the hand of a single artist or workshop. Their costumes and accoutrements are distinct from those of other figures in the same region and certainly suggest they were intended to be participants in ballgame scenes. Although there is not sufficient evidence to be certain of such arrangements, the grouped figurines from the El Opeño tombs and the platform models of ballcourts and village life from tombs in Nayarit and Jalisco indicate that this may have been the case.

Other groups of stylized ballgame figures dating from the Early Classic Period (A.D. 300–600) were found in the Huastec region of Veracruz. All of these slender figurines, both male and female, wear heavy, padded ballgame yokes (fig. 72). In addition, some wear protective arm- and kneepads or carry balls, but most simply stand erect with arms hanging at both sides. Again, there has not been sufficient excavation in this region to document the arrangement of these figures in the tombs. However, they form a distinctive, standardized group within the figurine tradition of the Veracruz region. Their great number and their padded yokes and equipment suggest that entire teams may have been made to compose ritual ballgame scenes in burials.

During the Classic Period (A.D. 300–900) finely made individual ballgame figurines with the appropriate gear are present throughout Mesoamerica, but generally we lack evidence that they were once grouped as sets or teams. An exception to this are several ceramic groups found in tombs in the Mexican state of Oaxaca.

One such group scene, now in the collection of the Denver Art Museum, comes from the Isthmus of Tehuantepec in southern Oaxaca (fig. 73). The figures were found as a group, and each is associated with elements of the ballgame. The scene consists of six ceramic figurines, two removable masks, and a throne. There are four male figures, one seated and three standing, and two female figures, one seated and one standing. The eyes of all six figures, as well as those on the two masks, are closed, as if dead, suggesting the scene is taking place in the Underworld.

The throne, or possibly a litter, could have been occupied by either of the two seated figurines. All the male figures wear a wide textile yoke-like belt, protective bands on their arms,

and elaborate jewelry consisting of nose rings, ear ornaments, and bead necklaces. Two of the standing males hold balls in their upraised right hands; the seated male figure probably also held a ball, but the hand is broken off from the upraised right arm. The fourth male holds a handstone, or *manopla*, in his left hand and what may be an *atlatl* (a type of spearthrower) in his right. The females wear skirts, wrist bands, and elaborate jewelry. The seated female has a rectangular implement strapped to her right hand, perhaps a *manopla*. The heads of both females are rudimentary, as the full head masks were meant to cover them.

The masking suggests performance; perhaps the two masked women played specific parts in a mythic drama. Interestingly the standing female figurine carries a large netted turtle (or turtle shell) on her back, held by a tumpline. The giant turtle often symbolizes the earth in Mesoamerican iconography.[12] This scene, in particular, may relate to an episode in the *Popol Vuh* when the Hero Twins assist the Maize God (their resurrected father) to emerge from a split in a giant turtle shell. In these resurrection scenes we commonly see the twins and the Maize God wearing ballgame yokes as they ascend to earth after defeating the Lords of the Underworld in a ballgame.[13]

It is interesting that certain elements such as ballgame yokes, protective arm and leg padding, *manoplas*, rubber balls, and the presence of females dressed as ballplayers, link the oldest group of figurines from the El Opeño ballgame scene with those that follow. The West Mexican miniatures, the simple, yet elegant figures from the Huastec region, and the ritual ballgame scenes from Oaxaca and Campeche all have similar characteristics. The teams or scenes represented are separated from each other by several thousand years, yet the continuity of ritual and equipment is clear. Perhaps many more ceramic groupings once existed, but the figurines that composed the scenes have been dispersed and removed from their original mortuary context. Probably only the most aesthetically pleasing figures were preserved for museums and the art market. In spite of this, the few known groups give us a concrete glimpse of teams and ritual events associated with the ballgame.

The ballgame continued to be a major ritual activity in Mesoamerica until the time of the Spanish Conquest in 1521. Maya pottery and stone sculpture, Teotihuacan wall murals, and the carved ballcourt walls at El Tajín all attest to the game's importance throughout the Classic Period. During the Terminal Classic (A.D. 800–1000), ballcourts proliferate at many

73 The masks worn by these figures suggest they were actors in a mythic pageant. The eyes of the figures are closed, indicating that this ballgame scene is taking place in the Underworld. Late Classic Period, Oaxaca, A.D. 700–900; Mexico, Isthmus of Tehuantepec; *pottery*; 8.25 × 4.5 × 3.5 in (21 × 11.5 × 8.9 cm) tallest figure; Denver Art Museum (cat. 59).

75 *(opposite)* The press-molded scene on this vessel shows a squatting ballplayer holding the head of a just-decapitated victim. Blood spouting from the neck of the victim has turned into serpents. Tripod vessel with ballgame sacrifice scene; Middle Classic Period; Maya, A.D. 400–700; Guatemala, Tiquisate; *pottery*; 7.6 × 5.4 in (19.4 × 13.7 cm); Denver Art Museum (cat. 128).

74 This relief from Chichén Itzá depicts an elaborate human sacrifice, probably staged in the ballcourt itself. Late Classic/Early Postclassic Periods, A.D. 800–1200. (See also figs. 36 and 40.)

sites; El Tajín has 18, Chichén Itzá 13, and Cantona 24 (see Taladoire). At the Terminal Classic Maya site of Chichén Itzá the side walls of the immense ballcourt are carved with two complete teams standing in long lines behind their captains. The captains face each other over the image of a large ball decorated with a human skeleton head. The standing captain holds in one hand the decapitated head of his kneeling opponent. From the beheaded captain's neck issue streams of blood represented by twining serpents (fig. 74). In the Middle Classic Period, the same scene is incised on the sides of tripod cylinder pots from Tiquisate on the Pacific coast of Guatemala (fig. 75), and similar decapitated figures with twined serpents representing blood are carved on ballgame stelae from the contemporary site of El Aparicio (cat. 132 and 133) in the state of Veracruz.

In the Late Postclassic Period (A.D. 1200–1519), scenes with players, patron deities, ballcourts, and sacrificial victims are frequently painted on the pages of the Mixtec codices (screenfold books) and, beginning in 1519, the Aztec form of the game starts to be well described by the first Spanish chroniclers. During the Postclassic Period the game seems to change from a mainly religious to a more secular form, but the teams, rituals, and bouncing rubber ball remain as constant and significant elements of Mesoamerican culture.

Performance on the Court

Ballcourt construction in Mesoamerica entailed a major commitment of resources by a community or an individual ruler. As far as we know, the courts were primarily dedicated to the playing of a ceremonial game of chance by two opposing teams. Nonetheless, I think we can speculate that other events might also have taken place there; surely the expensive stadiums were used more than the few times a year required for ceremonial games associated with seasonal and astronomical activities. Undoubtedly, the game was also played for fun and exercise by men, boys, and possibly some females, either in the courts or local fields. Perhaps aspiring athletes practiced on the ballcourts; and certainly some form of professional training or apprenticeship must have taken place. From the colorful Tepantitla Palace murals at Teotihuacan (see Uriarte) depicting a range of ballgames played with bats, sticks, and paddles,[13] and from figurines carrying various types of playing equipment and wearing protective padding on different parts of the body (see Scott), we can assume that diverse forms of the game must have existed. Particular games may have been linked with specific gods and played on the ballcourts during rituals honoring them.

The courts may also have been used for non-ballgame-related events. As mentioned above, one ballcourt model from Nayarit (see fig. 69) does not depict a ballgame; instead two figures are shown wrestling at center court and a third figure, not seen in the illustration of the model, stands behind the court wall as if waiting to be called onto the playing field. Also known from West Mexico are a number of pairs of fighting figures. Colima figurines sometimes depict pairs of ballplayers locked in combat with one player pinning the other to the ground ready to deliver a death blow. It is interesting to speculate that these figures might represent gladiators or scenes of punishment, or perhaps human sacrifice.[14]

What other ways might ballcourts have been utilized in the ceremonial life of kings and commoners during the pre-Columbian period? Obviously, the courts were intended above all for playing a ritual ballgame, but we should also consider the possibility of their use as stages for pageantry, festivals, and drama. Thought-provoking comparisons can be made to events in other parts of the world. For example, in the Roman empire gladiators fought wild animals and each other to a bloody death in order to entertain the public. Spectators spent entire days

at these sporting festivals diverted by rich feasting, music, drama, markets, and politics. The many sports arenas of the empire pulsed with the excitement and activity that tied the masses to Rome. Medieval Europe invites another comparison. As in ancient Mesoamerica, the general population was illiterate. Religious pageants brought the passion of Christ and the stories of the Bible out of the churches and into the streets. Usually referred to as "Mystery" plays,[15] these dramas, sometimes involving whole villages in their production, were an important ecclesiastical method of instructing people in the lessons and stories of the New Testament. Their vivid imagery provided both education and escape for the local masses. A modern-day example of this is the Bavarian town of Oberammergau, where the whole population still joins in acting out the story of the Passion of Christ for large groups of spectators and pilgrims (fig. 76). Not unlike ancient Mesoamerica, the reassuring iconography of a familiar tale helped medieval communities make sense of a confusing

76 "The Road to Golgotha," one of the dramatic scenes from the passion play at Oberammergau, Germany. This mythic pageant based on the life of Christ has been staged since the 16th century. Similar mythic plays revolving around ancient Mesoamerican stories of creation were no doubt regularly staged in ballcourts.

preparation for the staged contest against royal protagonists. The competition ended with the death of the captive players.

Other myths were also acted out on Maya ballcourts. As discussed earlier, relief carvings on the immense ballcourt at Chichén Itzá clearly illustrate a different ritual, one concerned with decapitation rites and fertility of the earth. On the great Chichén Itzá court, large teams competed against each other on a playing alley with stone ballgame rings on the walls at the center. The game ended with human sacrifice by decapitation. Both at Chichén Itzá and at Central Mexican sites, *tzompantli* (skull racks) were placed in the plaza outside the courts to hold the decapitated heads. The display must have provided a constant reminder of the basic significance of the ballgame, a dramatic debt offering to the gods of a human life in exchange for an orderly universe (fig. 77).

Elegant figurines have been recovered from burials on Jaina Island and nearby sites in the modern state of Campeche. These figures suggest other mythic dramas. Many of the Jaina-style figurines are costumed as warriors, kings, gods, and ballplayers (fig. 78), dressed perhaps to perform in a theatrical event; some of them have removable head masks, indicating they may have played more than one role in a dramatic presentation. A number of other figures in the Jaina tradition are depicted as hunters with blowpipes, or as dancers wearing a variety of human and animal masks. These surely reflect the mythic stories of the Hero Twins and recall their many adventures in the Underworld as they battled the gods of darkness and pestilence on the ballcourt. Figurines of Jaina women most frequently depict Ixchel, goddess of the moon, weaving, and fertility. Though considered the consort of the sun, in her role as the moon, ruler of the night sky, she was seen as his opponent who must be defeated to allow the sun to rise each morning. Perhaps when dressed as a female ballplayer she performed on the ballcourt in the reenactment of this cosmic drama. All of these dramatic rituals would have been accompanied by elaborate colorful parades of dancers, musicians, priests, and costumed attendants. The magnificent processional murals from the site of Bonampak in Chiapas, Mexico, clearly illustrate such performances, recording for us their importance in ceremonial activities at the royal courts of the Maya region.[17]

Another example worth consideration is carved on the walls of the South Ballcourt at the

77 Skull racks (*tzompantli*) are usually situated adjacent to ballcourts— the heads of decapitated victims would be displayed on the large platform. This detail is from a skull rack at Chichén Itzá, Yucatán, Mexico. Late Classic/Early Postclassic Periods, Maya, A.D. 800–1200.

world and brought them a feeling of spiritual and political unity.

Drama on the Courts

Mesoamerica's ancient ballcourts may also have served as theaters or locales for theatrical events. A number of scholars[16] have argued convincingly that among the Maya, the games, as well as other public events, were frequently more like stylized drama than sport—with music, dance, colorful ceremonies, and human sacrifices (see Miller). The ballcourts were seen as entrances to the Underworld, that dark region where the Hero Twins were called to play ball against the Lords of Death. The story of this legendary game, often painted on ceramic vessels or carved on stone panels, was dramatically acted out on the courts by Maya kings dressed as ballplayers. In the reenactment the kings played against captives taken in battle then tortured and weakened in

Terminal Classic/Early Postclassic (A.D. 800–1200) site of El Tajín in the modern state of Veracruz. Beginning around A.D. 800, this city experienced a population explosion. Numerous satellite communities sprang up around the central polity, probably as the result of an influx of emigrants from the Valley of Mexico after the fall of the massive city of Teotihuacan. The changing demographics at the site produced a need to solidify new alliances and legitimize the power of El Tajín's rulers. In light of this, several scholars have addressed the complicated iconography of the South Ballcourt.[18] Among them, Rex Koontz has interpreted a related complex of powerful images, positing that the El Tajín ballcourts were not only used for games but were venues for forging alliances between diverse groups of warriors, for legitimizing rulership, for enacting ceremonial pre- and post-warfare rituals, and for subsequent human sacrifices.[19] The images depicting this ceremony are found on six carved panels on the playing field walls of the main (South) ballcourt. According to Koontz, the sequence presents two men dressed as ballplayers meeting on the court to form an alliance. This is followed by one of these warrior/ballplayers receiving weapons (*atlatl* darts) from a deity that is associated with a feathered serpent image. This gift legitimizes his elite position as well as the pending battle. On his return from the successful battle, a victim is offered as a sacrifice to the gods. In exchange for the severed head of the ballgame sacrifice, the human receives the symbolic implements of rulership. These rituals, carried out on the ballcourt, presented a lavish spectacle, documented by the scenes of elaborate costumes, music, and dance shown on the ballcourt panels.

In addition to the reenactment of the above drama, it is also probable that the 18 ballcourts at El Tajín served as arenas for playing out pent-up aggression. Certainly the influx of new ethnic populations gave rise to new social pressures, tensions, and conflicts that may have been played out in ritual violence on the ballcourt. In this instance, ballgames may have acted as a catharsis for an ethnically diverse community, minimizing the possibility of internal warfare.

An elaborately carved pair of shell bracelets, also from the Gulf Coast region of Veracruz, echoes the warfare iconography of the El Tajín ballcourt (fig. 79). While size prohibits the depiction of the entire story, the delicately incised design on the bracelets clearly shows a warrior/ballplayer receiving weapons, probably *atlatl* darts, from a seated female who emerges

from the maw of a twining feathered serpent deity. These thematic elements are comparable, in shorthand version, with those portrayed on the sculptured walls at El Tajín's South Ballcourt.

Until recently, the 18 ballcourts at El Tajín were considered the largest number at any one site, but now excavations at the city of Cantona in the modern state of Puebla have revealed 24.[20] This amazing site flourished between A.D. 600–1000 and, like El Tajín, it appears to have received an influx of new populations during the Terminal Classic Period. Cantona sits midway on an ancient trade route running between the Central Highlands of Mexico and the Gulf Coast. What little has so far been published indicates that the site was located in dry desert country (*malpais*) and covered 12 sq. km (almost 5 sq. miles). It was a heavily fortified military citadel with access limited by stone fortifications and a moat. The numerous ballcourts at the site were enclosed within and among 3,000 elite living compounds, pyramids, and ceremonial plazas on a mountainside in the south unit of the city. Situated as it was on an important trade route, Cantona controlled commercial activities over a wide region.

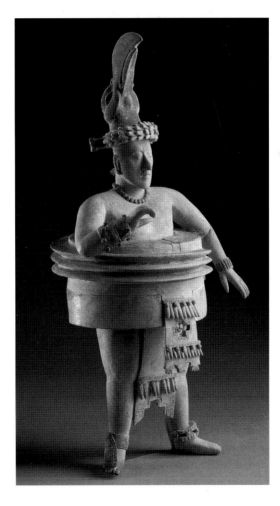

78 The elaborate costume of this ballplayer, with his three-part yoke and bird headdress, suggests a role in a ritual performance rather than an actual rough-and-tumble game. Late Classic Period, Maya, A.D. 650–850; Mexico, Jaina Island; *pottery*; 13.5 × 7 in (34.2 × 17.8 cm); The Art Museum, Princeton University (cat. 106).

79 Themes of the ballgame and warfare frequently overlap. On this pair of shell bracelets, a warrior/ ballplayer receives weapons from a female deity. Postclassic Period, Huastec, A.D. 900–1000; Mexico, Gulf Coast; *shell*; each 3 × 4.6 in (7.8 × 11.7 cm); Denver Museum of Nature and Science (cat. 92).

The presence of the 24 ballcourts, however, is still amazing and unexplained. Nevertheless, we can speculate that, like El Tajín, the city must have been occupied, or at least used in transit, by diverse groups of people who were probably different ethnically, linguistically, and certainly culturally. Conspicuous social differences among the elite personages of Cantona, wealthy traders, soldiers, porters, and slaves must also have been glaringly evident and, consciously or unconsciously, in such a situation it seems likely that escalating tensions and aggression between groups may have been addressed on the ballcourts rather than the battlefield. We can also speculate that in a large military trading center in the middle of the *malpais* both residents and transients would have looked to the ballgame for entertainment as well as for colorful ceremonies and rituals. As a result, the traditional gambling associated with ballgames during the Postclassic Period may have been a particularly attractive pastime in such an isolated situation.

Finally, let us look at the Aztec ballgame that took place on the great court in the central plaza of the capital city of Tenochtitlan. By the Aztec period (*c.* A.D. 1400) the game seems to have become largely secular, though religious pageantry still surrounded the event. From Spanish descriptions we know that the nobility of the Aztec world took great delight in the ballgame and either played it themselves or fielded professional competitive teams.[21] Betting formed a major aspect of the sport, and both spectators and players gambled heavily on the outcome of this ritual game of chance. The nobility never seemed to lack the wealth to pay their gambling debts, but addictive gambling by people of low status could bring disaster. In an early 16th-century chronicle, Fray Diego Durán reports:

> They … gambled their homes, their corn granaries, their maguey plants. They sold their children in order to bet and even staked themselves and became slaves to be sacrificed later if they were not ransomed. [22]

The stakes of the game were also high for the players. Blows from the heavy rubber ball could leave them badly injured, or even dead, but the dangers apparently paled in comparison to the glory enjoyed by the greatest heroic athletes. According to the Spanish chronicles, these professional players were awarded honors and special privileges at court, often becoming the intimates of kings. The most lauded player was he who actually managed to send the ball through one of the stone rings placed at the center of each wall of the ballcourt—a rare occurrence. Usually the game was won by the accumulation of points, as the passing of the ball through the ring was so difficult that as soon as it happened the game was over and

> The man who sent the ball through the stone ring was surrounded by all. They honored him, sang songs of praise to him, and joined him in dancing. He was given a very special award of feathers or mantles and breechcloths, something very highly prized. But what he most prized was the honor involved: that was his great wealth. For he was honored as a man who had vanquished many and had won a battle.[23]

The ballcourt spectacle in the city center of the Aztec capital of Tenochtitlan must have been noisy and colorful, and, as is indicated in the above quote, ceremonies surrounding the sport and its heroes must have included music and dancing by both the spectators and the players. This use of music, dance, and song at ritual events was recorded by Fray Bernardino de Sahagún, who tells of long lines of colorfully attired dancers moving through the city streets, and describes ceremonies in the sacred precincts as being accompanied by chanting and singers.[24] This relationship is reinforced by caches found buried near the court. One cache, found in the plaza near the main ballcourt, included a stone statue of Xochipilli, the god of flowers, music, springtime, and the ballgame (fig. 80). Associated with the deity figure were a group of miniature stone musical instruments, two small stone models of a ballcourt, two highly polished stone balls—one black and one white—and an obsidian knife.[25] These symbolic objects clearly indicate that despite a more secular approach to the game during the Late Postclassic Period, the rituals and original intent of the team sport remained intact: the black and white balls still reflecting the cosmic battle of the diurnal sun and the nocturnal sun, and the knife continuing to link the theme of human sacrifice to the sacred and political needs of the more secular Aztec empire.

It is evident that the ancient Mesoamerican ballgames expressed religious beliefs, were an arena for secular activities, and perhaps fulfilled psychological needs as well. Through drama and pageantry the team sport both reflected and influenced the culture from which it sprang— a stratified theocracy, rich with colorful ritual. This is particularly true in the area of human relationships where teams, or by extension Mesoamerican societies, committed themselves to group cooperation and strict governance according to set rules. In various roles, team games served as a substitute for war, as a showcase for the wealth and power of kings, as a vehicle for athletic contests, and as an outlet for gambling. In addition, the ballcourt itself was a stage for drama, music, dance, and entertainment.

Over its 3,000-year history however, the pre-Columbian ballgame always remained a ceremonial game of chance—a human team symbolically pitted against the gods and the frightening powers of the natural world. Through the reenactment of myths, cyclical rituals, and human sacrifice the people of pre-Hispanic Mesoamerica battled desperately to influence the universe and control the cosmic forces. At times, it was probably difficult to be certain where ritual ended and entertainment began. Although often unrecognized, this is still true in modern ballgames that also allow aggressive tendencies and unrestricted feelings to be acted out within the confines of the playing field.

Both today and long ago athletic heroes were so admired that they become the comrades of kings (or presidents) and wealth and honor are, and were, awarded to the winning teams. Even symbolic activities remain intrinsic in modern games, as songs and chants echo through the stadiums, and dancers and vendors of food and memorabilia vie with players on the field for the spectators' attention. Unlike pre-Columbian Mesoamerica, where the inherent religious significance of the game was clearly understood, modern audiences are less apt to recognize the ancient ceremonies lurking beneath the surface of sporting events. Nevertheless, the sacred and secular aspects still blend, and our human need for ritual and order, for spectacle and for bonding, is dramatically acted out on the ballcourts of both yesterday and today.

80 Xochipilli was the god of flowers, music, and dancing. He was also the patron deity of the ballgame. Ceremonies honoring Xochipilli were an integral aspect of Central Mexican ballgames during the Late Postclassic Period. Ballcourt offerings containing miniature musical instruments are a clear reference to this deity. Seated figure of Xochipilli; Late Postclassic Period, A.D. 1325–1521; Central Mexico, Tenochtitlan; *stone*; 38 × 14 in (95.5 × 35.5 cm); MNA (cat. 117).

MARY MILLER

6 THE MAYA BALLGAME: REBIRTH IN THE COURT OF LIFE AND DEATH

The Mesoamerican ballgame is a fascinating thing: both the game and the rubber ball have intrigued outsiders and observers ever since they set foot in the region more than 500 years ago. The courts of Europe were agog at their first sight of trained, muscular ballplayers from Mexico; Fray Sahagún's comments about this strange, exotic material inform the reader that it is "bouncing, noisy, noise-making," so that even its aural qualities were astonishing.[1] But the ballgame also absorbed the attention of ancient Mesoamericans. We know this because they left behind a set of material remains for the ballgame that differs both quantitatively and qualitatively from all others.

To understand what I mean, we might consider any other ritual of ancient Mesoamerica. We can think about the rites of passage of a Mesoamerican leader—an *ahau* among the Maya, for example, or a *tlatoani* among the Aztec. Much of the material imbued with value and power was actually perishable and probably much of it was particular. A great (but perishable, mind you) litter in which the king might be paraded around—the sort we know of from the graffiti at Tikal, Guatemala, for example—housed not only a king but also particular gods; it was refurbished and reused through time, but only ever to be sat in by the ruling king himself. The scaffold within which a new king was raised up at Piedras Negras, Mexico, may have emphasized its perishable, temporary nature, as well as the individual identity of the particular new lord, who is always named. Representations of the feature draw attention to rope lashings, swag curtains, and straw effigies, as well as to the sacrificed child at the base. None of these things lasts in the tropical rainforest and neither does the reign of any individual king.

Yet the material culture of the ballgame was to an unusual extent designed for eternity. The standard inventory of what we think of as the ballgame paraphernalia was both specific—it seems highly unlikely that *hachas* or *palmas* (see Scott) served any significant secondary purpose other than to identify winners or players—and yet generic, for such works may well have been designed to suit any winner. Most *hachas* and *palmas* that survive were made in Veracruz, but as Tatiana Proskouriakoff demonstrated half a century ago, that production was also robust in highland Guatemala (fig. 82), among the Maya, where such works were made into the Postclassic Period.[2] No example of such an object among the Maya has ever been found that names a particular owner: they emphasize, instead, the beauty of the ideal ballplayer, a young man at the peak of his powers. Additionally, the works that specify the ballgame have been more readily identifiable than much of Mesoamerica's other material culture. Since the works stand out—and for many years also seemed the province of good sport and fair play, unlike some of Mesoamerica's other rituals—they have been especially appealing to modern scholars.

The chief material remain of the ballgame among the

81 The rubber ball divides the scene on this cylinder vessel into two groups of opposing players. An additional player provides musical accompaniment. Late Classic Period, Maya, A.D. 600–800; Mexico, Campeche; *pottery*; 8.25 × 6.25 in (21 × 15.8 cm); National Museum of the American Indian (cat. 108).

82 Although most *hachas* and *palmas* come from Veracruz, they were made in the Maya region, such as this Maize God *hacha*. Late Classic Period, Maya, A.D. 700–900; Mexico, Chiapas, Palenque; *stone*; h. 12 in (30.5 cm); Art Institute of Chicago (cat. 136).

83 Two drawings of a graffito of a ballgame at Tikal, Guatemala. Palace observers scratched an image of the ballgame in play, although this particular palace building, 5D-43, did not provide direct observation of the court. Note in the lower version of the drawing that what looks like the plan of a ballcourt has also been attempted.

84 Incised scene of ballplayers along the wall of Structure K6-K at Piedras Negras, Guatemala. Two ballplayers are poised in play, while the ball itself is not represented. With the striking rendering of the back view of the figure at left, the artist has also understood how to capture the human body in various postures, almost as if a single individual posed for both views.

Maya is, of course, the ballcourt itself, the architectural setting where the game was played. As with all Maya architecture, the ballcourt varied dramatically in size, location, and scope at different Maya cities. At Tikal, the centrally located court seems almost marginal, given its relatively small scale, until one considers that the dominating feature of the Great Plaza, Temple I, forms one of its end zones, and that extensive viewing areas were created by the platforms of the Central Acropolis, Tikal's principal palace complex. Palace observers scratched the odd ballgame graffito into the walls, providing a more direct sketch of play than we find in works composed for more discerning clients, even though the palace wall where this particular image was found did not provide a direct view of the court (fig. 83). At Piedras Negras, ballcourts form part of the royal palace groupings, as if ballcourts, like sweatbaths, may have belonged to particular lineages. But the most dramatic

ballcourt belongs to Copán, Honduras. There, the main ballcourt (for there are other less grand ones) functions as a microcosm of both the entire site and the larger Copán valley. The ballcourt's long parallel and sloping sides mimic the valley, and its northern end guides the eye to the open saddle in the distance, the great cleft akin to the very form that the Maya gave to the personified mountains. In replicating such a space in the ballcourt, the Maya channeled the power of the earth into the space of humankind. The Copán court reveals the natural world to be the framing walls of nature's own court, with all of Copán its alleyway.

Despite the range of size of Maya courts, almost all evidence suggests that just two players saw action on a single team at once. The Tikal graffito shows a pair of opposing players, each with a reserve standing right behind him, much like the way play is shown on Maya pots (fig. 81). Incised into the slabs that form one of the walls for play at Piedras Negras is a pair of players, seemingly team-mates, who are rendered with dramatic foreshortening—and without a representation of the ball, forcing the viewer to conjure it up, in play (fig. 84). A few pots suggest that three players may have been engaged at once, but it is easy to imagine that no more than four players, two per side, may well have faced off in any given round of play.

Like most aspects of Maya culture, Late Classic (A.D. 600–900) ballgame

material is the best preserved, if only because the sample from the vastly expanded populations in the 7th and 8th centuries is so much greater. The subject of the ballgame certainly appeared during the Early Classic (A.D. 300–600) era, but even the noble title, *pits*, or "ballplayer," rarely appears until late in Classic times, although this may simply be a factor of the relatively fewer number of texts that survive from the period.[3] Particularly during the 8th century, Maya artists created all sorts of works celebrating the ballgame. Some of these were the most generic— say, *hachas*—while others range to the most specific, in which a particular Maya lord might be named as the winner or loser of ballgame play.

Rules of the Game

Players used their hands only to put the ball in play, and then otherwise ricocheted the ball off the walls using upper arms, hips, and thighs. But the balls themselves were dangerous: heavy and sometimes moving at great speed, such a ball could break a bone, if not a neck, or damage internal organs. The size of the ball must have varied greatly, although some representations, as, for example, at Chichén Itzá (see fig. 74), can have no relation to the size of the actual ball used in the very court where the representation occurs. The huge ball of the Chichén Itzá Great Ballcourt could not have been bounced high enough even to make contact with the diminutive rings set 20 ft (6 m) above the alley—not to mention actually passing through them! No Maya rubber ballgame balls have survived archaeologically, but modern balls of northern Mexico and archaeologically excavated Olmec balls provide evidence for a ball never more than 12 in (30 cm) in diameter and sometimes quite a bit smaller. The representation of human skulls on the ball, as at Chichén Itzá, may suggest that the Maya made hollow balls by placing skulls in the center—thus lightening them and improving their bounce.

Some works of art provide rich detail of the protective armor that ballplayers donned. Because the most powerful strokes emanated from the hips, players wore their most extensive padding at the middle of the body, usually wrapped around waist yokes. These yokes were probably made of wood, since few survive from the Maya lowlands, although they commonly survive in stone elsewhere. But the Maya padding is usually represented as if quilted— perhaps cotton cloth filled with unspun cotton or with kapok, the silky product of the ceiba tree that until recently filled life-preservers.

Long hipcloths are deer hides, brightly painted and trimmed with feathers; these provided additional protection. On some works Maya players are shown with wrapped legs and lower arms, and at least on the highly life-like figurines from the island of Jaina, players are almost always revealed as right-handed, although presumably a left-handed player, like a modern baseball pitcher—or, in fact, an Aztec warrior armed with a *macana* (obsidian-spiked club)—would have had some advantage. Because players lunged to make contact with the ball, a posture represented particularly vividly by some Jaina figurines, an important piece of equipment was the kneepad (fig. 85), a protective element that was probably difficult to keep in place during hard-fought play.

Most carved stone ballplayer representations feature the headdresses of Maya gods. The Art

85 Ballplayer wearing a bird headdress; Late Classic Period, Maya, A.D. 600–800; Mexico, Campeche, Jaina Island; *pottery*; 7.8 × 3.6 in (19.7 × 9.2 cm); Mint Museum of Art (cat. 104).

86 Dressed in balloon headdress, skull pectoral, and skeletal Tlaloc waist figure, the player at left on this panel appears as the victorious warrior destined to defeat the fallen player at right, whose sacrifice is prefigured by the punched cloth cut-outs that he wears. Carved panel with ballplayers; Late Classic Period, Maya, A.D. 700–900; Guatemala, Usumacinta River region; Art Institute of Chicago.

87 This lively ballplayer vessel features two teams of two players each, who face off, while a conch shell trumpeter and two dancers with rattles provide musical accompaniment. The fallen player with deer headdress may have met his demise. Late Classic Period, Maya, A.D. 700–900; Guatemala, northern Petén region; *pottery*; St. Louis Art Museum.

Institute of Chicago panel from Site Q shows the victorious player at left in what can be recognized as the headdress of a god of war and sacrifice, even though that part of the panel is damaged (fig. 86). At least one other ballplayer panel from the Site Q sequence wears the headdress of Chac, often mistakenly thought of as a benign god of rain, but who frequently wielded his lightning axe as a god of human sacrifice. Yet most Jaina figurines and ballplayers on painted ceramics don deer and vulture headdresses, or sometimes the broad-brimmed sombrero—what is usually called the "hunter's hat."[4] As Nicholas Hellmuth has shown, hunters of deer wear their prey. The deer headdress is the most common headgear in painted ballgame ceramics. The hunter's hat is

characteristic of the Hero Twins, the great mythic ballplayers and blowgunners (in other words, hunters of birds) about whom I will have more to say below. What links these two sets of headdresses—Maya gods of war and sacrifice and hunting garb—is that war and hunting were linked in the Mesoamerican mind: war was sometimes called the "hunting of men," and the dry season was the time for both activities. Both hunting and making war were the province of noble young men, and these events could culminate in the ballgame.

Architecture of the Ballgame

One of the more puzzling features of the representations of the Maya ballgame is the way

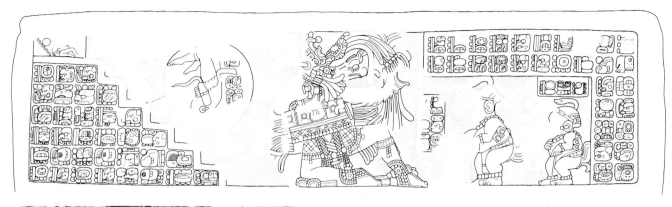

the architectural setting is portrayed. As we have already noted, the ballcourt can be center stage of Maya public space. With its two parallel walls, generally with sides that slope toward one another, the ballcourt would seemingly be a straightforward subject for representation—as indeed is sometimes the case (see fig. 83). But, in fact, when architecture is represented, artists typically sketched in what would seem to be stairs, rather than the sloping walls. Some such representations may feature the flight of steps in the end zone, which were constructed, for example, at both Yaxchilan and Copán. The St. Louis ballgame pot may feature one of these end zone constructions, where the musicians provide musical support and the scorekeepers or referees may have the best vantage points (fig. 87). The artist of this pot strives also to show that play of the game, in front of these stairs, and presumably within the court itself, is ongoing. In an innovation that we may read as only partly successful, the animated squiggles at the feet and around the body and ball reveal both sound and active movement. Such conventions are common in modern cartoons but exceedingly rare in any earlier means of representation.

Some other representations of play of the game against stairs explicitly show the stairs to be the risers of pyramids, where two players face off against what looks like a lopsided wedding cake. Presumably such representations relate to that of

88 Step 7, Hieroglyphic Stairs 2, Mexico, Chiapas, Yaxchilan, Structure 33. Dated A.D. 744, probably executed *c.* A.D. 755. Bird Jaguar the Great plays ball against the steps of a great pyramid, probably Structure 33 itself, and defeats a captive rendered as the ball. Note the miniature scene inset at upper left (*detail, left*).

Step 7 of Yaxchilan Hieroglyphic Stairs 2, where King Bird Jaguar the Great poises to strike a ball that features a trussed captive on its surface, upside-down and perhaps with a broken neck (fig. 88). This captive—and others, such as the captive described in the text of Tikal Altar 8—are the captives of war, captives who were dispatched in a public ritual that probably brought the ballgame to an end.

Like the Yaxchilan step, the Chicago ballgame panel (see fig. 86) was probably a central step in an assemblage of related but individual scenes, including the National Museum of the American Indian and the Kislak panels (figs. 89 and 90), and these may have been set into a flight of stairs or perhaps directly into a ballcourt. The Yaxchilan step comprises the top riser of Structure 33, whence the king would have surveyed the plaza below, including the ballcourt. In fact, with its inset miniature representation of a player and a ball against a flight of steps, the step seems explicitly to point out that the representation pertains to this very place, atop Structure 33. And this trussed unfortunate soul is being bounced to his death on the steps of Structure 33, the temple Bird Jaguar dedicated to celebrate his own rise to power. The Chicago panel portrays the victor at left in the costume of a victorious warrior, signaled in part by the skull around the neck and the balloon headdress. Sprawled in front of him is a warrior in defeat, his legs too tangled to move, the ball heading straight for his head. The many birds of his costume signal his demise and preparation for death, as does the cut and punched cloth that

swaddles him. Other captives, too, prepare for either life or death in the ballgame. A Jaina figurine who holds a ball (fig. 91) has been shorn and tonsured, indicating, as it did for Samson in the Bible, a certain death.

Sacrifice, Death, and the Maize God

For many years the Maya ballgame of the southern lowlands had been thought to be different from the ballgame portrayed at Chichén Itzá, where human sacrifice is depicted explicitly.[5] But what the Yaxchilan and Chicago panels reveal is that the Maya game had the potential to end in sacrifice throughout the 1st millennium A.D., and not just at Chichén Itzá.

The role of human sacrifice in the ballgame is also evident in the great Maya religious and

89 Panel with Hero Twin ballplayer; Late Classic Period, Maya, A.D. 600–800; Guatemala, Usumacinta River region; *stone*; 10.9 × 15 × 0.8 in (27.6 × 38.1 × 2 cm); National Museum of the American Indian (cat. 112).

ballplayer, but his progeny, the demigod heroes that humans emulate in defying the gods of death, are masters of the game. Life is both taken and renewed in the ballcourt. The ballcourt is the place where fortunes are reversed, and then reversed again. It is the ultimate place of transition, and the Maya seem to have found this

historical narrative, the *Popol Vuh*, recorded by a Quiché nobleman in the mid-16th century. There, following the story of the sequential attempts by the gods to create a sentient being, the reader learns of the story of first a pair of brothers, Hun Hunahpu and Vucub Hunahpu, and later the pair of twin brothers, Hunahpu and Xbalanque, born to Hun Hunahpu by a princess of Xibalba, the Quiché Underworld. Expert ballplayers on earth, Hun Hunahpu and Vucub Hunahpu accept the call from the Underworld gods to join them in the ballgame, but the boys from earth are no match for the wily old gods. Quickly dispatched both by guile and in play of the ballgame, the brothers are sacrificed.

The decapitated head of Hun Hunahpu is stuck in a calabash tree, where its spittle impregnates a young goddess, who must then flee to earth. She bears the Hero Twins, Hunahpu and Xbalanque, who grow up to surpass their father and uncle in skill and wiliness. Called once again to Xibalba, they outwit the old gods and eventually resurrect their father, whose body was buried in the ballcourt. According to the story, the Hero Twins ascend to the heavens, becoming the sun and possibly Venus.

Although the story is not transparent, scholars have realized in recent years that Hun Hunahpu, who is decapitated and then brought back to life, is the Maize God, and so the story of the life cycle of maize also lies at the heart of the matter.[6] Hun Hunahpu himself is not the greatest

90 *(left)* Panel with God N ballplayer; Late Classic Period, Maya, A.D. 600–800; Guatemala, Usumacinta River region; *stone*, 10.9 × 15 × 0.8 in (27.6 × 38.1 × 2 cm); Kislak Foundation, Inc. (cat. 113).

91 War captive ballplayer; Late Classic Period, Maya, A.D. 700–900; Mexico, Campeche, Jaina Island; *pottery*; h. 9.3 in (23.7 cm); New Orleans Museum of Art (cat. 124).

92 Hero Twin ballcourt marker; Late Classic Period, Maya, A.D. 550–850; Mexico, Chiapas; *stone*; 23 × 24 in (59.8 × 61 cm); North Carolina Museum of Art (cat. 39).

93 Drawing of a detail of a mural from Room 1, Bonampak. Here the young Maize God sits in front of two hooded ballplayers. They stand behind him, preparing for a ritual maize sacrifice. The young Maize God is reborn at the ballcourt and sacrificed there again as mature, ripe corn.

particular characteristic of the game absorbing. The round markers that studded the alleyway of the Maya ballcourt emphasize the liminal and dangerous qualities of the space itself (fig. 92). Most are framed by the quatrefoil that marks an opening, or portal, and the scene within is then happening elsewhere, in another time, or space, but revealed transparently to those on earth— what David Freidel, Linda Schele, and Joy Parker have called the "glass-bottom boat" effect.[7]

At Copán, heroes face off against death gods, but growing in the background is maize. The victory of the Hero

Twins liberates maize and allows the story of humankind to proceed—as in fact it does in the *Popol Vuh*, moving quickly from this supernatural era to the historical one. The ballgame seems to situate all the pieces in their appropriate places: heavenly bodies rise; humanity's required foodstuff becomes available, if seasonal, for the life cycle of maize requires annual "decapitation," or harvest; and humans themselves emerge smarter, able to parry successfully with gods, who are then often represented at a small scale.

Where modern ballgames depend on instant replay, the Maya ballgame guaranteed eventual rebirth for maize and humanity. The story of the ballgame is also one of the stories of the Maize God. In the murals at Bonampak, Mexico, the Maize God sits with ballplayers, presumably before reenacting their shared story (fig. 93). It is the Maize God who returns from the dead, and it is he that Maya kings emulate at their death. He summed up human perfection in his physiognomy and attire: he was the ideal young man, the man of the hunt or the battlefield. For many Maya kings, the Maize God epitomized the resurrection they sought in death, as, for example, on Copán Stela 11, or on the surface of King Pakal's sarcophagus at Palenque—where deceased kings rendered as the Maize God (and also as K'awil, the Maya god of lineage) rise up from the black hole, the visual presentation of Xibalba. In numerous tombs, a plate with the image of the lively Maize God, either as a whirling dancer or as a chief scribe, was placed face down over the head of the deceased, as for example at Altar de Sacrificios.[8] Those who interred the noble dead created a small breathing hole in the plate that can be likened to the "psychoduct" that linked the dead King Pakal's tomb to the outside. In this way, a king was not reborn as a Hero Twin but rather as the Maize God, young and beautiful, in whose regeneration in the ballcourt humanity would see its own cyclical rebirth. Consistently, plates feature the Maize God

or a related entity (figs. 94 and 95). In life they may have served up the first fruits of renewal; in death they offered the promise of resurrection.

Representing the Ballgame

Finally, a return to the question about the nature of the representation itself. Certain ballgame scenes are among the most complex Maya representations. Explicitly, in some of these scenes a subsequent event is implied. On the Chicago panel, for example, the fallen ballplayer is represented in the garb of the sacrificial victim, as if the next stage is foreshadowed—and presumably understood by an educated observer within the culture. In this way, the visual—where so clearly the verbal action is play—obviates the necessity for the next verbal reference, which would be death. This also makes it possible for the image to be polyvalent, and to make intelligible within a single scene what requires a series of sequential verbal statements. In this way, the Maya artist began to exceed through visual means what could be achieved textually.

Other representations call on us to conjure up some missing piece of the action. The Hudson Museum figurine (cat. 105) has taken the ball under his arm, and he looks around alertly, as if scouting for a team member to whom he can launch the ball. For another Jaina figurine, found nearly 40 years ago on the island, there is no ball in sight, yet the player remains in eternal play; the ball is absent—yet the viewer knows that it is there, somewhere. Here the artist makes us see the invisible. Were the ball to be in evidence, the motion would come to an end, so the artist has realized that only through absence can he make us see motion. At Piedras Negras (see fig. 84) the two players are carved into a single side of the court, with no ball in evidence here either. But we see their outlines almost as if we were seeing shadows or silhouettes, keeping the space in play, especially when not in use. No ball is in evidence: were it, then the scene would be frozen, instead of ever-pregnant with action. When the Maya set carved ballplayers on the sides of staircases, as they did at La Amalia or Seibal in Guatemala, they kept the play suspended. But those players framed against stairs also remind us of the sacrificial death on stairs, sometimes emphasized by the carving of captive bodies on risers or treads.

Perhaps this is, in the end, the source of the fascination of the ballgame: in this lively group of representations among the Maya there is also the raw anxiety of a contest that ends in death. But the works themselves, even where death is

94 The fully resurrected Maize God is dressed as a ballplayer, completing the cycle of death and rebirth. Detail drawing of plate with Maize God ballplayer; Late Classic Period, Maya, A.D. 600–900; Guatemala, Petén Region; *pottery*; 2.75 × 14 in (7 × 36 cm); Mint Museum of Art (cat. 137).

95 *(below)* Dancing in the center of this plate is the resurrected Maize God. In the circular band surrounding him are the 20 day signs of the Maya calendar. Plate with Maize God; Late Classic Period, Maya, A.D. 600–900; Guatemala, Petén Region/Tikal; *pottery*; 4 × 12 in (10.2 × 30.5 cm); Mint Museum of Art (cat. 135).

explicit or implicit, insist on a living presence, on a vibrancy rarely seen in ancient works of art—in part because what we see goes beyond what is represented, and because an anticipated rebirth is inherent in death itself. These works are alive and vivid, and in that quality, they take the viewer from the 21st century into a world of the past.

EDUARDO MATOS MOCTEZUMA

7 THE BALLCOURT IN TENOCHTITLAN

The complementary disciplines of archaeology and history are important tools in understanding societies such as the Aztec of Central Mexico. Archaeology, with its emphasis on the interpretation of material remains, and history, incorporating both the oral and written indigenous and European traditions, can together greatly illuminate our general knowledge of the Aztec, Mexico's last, great civilization vanquished by the Spanish in the early 16th century. Specifically, they can be used to further our understanding of the great ballcourt of the Aztec imperial capital Tenochtitlan—a metropolis buried underneath the sprawl of modern Mexico City.

A logical beginning is with the historical record, following the writings of the Franciscan chronicler Fray Bernardino de Sahagún. His monumental work *General History of the Things of New Spain* was written around 1560 as a tool for Spanish missionaries to understand, and ultimately suppress, native religious practices. Using Aztec informants and artists, Sahagún described and illustrated the numerous buildings that comprised Tenochtitlan's ceremonial precinct (an area known today as the Templo Mayor), a district that included two ballcourts. Sahagún's description of Tenochtitlan has proved fairly accurate. Of the 78 buildings listed in *General History of the Things of New Spain*, archaeologists have detected at least 40 inside the ceremonial precinct perimeter, with the hope of new structures yet to be discovered.

Archaeological data come from several projects undertaken throughout the 20th century. One of the most useful has been the Urban Archaeological Program (UAP), associated with the Templo Mayor project. Its purpose of

analyzing the developmental process of the ceremonial precinct has resulted in valuable information regarding the growth of Tenochtitlan.[2]

The Ballcourt According to Sahagún

In *General History of the Things of New Spain*, Sahagún described a number of the buildings within Tenochtitlan's great plaza. Included among the 78 structures, he lists two ballcourts:

> The 32nd edifice was called *Tezcatlachco*; this was a ballcourt, in it they killed some captives as devotion when the sign named *omacatl* [an Aztec deity associated with specific calendar dates or signs] reigned.[3]

96 This ballcourt offering contained a miniature rubber ball and three tiny shell carvings in the form of a flower, or a hand with four fingers, and a human femur and hand. Ballcourt Offering One; Late Postclassic Period, Aztec, A.D. 1400–1520; Central Mexico, Tenochtitlan/ Templo Mayor; *rubber, shell*; 1.4 × 0.7 × 0.1 in (3.5 × 1.7 × 0.1 cm) to 1.8 × 3 in (4.5 × 7.5 cm); Museo del Templo Mayor (cat. 118).

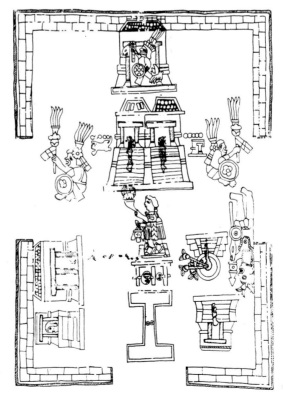

97 The Templo Mayor according to Sahagún, from the *Primeros Memoriales*. The I-shaped ballcourt is opposite the twin temples of Huitzilopochtli and Tlaloc.

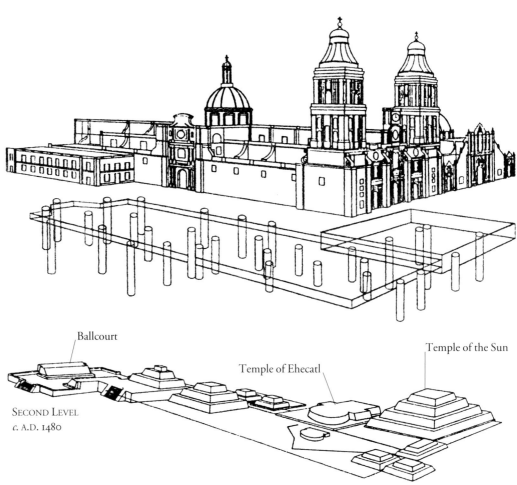

98 Drawing showing the Metropolitan Cathedral of Mexico City and the two levels of Aztec structures that lie beneath.

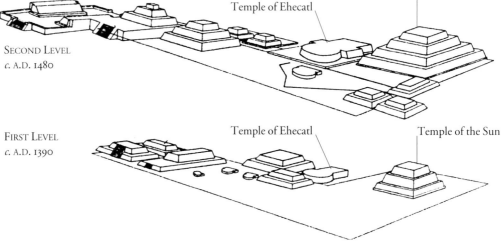

Ballcourt

Temple of the Sun

Temple of Ehecatl

SECOND LEVEL
c. A.D. 1480

FIRST LEVEL
c. A.D. 1390

Temple of Ehecatl

Temple of the Sun

99 Mexico City's Metropolitan Cathedral. Foundations of the Aztec ballcourt and associated offerings were found in the area located at the middle left section of the photograph.

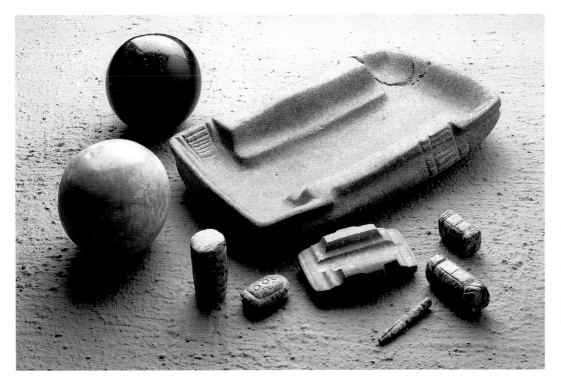

100 This ballcourt offering group consists of miniature ballcourts, replicas of musical instruments, and stone balls. Late Postclassic Period, Aztec, A.D. 1325–1521; Central Mexico, Tenochtitlan/ Templo Mayor; *stone*; 0.8 × 1.4 in (2 × 3.5 cm) to 2 × 14.2 in (5 × 36 cm); MNA (cat. 121).

As to the second ballcourt he writes:

> The 39th edifice was called *Teotlachco*; this was a ballcourt found in the same temple; they killed here some captives that they named *amapanme*, in the *panquetzaliztli* festivity.[4]

I believe that this second ballcourt described by Sahagún is the one illustrated in *Primeros Memoriales* (fig. 97). The evidence for this is compelling. Sahagún writes that the great ballcourt was "in the same temple." This probably refers to the Templo Mayor— Tenochtitlan's great dual pyramid complex dedicated to the supreme deity Huitzilopochtli and to Tlaloc, the rain god. Sahagún also refers to the deity Amapam. During an annual festival known as *panquetzaliztli*, four captives were sacrificed in the Teotlachco, or ballcourt. Two were sacrificed in honor of Amapam, and the other two were sacrificed in honor of the god Oappatzan. Sahagún also describes the great *tzompantli*, or skull rack, where the skulls of sacrificed victims were displayed. It was located, he writes, opposite the temple of Huitzilopochtli, and sacrifices took place during the *panquetzaliztli* ceremony.

The illustration in *Primeros Memoriales* shows the ballcourt oriented from east to west, next to the *tzompantli*. And both structures were located in front of the Templo Mayor. This architectural relationship of *tzompantli* to ballcourt can be seen in at least two other Postclassic sites: Tula (Ballcourt 2) and Chichén Itzá (see Taladoire).

It is well known that there was a close relation between ballcourt, *tzompantli*, and beheading. Interestingly, on a map ascribed to Cortés, no ballcourt is listed, but there is a *tzompantli* shown opposite the Templo Mayor. This is not surprising since thousands of skulls arranged on racks must have had a strong impression—to say the least—on the Spanish.

Archaeological Evidence

Leopoldo Batres was the first archaeologist to provide information about the possible existence of a ballcourt in front of the Templo Mayor. In his book *Exploraciones Arqueológicas en la Calle de las Escalerillas*, Batres describes how, on November 28, 1900, a large stone sphere with a striated circular base 22 in (57 cm) in diameter was discovered.[5] The next day, workers found five smaller stone spheres (6 in (15 cm) in diameter); one of these was painted red, another blue. These probably symbolized rubber balls used in the ballgame. They were found near the northeast corner of the Chapel of Souls (Capilla de las Ánimas), behind the Metropolitan Cathedral. Other archaeological remains have since added evidence relating to the existence of the ballcourt and coinciding with Sahagún's description of its position (figs. 98 and 99). In 1967, at the same site, an archaeological rescue project was undertaken as a result of finds encountered during the construction of Mexico City's Metro subway system. Here, archaeologists found two stone ballcourt models (fig. 100), as well as two stone balls, one black and one white. These almost certainly symbolize night and day. Among the many metaphorical layers embodied in the ballgame was the daily battle between night and day, represented by the deities Tezcatlipoca (Smoking Mirror) and Quetzalcoatl (Feathered Serpent).

As a result of the Urban Archaeological Program begun in 1991, an architectural feature was found behind the Cathedral that from the outset I believed to be the possible end-zone of the great ballcourt.[6] The excavations undertaken by Francisco Hinojosa and, subsequently, Álvaro Barrera, confirmed this. Furthermore, the remains of the two end-zones of the court and several substructures were recorded, including a talus (a sloping wall) oriented east–west, with sculpted skulls painted red, black, and white. The identification of these elements has illuminated where the five stone spheres described by Batres must have been situated— exactly at the center of the court.

Based on the architectural data recovered, we can say that the playing field was around 165 ft (50 m) long. The court was constructed in several phases. It consisted of a bench with a talus or slope oriented east–west, which turned at right-angles at the ends. The bench joined the wall of the court by a horizontal floor. The parapet or wall also had a talus. Based on these features, it can be assigned to Taladoire's Type VI or VIII (see p. 108).[7] It was oriented east–west and not north–south as Marquina showed it in his reconstructed model and map of the Tenochtitlan ceremonial precinct.[8]

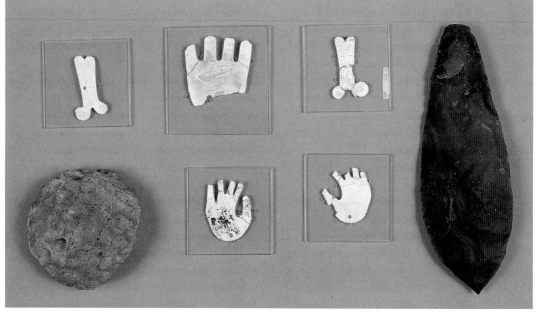

101 A flint knife accompanies the rubber ball and shell ornaments in this offering. The presence of the knife hints at the sacrificial aspects of the ballgame. Ballcourt Offering Four; Late Postclassic Period, Aztec, A.D. 1400–1520; Central Mexico, Tenochtitlan/ Templo Mayor; *shell, rubber, flint*; 1.2 × 0.7 × 0.1 in (3.1 × 1.7 × 0.1 cm) to 5.5 × 1.9 × 0.5 in (14 × 4.9 × 1.2 cm); Museo del Templo Mayor (cat. 120).

102 Among the variety of
items in Ballcourt Offering
Two were miniature
censers, vessels, beads,
ornaments, pendants,
and musical instruments.
Late Postclassic Period,
Aztec, A.D. 1400–1520;
Central Mexico,
Tenochtitlan/Templo
Mayor; Museo del Templo
Mayor (cat. 119).

This orientation agrees with that given by
Sahagún in *Primeros Memoriales*.

In addition, several offerings were found
associated with the ballcourt, further confirming
its existence. Two very important, very similar
offerings were discovered in the eastern and
western end-fields. The first, Offering One
(fig. 96), was found 17.8 ft (5.42 m) underneath
the floor of structure 1, at the eastern end-zone of
the court. Inside a stone box covered by a stone
slab were a flint knife, a small rubber ball, and a
mother-of-pearl pendant in the form of a human
hand with four fingers (or a flower?). After the
artifacts were removed from their stone
receptacle, the sediments at the bottom of the
box were sent to the laboratory for analysis.
In examining this material, biologist Aurora
Montúfar discovered two additional artifacts:

small shell carvings in the form of a human hand
with five fingers and a femur. She also detected
carbonized remains of cotton seeds (*Gossypium* sp.).

Offering Four (fig. 101) was found in the
western end-zone of the court. In a box
constructed of dressed stone were a flint knife,
a rubber ball, and five small shell pendants;
three in the form of a human hand or glove
(one with four fingers, possibly a flower) and
two depicting femurs. Also recovered were two
greenstone beads and seeds, probably of cotton.
The similarity of both discoveries would seem
not coincidental. No doubt one day the northern
extremity of the end-fields will be excavated and
two other similar offerings will almost certainly
be found.

These were not the only offerings found inside
the ballcourt. Partially destroyed by Colonial-era

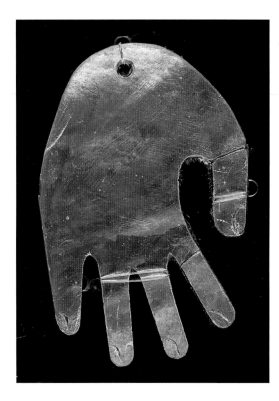

construction, Offering Two was discovered at a depth of 16.25 ft (4.95 m). It consisted of pottery vessel fragments, carbonized cotton seeds (*Gossypium* sp.), and human skull remains. Two other offerings were also found in the western part of the court, although they belong to later phases of construction and their contents are different from the first two.

One of these offerings contained two tubular whistles with bird-head finials, two flint knives, and three marine snail shells. The other offering (fig. 102) consisted of five miniature drums (*teponaztli*) and seven tubular whistles, four with bird-head finials and the rest with finials of human heads. Additionally, this offering contained seven miniature vessels, two braziers, ten flint knives, one shell, and 78 greenstone beads. It is clear that in both offerings, miniature musical instruments were emphasized.[9]

What was the significance of the materials in these offerings? The first two clearly contain elements associated with the ballgame, most prominent among them actual rubber balls (fig. 103). Numerous scholars have commented on the metaphor of the movement of the rubber ball in the court as relating to the sun and planets moving through the firmament.[10] Interestingly, among some societies this metaphor is illustrated much more dramatically.[11] Today, in the Western Mexican state of Michoacán, a game is played with a burning ball, made out of thick, dry maguey or red linnet root. The ball is kept in play with sticks used as bats. Players practice at night, coating the ball with petroleum and then igniting it (see Uriarte, fig. 34). This modern Michoacán game represents the battle between the Old Sun and the Young Sun, that is of night and day.[12]

The ballgame can thus take place on multiple levels: celestial, terrestrial, and subterranean, in the realm of the Underworld.[13] This is epitomized in the great Maya epic, the *Popol Vuh*, in which the Hero Twins Hunahpu and Xbalanque journey to the Underworld of Xibalba and play the ballgame against the Lords of Death. For the Aztec, the rubber ball also symbolized the sun as it dipped below the horizon, to be devoured by the Lord of the Earth, Tlaltecuhtli, thus beginning its nightly journey through the Underworld. The sun continued its travels through the world of the dead to be reborn from the earth every morning in the east.

On the earthly plain, some of the offering items depict equipment and paraphernalia used in the game and by the players. The shell pendants possibly to be interpreted as gloves (fig. 104), represent protective devices worn by ancient ballplayers exactly as seen in the ballcourt reliefs at El Tajín, in the men's procession in the Huijazoo tombs, or worn by the players depicted at Dainzú, the last two sites located in Oaxaca.[14] Sahagún writes that gloves were used by ballplayers to protect their hands.[15] Durán describes similar protective equipment, but also adds that, "at night, they took the ball and placed it over a clean dish, and the leather truss and the gloves that for their defense they used."[16]

Associated with the ballgame's elements of sacrifice and death are flint knives. It is interesting how that found in Offering One was oriented east. The small shell femurs probably have the same symbolic relationship to death. López Arenas identifies these with *malteutl*, the dead, captive god of the battlefield, which again brings to mind the struggle that prevails during the ballgame.[17] A large number of miniature musical instruments are represented in the ballcourt offerings (fig. 105). These are related to Xochipilli-Macuilxochitl, overlapping gods considered the patron deities of the ballgame and of music and dance.

103 Rubber balls from the Ballcourt Offering groups. Late Postclassic Period, Aztec, A.D. 1400–1520. Central Mexico, Tenochtitlan/ Templo Mayor; Museo del Templo Mayor, Mexico City.

104 Shell pendant in the form of a hand or glove from Ballcourt Offering One. Late Postclassic Period, Aztec, A.D. 1400–1520; Museo del Templo Mayor, Mexico City.

Last Reflections

As a result of archaeological investigations at the site of the present Metropolitan Cathedral of Mexico, there is no doubt that this 16th-century sacred building was constructed on top of one of the great ballcourts of Tenochtitlan: the one Sahagún listed as *Teotlachco*. This public space served as a stage for specific rituals such as the sacrifice of war captives, in addition to being the playing field for the ballgame.

It is perhaps appropriate to conclude with a song, since music—judging from the numbers of miniature musical instruments included in the offerings—was an important feature of the ballgame. The lyrics of the following song describe a ballgame between Huemac—a deity related to both Tezcatlipoca and Quetzalcoatl— and the Tlaloques—supernatural beings who assisted Tlaloc, the Rain God. The Tlaloques bet jades and quetzal feathers on their victory in the game. But they lost, and tried to cheat, giving Huemac ears of corn instead. When he complained, the Tlaloques relented, giving him the jade and precious feathers. In revenge, however, the Tlaloques sent a four-year drought to punish the Toltec people.

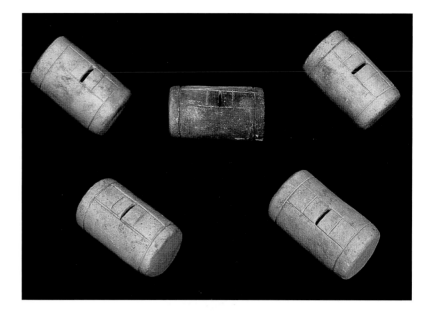

> Huemac plays ball; with the Tlaloques he played.
> The Tlaloques told him:
> What do we win playing?
> Huemac told them:
> My jades, my quetzal feathers.
> Later the gods said:
> You win the same thing: our fine green stones, our
>   quetzal feathers.
> Now they play ball: Huemac won the game.
> Now the Tlaloques go to change what they will
>   give Huemac:
> Quetzal for maize; precious feathers for corn cobs
>   in which the ear of corn is inside.
> He didn't want to receive them, and said:
> Is that what I bet? Aren't they perchance jades?
> Aren't they quetzal feathers? That … take it away
>   from here!
> The gods say:
> Very well, give him jades, give him feathers
> and they took and left taking their own jades
>   and their feathers, they said:
> Let's hide our jades … For four years distress and
>   difficulties the Toltec will suffer! [18]

This constant struggle of the gods and men is at the core of the symbolism of the Mesoamerican ballgame.

105 A selection of musical instruments from Ballcourt Offering Two. Late Postclassic Period, Aztec, A.D. 1400–1520. Central Mexico, Tenochtitlan/Templo Mayor; Museo del Templo Mayor, Mexico City.

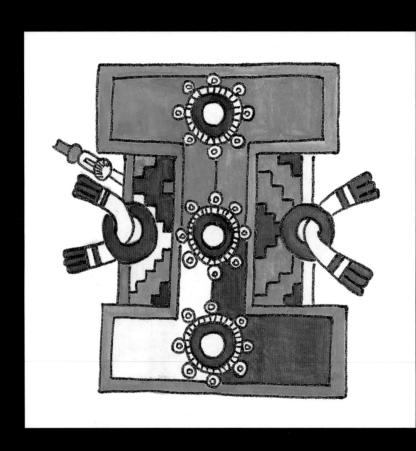

ERIC TALADOIRE

8 THE ARCHITECTURAL BACKGROUND OF THE PRE-HISPANIC BALLGAME: AN EVOLUTIONARY PERSPECTIVE

From their earliest encounters with indigenous Americans, the Spanish Conquistadors were fascinated by a game they saw being played with a bouncing rubber ball.[1] The numerous written narratives of these European conquerors provide us with marvellous insights into *ullamaliztli*, the game they saw played by the Aztecs, and the *tlachtli*, or court, where the sport was played. Through the complementary disciplines of archaeology, ethnology, and ethnohistory sufficient data have now been accumulated to allow the first scientific studies of these games and courts, and to achieve an overall perspective of this unique feature of Mesoamerican culture.[2] Until recently, study of the ballgame might perhaps have been considered a specialized, narrow field, compared with apparently more significant areas of inquiry such as religion, economics, or social structure. But the recent growth of interest in pre-Hispanic ballgames has in many ways changed this perspective.

In the past 20 years, exhibitions in Mexico, Europe, and now in the United States, have given rise to catalogues, symposia, and numerous publications.[3] The growing interest in this theme stems first and foremost from the astounding number of identified ballcourts: 1,560 on some 1,275 archaeological sites. This means that almost every archaeologist working in Mesoamerica has discovered or excavated at least one. And investigators working in other fields of study have also contributed to our knowledge. Epigraphers have deciphered the Maya glyphs for the ballgame, ballcourts, and ballplayers.[4] Specialists working on the codices have identified representations of ballcourts, and ballgame symbolism (fig. 106). Iconographic studies have revealed representations of ballplayers or ballgame rituals, both in ballcourts themselves and also on other buildings, such as Yaxchilan Structure 33 stairway (see fig. 88).[5] Even at sites without ballcourts, such as El Resbalón or Ichmul, players may be represented.[6]

Many works of art depict rulers costumed as ballplayers, suggesting that playing the ballgame was one of the king's ritual responsibilities. At Copán, the king is shown in player's attire confronting the Lords of the Underworld to secure the rebirth of vegetation and thus ensure the survival of his people.[7] We know also that Aztec emperors played the game: Moctezuma played against the king of Texcoco, Nezahualpilli, to determine the fate of the empire, on the verge of conquest. Thus, the ballgame may be considered an attribute or a symbol of power.

Moreover, the game could be used as an instrument of conquest. When the Aztec emperor Axayacatl wanted to annex the rich chinampas (raised field systems separated by canals) of Xochimilco, instead of going to war, the issue was resolved by a game against the Lord Xihuitlemoc of this city-state. Through treachery, Mexico-Tenochtitlan succeeded in acquiring these valuable economic resources.[8] Thus the various themes of the ballgame are far reaching, making it fundamental for our comprehension of the cultural evolution of Mesoamerica.

What makes the ballgame most important is its long history in Mesoamerica.[9] From the ancient origins of the game at the site of Paso de la Amada on the Pacific coast of Chiapas in

106 Representation of an I-shaped ballcourt from the *Codex Nuttall.*

States	Number of known courts in 1981		Number of known courts in 1995		Number of known courts in 2000		Growth of data
	Courts	Sites	Courts	Sites	Courts	Sites	
Yucatán	11	3	32	19	32	19	× 2.9
Quintana Roo	7	6	8	7	9	8	× 1.3
Campeche	10	10	30	27	36	32	× 3.6
Tabasco	2	2	5	3	5	3	× 2.5
Petén	23	16	47	37	56	46	× 2.4
Chiapas	15	12	21	15	23	16	× 1.5
Belize	17	14	42	32	46	33	× 2.7
Quiché		0	1	1	1	1	× 1
Izabal	1	1	2	1	2	1	× 2
Honduras	3	1	10	6	15	11	× 5
Total	89	65	198	148	225	170	× 2.5
Proportion		1.3		1.3		1.3	

Table 1 (above) Growth in the number of documented ballcourts and related sites in the Maya Lowlands from 1981 to 2000. The proportion evaluates the mean quantity of ballcourts per site. Growth of data shows the increase of the sample size.

Mexico (1400–1250 B.C.),[10] to the present-day game,[11] this Mesoamerican cultural feature has persisted for over 3,000 years. Not many human ritual activities can demonstrate such an unbroken tradition.

Distribution of Ballcourts

As mentioned above, ballcourts are nearly ubiquitous at Mesoamerican archaeological sites and, almost every month it seems, new examples are discovered and excavated.[12] In 1981, our research accumulated data for some 632 courts, dispersed on 518 sites throughout Mesoamerica,

northern Mexico, and the American Southwest (Arizona and New Mexico).[13] A recent evaluation brought this total to 1,560 ballcourts, scattered over 1,275 sites (Tables 1 and 2). This means that, apart from a few instances such as Teotihuacan, almost every large site in Mesoamerica has at least one ballcourt. Some sites have multiple ballcourts—El Tajín and Cantona, both in the modern day state of Veracruz, have 18 and 24 respectively (figs. 107 and 108).[14] But even very small sites may have a court.[15] Over the last 20 years, our corpus of archaeological sites with ballcourts has more than doubled. In some areas

Cultural areas	Number of known courts in 1981		Number of known courts in 1995		Number of known courts in 2000		Growth of data
	Courts	Sites	Courts	Sites	Courts	Sites	
Southwest	75	68	206	165	206	165	× 2.7
Northern Mexico	8	8	30	26	35	29	× 4.3
Western Mexico	5	4	83	74	86	77	× 17.2
Michoacán	5	5	28	28	29	29	× 5.8
Guerrero	16	13	34	30	36	32	× 2.2
North-Central Mesoamerica	8	4	46	36	50	40	× 6.25
Huasteca	20	20	24	21	24	21	× 1.2
Central Mexico	59	53	71	60	79	66	× 1.3
Gulf Coast	31	20	126	73	128	75	× 4.1
Oaxaca	34	32	77	67	100	90	× 2.9
Chiapas-Tabasco	102	80	225	188	226	189	× 2.2
Pacific Coast	10	10	34	30	37	33	× 3.7
Maya Highlands	158	125	236	201	262	226	× 1.65
Maya Lowlands	89	65	198	148	225	170	× 2.5
Central America	12	11	37	33	37	33	× 3
Total	632	518	1,455	1,181	1,560	1,275	× 2.5

the growth of data is still more significant: in northern and western Mexico, recent investigations have brought the number of documented courts from 26 to 166, while in Veracruz, it rose from 31 to 126. In other areas, such as the Maya Lowlands, a steady flow of research has resulted in 225 known ballcourts, as compared to only 89 recorded in 1981.

Despite this general increase in information, there are still many gaps in our knowledge, which reflect a lack of research rather than a lack of ballcourts. In the Maya Lowlands, northwestern Petén, central Campeche or Quintana Roo are all areas where there is a need for such research. The same would be true for the Oaxaca coast and many parts of Veracruz.[16] The problem is somewhat different for other sites or regions. Why are major Maya sites such as Bonampak or Tortuguero devoid of ballcourts? Is it only a lack of proper research? How can sites such as Itzan,

Ichmul, or El Resbalón, where ballgame iconography is known, lack such structures? In Central Mexico, no court is known from the most important site of Teotihuacan, although this, as we see later, can be explained. Indeed, very few ballcourts have been documented in the Valley of Mexico, despite intensive archaeological research and the Spanish chroniclers' testimonies. This may partly be explained by the destruction following the Conquest, since Colonial buildings were constructed over ballcourts and other public structures.[17] Representations in the codices confirm the existence of these ballcourts. But there may be other, more specific reasons, as we shall see below. In the next few years there will quite likely be a steady growth of new data resulting in the discovery of more ancient Mesoamerican ballcourts.

Given its 3,000-year history and the large territory over which it was played (fig. 109), some

107 The South Ballcourt at El Tajín, Veracruz, Mexico. This Late Classic Period site has 18 known ballcourts.

Table 2 *(opposite)* Growth of the number of recorded ballcourts and related sites in Mesoamerica and adjoining areas from 1981 to 2000. Growth of data shows the increase of the sample size.

108 Type VII, Enclosed
Late Classic court from
Cantona, Veracruz,
Mexico.

109 Major Mesoamerican
sites with ballcourts.

diversity in the Mesoamerican ballgame is only to be expected. Obviously, games played on Tikal's small ballcourt, with a playing field measuring just 52.5 by 16.5 ft (16 by 5 m), and games played on the gigantic ballcourt at Chichén Itzá, which measures 316 by 98 ft (96.5 by 30 m), must have

had different rules (figs. 110 and 111). The introduction in Postclassic courts of rings through which the ball had to be hurled, such as at Chichén Itzá, Uxmal (fig. 112), Xochicalco, and Tenochtitlan, obviously modified the scoring method. And the disappearance of formal courts

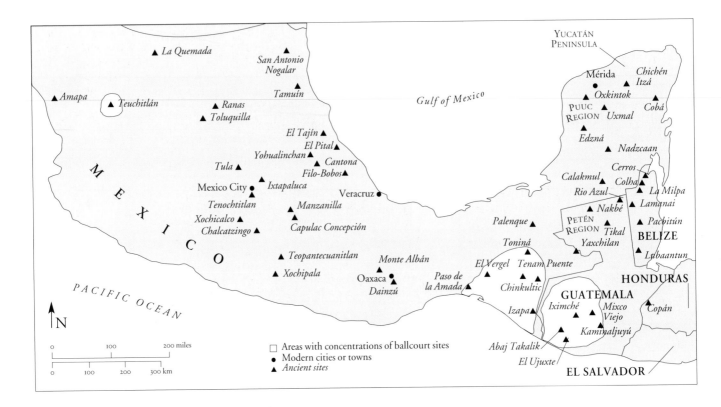

altogether for present-day games has certainly changed play from pre-Hispanic times. But, in spite of such differences, the Aztec game of *ullamaliztli* has maintained a basic unity throughout its history.[18] Ethnological studies demonstrate that the present-day game of *ulama* played in Sinaloa basically corresponds to the Aztec game described by the Spanish chroniclers (see Leyenaar).[19] Representations of players in the codices, on pottery ballgame models from Western Mexico, and on some Classic Maya monuments are consistent with the equipment

110 The Great Ballcourt at Chichén Itzá, Yucatán, Mexico. This Late Classic/Early Postclassic Period court conforms to Type III, Variation 1.

111 Interior of the Great Ballcourt at Chichén Itzá, Yucatán, Mexico. This huge court measures 316 by 98 ft (96.5 by 30 m).

112 A tenoned ring in the ballcourt at Uxmal, Yucatán, Mexico. Such rings were an innovation of the Late Classic/Early Postclassic Periods.

The Ballcourt and the Game

The basic rules of the game can be briefly summarized. It was played in a formal court, consisting of three main elements: a playing alley, two long parallel buildings or lateral structures bordering the alley, and a steep slope or apron-like feature on their interior side (fig. 113). The alley is usually long and narrow, with a flat plastered or stone floor. The lateral structures, several meters high, have flat tops on which small buildings sometimes stand. On the inner side of each structure a steep slope, or apron, extends from the summit to the playing field. This is topped by a cornice or a high wall, the base of the apron falling vertically to the alley. In many courts, the apron is bordered by a bench with a vertical or subvertical wall and a flat or slightly rising top. Often the playing field is open-ended, but it might also be partially limited at one or both ends by small walls, altars, or even structures (fig. 114). In other courts, end zones are more strictly defined by walls. These are attached to the lateral structures, giving the court the I-shape form so frequently depicted in the codices.

Two teams, consisting of between two and seven players each, faced off, separated by a center line in the ballcourt. It is possible (see Miller) that only two players were engaged in the game at any one time. The best players took positions along the alley, while others worked the end zones. They prevented the ball from going dead by deflecting it and sending it back to the other team. The ball was struck with particular parts of the body, such as the arms, shoulders, or buttocks. Players were prohibited from using their hands, feet, or head to hit the ball. This was probably

worn by modern players.[20] One can also easily compare attitudes and positions of players as represented on Maya monuments with those of players from Sinaloa and Nayarit. Finally, even in the absence of formal courts nowadays, the plan of the playing alley fits with the general form and proportions of pre-Hispanic antecedents.

113 Ballcourt terminology.
   A Lateral Structures
   B Cornice
   C Apron
   D Bench
   E Bench Wall
   F Playing Alley
   G End Zones
   H Outer Surfaces
   I Terminal
      Structures

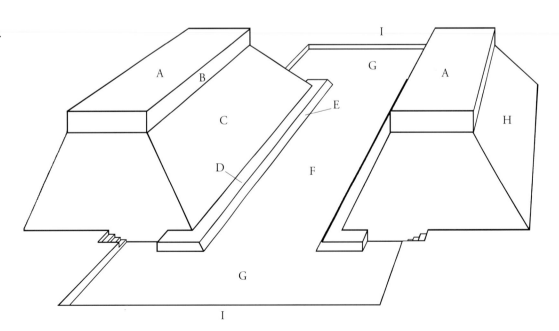

a matter of safety, since a simple blow from the heavy ball could injure or even kill a player. To protect themselves from the impact of the ball and the rigors of play, the almost naked players wore protective belts, gloves, and sometimes kneepads and sandals. Scoring was mainly the result of faults, as in tennis: touching the ball with a prohibited part of the body; failing to catch or to return it; or sending the ball outside the court. Due to the complex scoring method, games could last for long periods—sometimes the entire day.

Classification of Ballcourts

The general form and basic common elements of ballcourts allow them to be classified according to the criteria of floor plan, and transversal and longitudinal profiles.[21] Former classifications were mainly based either on the floor plan or on the combination of plan and transversal profile, but this does not seem adequate.[22] For instance, these methods do not allow simple open-ended courts and partly enclosed ones to be distinguished, a difference which may be chronologically significant. Using the sole criterion of the plan may lead to erroneous identifications, as exemplified by the El Tigre

114 Type II, Variation 2, Late Classic court at Edzná, Campeche, Mexico. End zones are defined by the small walls at both extremities of the playing alley.

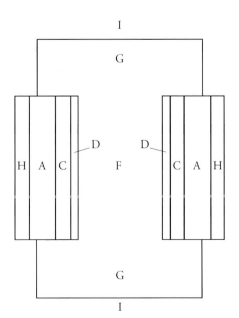

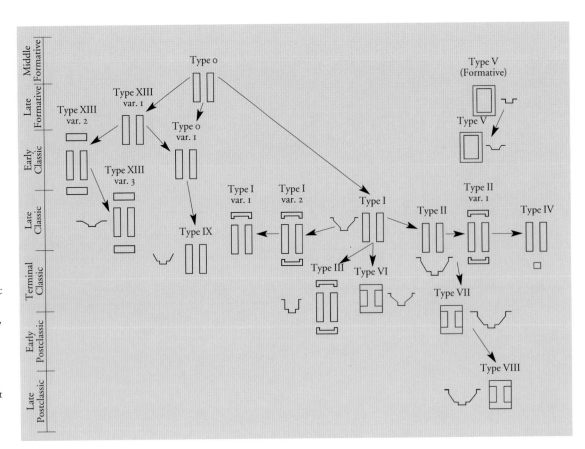

115 (right) Proposed chart of the evolution of ballcourt types in Mesoamerica.

116 (below) Type I, Variety 1: the Late Classic Period ballcourt at Copán, Honduras.

117 (opposite above) Type VI, Late Classic enclosed court at Xochicalco, Morelos, Mexico.

118 (opposite below) Type VIII, enclosed, Late Postclassic court at Iximché, in the Highlands of Guatemala.

119 Type V, Early Classic, type V *Palangana* court from La Lagunita in the Highlands of Guatemala. Its rounded profile is quite unusual, and very different from most other known profiles.

court in Campeche, whose proportions do not correspond to the usual norm.[23] In the classification developed in 1981 for Mesoamerica, we identified 12 types and 7 varieties, mostly defined by the longitudinal profile (fig. 115). Open-ended courts, Types I (fig. 116), II, and IV, seem to be the most ancient, while Types III, VI, VII, VIII, and IX (figs. 117 and 118) correspond to later periods. Types X and XI comprise only ballcourts from the American Southwest, while Type XII refers solely to courts from the Caribbean area.[24]

Although it is possible to trace an evolution from the earliest open-ended courts to the latest types, and from Mesoamerican courts to those of the American Southwest, two types stand apart from this scheme. Type XII courts are restricted solely to the Caribbean Islands and may be related to South American influences. Type V enclosed courts, usually called *palangana*

120 Reconstruction drawing of Type V, Early Classic, type V *Palangana* court from La Lagunita in the Highlands of Guatemala.

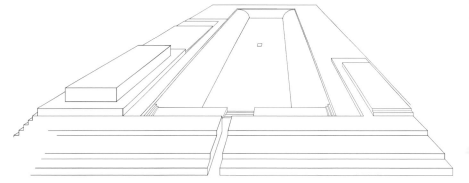

(Spanish for basin), after their bowl-shaped form which lacks end zones, cannot be related logically to other identified types (figs. 119 and 120), an anomaly that remains to be explained.

This classification based on form and chronology initially proposed in 1981 has been successfully tested over the past 20 years. Research in different parts of Mesoamerica, such as the Maya Lowlands and Michoacán, has generally confirmed its validity and usefulness.[25] Of course, the increasing amount of new data necessitated some revisions and modifications, especially in areas where data were deficient in 1981. In western Mexico, recent research has revealed the existence of numerous ballcourts generally associated with circular structures called *guachimontons*.[26] These have been dated from the Middle Formative (900–400 B.C.) through the Late Classic (A.D. 600–900) Periods. Their unique form led Phil Weigand to identify them as a specific type, with three corresponding sub-types. We agree with his proposal and number this new type XIII (fig. 122). The most important critical revision to the typology was offered by Beatriz Braniff, who took into consideration the known courts from western and northern Mexico.[27] Although she mainly accepts the proposed types, she considers western Mexican examples as a special group and proposes the creation of a new type, 0, which would include open-ended Formative Period courts (fig. 121), as well as the very simple later cases from northern Mexico. Although we accept her criticisms and proposals, we would rather differentiate the earliest Formative courts (her Type 0), from the northern examples, of a later date, which would be considered as Type 0, Variety 1.

This modified classification of 13 types, with varieties (Table 3), for Mesoamerica and the American Southwest covers almost all identified and excavated ballcourts. Of course, some lesser-known examples still remain to be properly described, and many areas of Mesoamerica still remain *terra incognita*. Future research in Guerrero, Oaxaca, and northern Mexico might make it necessary to amplify recent revisions. For the moment, however, the modified classification presented here allows us to trace the general evolution of ballcourts in Mesoamerica and adjoining areas.

History and Development

The Olmec are often credited as the creators of the ballgame, from tenuous, often over-interpreted evidence I would argue. Whereas there can be no doubt that the Olmec had knowledge of rubber and its use, iconographic interpretation of figurines or gigantic heads as ballplayers remains, in my view, hypothetical.[28]

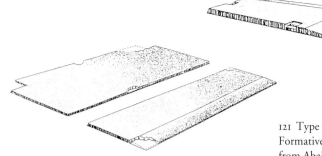

121 Type 0, Middle Formative earth ballcourt from Abaj Takalik, Pacific Coast of Guatemala. After a reconstruction drawing by Schieber de Lavarreda.

Additionally, the proposed identification of ballcourts at the sites of San Lorenzo and La Venta is yet to be confirmed.[29] As mentioned above, the oldest excavated ballcourt was discovered at the site of Paso de la Amada on the Pacific Coast of modern Chiapas, Mexico.[30] Parallel structures 260 ft (80 m) long, but only 14 in (35 cm) high, line each side of the playing alley. Archaeologists who excavated the site have proposed a date of 1400 to 1250 B.C. for this ballcourt. This would be before any possible Olmec influence at the site. Probably more significant is the abandonment of the court in the following phase (1250–1100 B.C.), corresponding to the height of Olmec influence in that area. This could suggest that the origins of the ballgame on the Pacific Coast must be predate the Olmec horizon. By the Middle Formative,

122 Type XIII, open-end ballcourt at Los Guachimontones, Jalisco, Mexico.

Types	Plan	Transversal profile	Axial structures	Chronological period	Location
0	Open-ended	Low apron	Possible end structures	Formative	Pacific Coast, Maya Lowlands, Chiapas, Oaxaca, West Mexico
0 var. 1	Open-ended	Low apron or wall	No axial structures	Early/Late Classic	Maya Lowlands, Honduras, Huasteca, Northern Mexico
I	Open-ended	Apron, cornice	No axial structures	Late Classic	Maya Lowlands, Central America, Veracruz
I var. 1	Open-ended	Apron, cornice	One axial structure	Late Classic	Maya Lowlands
I var. 2	Open-ended	Apron, cornice	One U-form axial structure	Late Classic	Maya Lowlands
I var. 3	Open-ended	Apron, cornice	Two U-form axial structures	Late–Terminal Classic	Maya Lowlands
II	Open-ended	Bench, apron, cornice	No axial structure	Late Classic	Maya Lowlands and Highlands
II var. 1	Open-ended	Bench, apron, cornice	No axial structure	Late Classic	Maya Lowlands and Highlands
II var. 2	Open-ended	Bench, apron, cornice	Two U-form axial structures	Late–Terminal Classic	Maya Lowlands and Highlands
III	Open-ended	Bench, high wall	No axial structure	Late Classic	Yucatán
III var. 1	Enclosed	Bench, high wall	Two U-form axial structures	Late–Terminal Classic	Yucatán, West Mexico
IV	Open-ended	Bench, apron, cornice	Axial altar	Late Classic	Maya Highlands, Chiapas
V	Enclosed	Unknown	High end structure	Early Classic	Maya Highlands, Chiapas, Oaxaca
VI	Enclosed	Apron, cornice	End structure	Late Classic	Maya Lowlands and Highlands, Central America, Chiapas, Oaxaca, Puebla, Veracruz, Central Mexican Highlands, Michoacán, Northwest Mexico
VI var. 1	Enclosed	Apron, cornice	End structure	Late Classic	Maya Highlands
VI var. 2	Semi-enclosed	Apron, cornice	Unknown	Late Classic	Maya Highlands
VII	Enclosed	Bench, apron, cornice	Large end zones	Late Classic	Maya Lowlands and Highlands, Central America, Chiapas, Oaxaca, Puebla, Veracruz, Central Mexican Highlands, Michoacán, Northwest Mexico
VIII	Enclosed	Bench, apron, cornice	Small end zones	Postclassic	Maya Highlands
IX	Open-ended	Steep apron	End structures	Late Classic/Postclassic	Northern Mexico
X	Enclosed	Low apron	Small end zones	Late Classic/Postclassic	Arizona
XI	Enclosed	Low apron	Small end zones	Late Classic/Postclassic	Arizona
XII	Enclosed	None	Wall		Caribbean
XIII var. 1	Open-ended	Low apron	No structures	Formative/Early Classic	West Mexico
XIII var. 2	Enclosed	Low apron	Axial structure	Formative/Early Classic	West Mexico
XIII var. 3	Enclosed	Low apron	Axial structure	Late Classic	West Mexico

on the Pacific Coast of Chiapas and Guatemala, ballcourts appear on several sites, including Abaj Takalik.[31] At the end of the Middle Formative, and during the Late Formative (400–100 B.C.), ballcourts began to be popular all over Mesoamerica, with examples in Chiapas, the Maya Lowlands, Guerrero, Oaxaca, and Honduras.[32] The most surprising occurrence comes from western Mexico, where a Middle Formative date has been proposed for the first ballcourts constructed in that region. There can be no doubt that many Type XIII, Variety 1 courts existed in that region during the Late Formative. Considering the absence of rubber in western Mexico, it is utterly improbable that its ballgame was indigenous. This suggests that the western Mexican ballgame was introduced from Central Mexico or the Pacific Coast. Archaeological data from the coast of Oaxaca and Guerrero will be key to answering this question.

The situation changes drastically during the Early Classic Period (A.D. 300–600). All over Mesoamerica, ballcourts fall into disuse and no new courts are constructed. None have been documented in the Maya Lowlands or in most other cultural areas. The absence of ballcourts at Teotihuacan has already been noted, but the same is true of many sites at the time. There are only two exceptions to this. The first relates to Type V courts, known only in Oaxaca, Tehuacan, Chiapas, and the Guatemala Highlands, most of which date from this period. Few of these have been excavated and this type remains distinct. Given the specificity of those courts, and their relatively restricted distribution, it may be possible that they belong to another game.[33]

The other exception concerns marginal areas in Mesoamerica. During the Early Classic, ballcourts continue in use in northern Veracruz and in the Huasteca, as at San Antonio Nogalar.[34] In western Mexico, Type XIII reaches its peak, while in northern Mexico, Type 0, Variety 1 ballcourts multiply.[35] This is quite possibly the era when the game and ballcourts were introduced to the American Southwest.[36] It is notable that the Teotihuacan influence was minimal in that area. Whatever the case, one cannot escape the fact that in Teotihuacan-influenced or -related areas, the ballgame seems to be abandoned during the Early Classic.

After Teotihuacan's decline in the Late Classic, the situation changed radically. The ballgame reached its apogee and more than half of all the known ballcourts were constructed during that

123 Type VII, enclosed Late Classic court from Dainzú, Oaxaca, Mexico. Its form is quite similar to most other documented ballcourts from Oaxaca.

Table 3 *(opposite)* A summary description of identified types of ballcourts, according to the three criteria of plan and transversal and longitudinal profiles, with tentative chronological periods and geographic location.

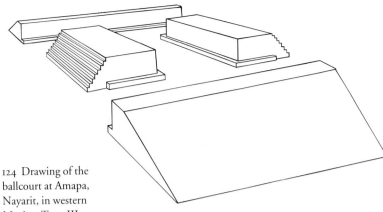

124 Drawing of the
ballcourt at Amapa,
Nayarit, in western
Mexico; Type III,
Variation 1. This type
of court is unusual for
western Mexico and it
is the only known example
in that area.

125 Type I, Late Classic,
open-ended ballcourt
at Calakmul, Campeche,
Mexico.

era. At some sites reconstruction of ballcourts may have started somewhat earlier, as at Copán or Río Azul. But, during the Late Classic, every major site in Mesoamerica has at least one ballcourt. The great majority of the Maya Lowland courts belong to this period. Courts start multiplying at almost every site in the Central Mexican highlands,[37] as well as on the Gulf Coast (fig. 123).[38] Others begin to appear in areas previously lacking them, such as Michoacán and Guanajuato/Querétaro.[39] In western Mexico,

local Type XIII courts fall into disuse and give way to new Mesoamerican types—evidence of the mesoamericanization of that area (fig. 124).[40] Still more significant was the construction of courts at sites such as Matacapan, formerly under Teotihuacan influence. And lastly, at cities such as Pacbitún, Colha, and Monte Albán, earlier Formative Period ballcourts were rebuilt.

This tremendous growth in construction was paralleled by a formal diversification—most varieties of courts were elaborated then. If the open-ended courts, Types I (fig. 125) and II, seem to be earlier than the enclosed ones, Types VI (fig. 126), VII, VIII, it is possible to propose a gradual evolution. In the Maya Lowlands, for instance, open-ended courts give way to partly enclosed ones, such as Edzná, with the appearance of new varieties. In Copán, apart from the old open-ended court, an enclosed one was built.[41] In the state of Chiapas, at the sites of Toniná and Chinkultic, Type VII enclosed courts, with asymmetric end-zones, appear (fig. 127). Without any doubt, the Late Classic Period was the heyday of the ballgame.

126 Type VI, Late Classic, enclosed court at Teotenango, Mexico.

In spite of several changes, this tradition was sustained into the Postclassic Period (A.D. 1000–1519) and ballcourts were now permanent features of every major archaeological site in the Guatemala Highlands (fig. 128), Oaxaca, and Central Mexico. Mesoamerican-type enclosed ballcourts are built in some of the major sites of the Huasteca. However, the game seems gradually to lose some of its importance, and tends to fall into disuse in other areas. In Michoacán, for example, although the ballgame is referred to in the *Relación de Michoacán* (1541), no court is known for late Tarascan sites. The most obvious example comes

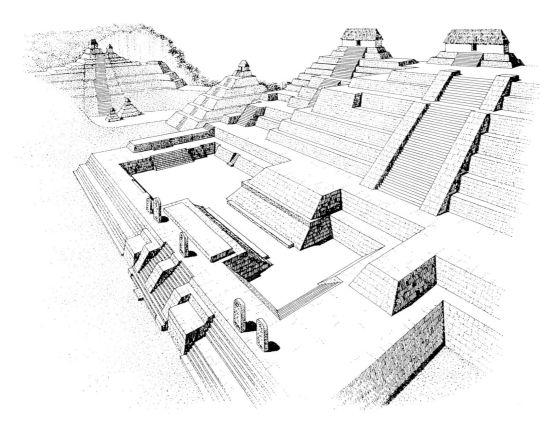

127 Reconstruction drawing of the Type VII, enclosed, Late Classic court at Chinkultic, Chiapas, Mexico, with irregular or asymmetric end zones.

128 Type VIII, enclosed
Late Postclassic court
at Mixco (Jilotepeque)
Viejo, in the Highlands
of Guatemala.

from the Maya Lowlands: although almost every major Late Classic Maya site has a court, during the Terminal Classic Period (A.D. 800–1000) the situation evolves gradually.

Chichén Itzá is preeminent, with 13 courts; at other sites, in northern Belize for instance (Nohmul, Lamanai), the building of courts can be interpreted as inspired by the political or cultural influence of Chichén Itzá, and they appear along with other elements of Yucatec Maya influence such as new ceramic styles.[42] But the ballgame passes completely into oblivion after the fall of Chichén Itzá, and no court is documented at any Late Postclassic site, such as Mayapan or Tulum. The reasons for such a complete disappearance are yet to be understood, and the situation is all the more puzzling since the game becomes quite popular in the Maya Highlands at this time.

Teotihuacan

This survey of the history of ballcourts provides an understanding of their general evolution, but it does raise one major problem: the cessation of ballcourt construction at the period when

Teotihuacan was at its peak. Until A.D. 100, when this great Central Mexican city began to expand, the ballgame seems to have experienced a steady and regular growth. Indeed, with over 30 courts documented from Honduras to western Mexico, it could even be considered an established tradition. But suddenly in the major urban centers, ballcourts ceased to be used.

Significantly, no court has ever been found at Teotihuacan itself. This does not mean that *ullamaliztli* was unknown there. Indeed, an open-ended court is depicted in the Tlalocan murals painted on the walls of the Tepantitla Palace at Teotihuacan (fig. 129). But this version of the ballgame seems to be more of an evocation of a foreign tradition of the tropical lowlands where it was still practiced, than a specifically Teotihuacan activity. In fact, the same paintings depict another game in much more detail, in which two teams of players strike a small ball with sticks. This activity takes place on an open field, whose end zones are marked by stone monuments. A similar monument has been discovered at the La Ventilla compound at

Teotihuacan, suggesting that this game was indeed played there. Other examples have been discovered at Matacapan in Veracruz, in Guerrero, Chiapas, Kaminaljuyú, and, recently, at Tikal.[43] The Tikal monument was associated with Teotihuacan-related remains and structures that replicate the distinctively Teotihuacan talud-tablero architectural forms. It seems as if another ballgame was favored at Teotihuacan, from where it was diffused, bringing about a temporary disappearance of *ullamaliztli*—at least in sites and areas where Teotihuacan influence was sufficiently strong.

The decline and fall of the great metropolis occasioned, in turn, the abandonment of this game, which may have survived in certain parts of the Central Mexican highlands. A ballgame using sticks, called the *Pelota Tarasca,* is still played in Michoacán, which may represent the last descendant of the ancient Teotihuacan game. It is significant that the same sites where the Teotihuacan game has been documented, such as Matacapan and Tikal, started to build ballcourts after that city's decline. During the Late Classic, other cities such as Colha and Pacbitún began rebuilding formerly abandoned courts.[44] The replacement of one game by another has yet to be properly explained, but it is consistent with numerous other characteristics that give Teotihuacan its distinct originality.

The Siting of Ballcourts

Throughout the ballgame's long and complex evolution, it has preserved its identity and its symbolism. The renaissance of the game after its abandonment during the Teotihuacan period is proof of its deep significance. The rebuilding of ballcourts at the same sites, and even on the same spot, further underlines its importance. Technical considerations might, of course, have contributed to the decision to rebuild courts on the same locations, since unlike pyramids and palaces, ballcourts have specific site requirements. Whereas pyramids or other tall buildings might utilize rocky outcrops, ballcourts need large, flat surfaces for their playing alleys. In order to minimize unnecessary site preparation, such areas were preferred, thus limiting site selection to the lower flatlands. But technical requirements alone do not always explain site selection. At Toniná, for example, where such areas were readily available, the inhabitants instead invested a huge amount of time and energy to build a sunken court with high reinforced walls on one side of the main plaza.[45] At Copán, as at many other sites, the periodic rebuilding of a ballcourt might be explained as routine maintenance, but also by ritual or symbolic necessities.

Several hypotheses have been suggested to interpret the meaning of ballcourts. Foremost

129 This Middle Classic, open-ended ballcourt—corresponding to types 0, I, or II—is depicted in the Tlalocan murals in the Tepantitla Palace at Teotihuacan, Mexico.

among these are theories relating to the orientation of the courts—their alignment from north to south, or east to west, connected with astral cults or solar symbolism respectively. A precise and detailed study, however, has shown that no consistent orientation can be identified.[46] The orientation of ballcourts depends mostly on the site itself and on the proximity of the court to other buildings.

This leads to another set of hypotheses: the association of ballcourts with specific categories of buildings and their relationship to the site itself. Spatial relationships have been identified between ballcourts and several specific types of buildings. This sample, however, is as yet too small to provide general conclusions. *Temascals* (sweatbaths) and ballcourts are associated at the sites of Piedras Negras, Chichén Itzá, Toniná, and San Antonio.[47] *Tzompantli* (skull racks) are closely related to courts at Tula and Chichén Itzá. But this amounts to a handful of examples that may have meaning only at these specific sites. The relationship between ballcourts, circular structures, and *sacbeob* (raised roadways) may prove more promising. Several instances have been documented at the sites of Ek Balam and Yaxuna in Yucatán, in Belize, and at the site of Seibal in the Petén.[48] It is possible, however, that this relationship is specific to the Terminal Classic Period of the Maya Lowlands.[49]

From a different perspective, it is interesting to consider how ballcourts are distributed within a site. Although many sites have only one court, others have dual and multiple courts: Tikal has 5, Cantona 24, and Chichén Itzá 13. Previous scholars have sought to explain this phenomenon.[50] The most likely explanations are either that there were distinct varieties of the game, or that there were different functions for each court, such as ritual activity as opposed to practice. Why then are dual courts so close to each other in the center of a site? If the range of sites with dual ballcourts, is examined, no patterns can be identified to assist in interpreting them. Courts may belong to the same or different types, be similarly oriented, or oriented at angles to one another. They may be located in the same part of the site or quite apart from one another.

An alternative explanation looks at the relationship of each court to a specific socio-political group. Just such an argument has been proposed for the construction of Copán's second ballcourt.[51] Since ballcourts and the ballgame are related to power and can be considered instruments of prestige, the building of a court

by a wealthy or noble lineage would contribute greatly to its rank at the site. This might justify the building of a second court at Copán, but also the existence of smaller courts on secondary sites such as Petulton in the Ocosingo Valley. It would also explain the late building of courts by emerging powers in northern Belize during the Terminal Classic. If we consider sites such as Cantona or Chichén Itzá, such a hypothesis gains more credibility. At Chichén Itzá, there are associations between ballcourts, temples, halls, and circular buildings, thus defining several similar but stratified groups.[52] At Cantona, there is a very similar arrangement composed of a pyramid, altar, sunken plaza, and a ballcourt, each set of buildings forming a specific unit.[53] Such units might indeed correspond to a particular socio-political entity. Thus, the exceptional density of courts at certain sites could indicate a political confederacy, while in Lowland Maya sites, for example, the existence of only one ballcourt would correspond to a society ruled by a single individual. If this hypothesis proves correct, it would lead to the idea of a systematic association between three types of structures: the pyramid, the palace or residential buildings, and the ballcourt.

130 Type I, Late Classic ballcourt at Uxmal, Yucatán, Mexico. This court has tenoned rings and very high walls instead of cornices.

Ballcourts and the Underworld

The spatial relationship between pyramids and ballcourts has often been noted, with many authors insisting on the symbolism of pyramids as celestial representations. Numerous arguments can be put forward to confirm the relationship of pyramids to the upper world: the architectural structure itself, the symbolic value of tiers and stairways, and iconography and mythological significance. At Copán, on the other hand, ballcourt markers depict the ruler confronting the Underworld Lords of Death in a ballgame. It is possible that all ballcourt iconography may be related to the Underworld.[54]

The ballcourt could thus be interpreted as an architectural representation of the Underworld itself, instead of simply the entrance to it. When the Hero Twins of the *Popol Vuh* play against the Lords of Death, the ballcourt is located in the Underworld. The Hero Twins dressed as ballplayers are painted on the walls at Naj Tunich, a large cave in the southeastern Petén region of Guatemala, If, in addition to the simple association between ballcourt and pyramid, we include the plaza/palace complex, a much more fruitful interpretation may be proposed. The pyramid would symbolize the upper celestial level, the ballcourt would represent the Underworld, and the palace, plaza, and associated buildings would correspond to the terrestrial level. Thus is created an architectural representation of the universe itself.

One of the best examples of this hypothesis is Uxmal, in the Puuc region of northern Yucatán. The site is dominated by the Pyramid of the Magician, a structure crowned by dual temples. The Nunnery and the Palace of the Governor are ritual and political centers, corresponding to the terrestrial level of humanity. The ballcourt is situated between these complexes, in the lower part of the site center, much like an opening in the earth (fig. 130). The model of the cosmos is complete.

If, indeed, ballcourts represent the Underworld, their placement in the lower parts of many sites would be justified, and their association with pyramids and other types of buildings more easily understood. Moreover, since such associations are to be found in Central and western Mexico, Oaxaca, and the Gulf Coast or the Maya area, it would again confirm the deep and fundamental unity of the ballgame and explain its central position in Mesoamerican life for more than three millennia.

MICHAEL J. TARKANIAN AND DOROTHY HOSLER

9 AN ANCIENT TRADITION CONTINUED: MODERN RUBBER PROCESSING IN MEXICO

Ancient Mesoamericans were processing rubber by 1600 B.C., predating modern vulcanization by 3,500 years. Mesoamericans used natural rubber for a wide variety of purposes, the most important being the manufacture of the solid rubber balls for the Mesoamerican ballgame. The raw material for Mesoamerican rubber balls and for other Mesoamerican rubber artifacts is latex, acquired from the *Castilla elastica* tree. In the *Florentine Codex*, Fray Bernardino de Sahagún identifies this tree, in the Nahuatl language, as *olquauitl*.[1] In Nahuatl, rubber is known as *olli* or *ollin*. The Spanish word for rubber, *hule*, is said to derive from *olquauitl*.

Castilla elastica, the species of tree whose latex was used by ancient Mesoamerican peoples, is indigenous to tropical lowland Mexico (see Filloy, fig. 8), and grows primarily in the states of Chiapas, Yucatán, Tabasco, and Veracruz, below altitudes of 2,300 ft (700 m).[2] The tree also grows along the coasts of Central America and on the western side of the Andes in Peru and Ecuador.[3] *Castilla elastica* thrives in open, well-drained, porous soil, but prefers to grow among other trees in a lightly shaded environment.[4] Adult trees will grow to heights of 65 ft (20 m) or more.

Ancient Mesoamericans also had access to at least two other potential sources of rubber: *guayule* and *Euphorbia elastica*. However, no evidence for the ancient use of either of these types of rubber has been found in the archaeological record or historical documents. *Parthenium argentatum* Gray, commonly known as *guayule*, is a shrub particular to the Chihuahuan desert. *Guayule* is a non-renewable source of rubber, as latex can only be extracted by

grinding, and thus killing, the entire plant. Latex is contained in all parts of the guayule shrub, and grinding achieves the separation of latex from the plant matter. There is secure evidence of the use of *guayule* beginning in the mid-1800s by inhabitants of northern Mexico and the southwestern United States.[5] *Guayule* may also have been used before the Spanish invasion. *Euphorbia elastica* is a rubber tree found primarily in Western Mexico. Much smaller than *C. elastica*, *E. elastica* grows to 26 to 33 ft (8 to 10 m) in height.[6] We have no evidence of modern or ancient exploitation of *E. elastica*.

The latex that *C. elastica* produces is a sticky white liquid that when dried is too brittle to retain its shape, nor does it have the strength, toughness, or elasticity for use in balls, or for other ancient applications such as hollow figurines or hafting bands. Sixteenth-century Spaniards relate that ancient Mesoamerican peoples processed the raw material by mixing the *C. elastica* latex with juice from *Ipomoea alba*, a species of morning glory vine (fig. 131). Fray Toribio de Benavente (Motolinía), one of the first 12 Franciscans to arrive in the New World, recorded some of the earliest known data on rubber:

> Rubber, is the gum of a tree that grows in the hot lands, when [this tree is] punctured it gives white drops, and they run into each other, this is quickly coagulated and turns black, almost soft like a fish; and of this they make the balls that the Indians play with, and these balls bounce higher than the wind balls used in Spain, they are about the same size and darker; the balls of this land are very heavy, they run and jump so much that it is as if they have quicksilver within.[7]

131 *Ipomoea alba*. Liquid extracted from this species of morning glory is used to coagulate and improve the strength and elasticity of *Castilla elastica* latex.

132 Luis Guillén incises a vertical channel into a *Castilla elastica* tree with a tool specifically made for rubber collection.

into the desired form … but I don't understand how when the balls hit the ground they are sent into the air with such incredible bounce.[8]

It was this quote, indicating that ancient Mesoamerican rubber was made with a certain type of vine, that allowed Paul C. Standley, a botanist from the Field Museum of Natural History, Chicago, to identify the vine as morning glory. Standley had observed the use of morning glories in modern indigenous rubber processing, and discusses the processing technology and Spanish accounts of it in a 1942 publication:

> After *Castilla* sap is collected, various substances often are added to it to make the rubber coagulate. The usual one is the juice of certain morning-glories (*Ipomoea*), or especially the juice of the moon-vine (*Calonyction*). In the account of rubber preparation doubtless these vines were mentioned and someone misunderstanding—probably through faulty knowledge of the Nahuatl language—got the idea that it was the vine that really furnished the rubber.[9]

133 The tool made for latex collection has a curved metal blade attached to a wooden handle. The handle is approximately 12 in (30 cm) in length.

While Motolinía described the behavior of rubber, Peter Martyr d'Anghiera, an official royal chronicler of the Spanish court of Charles V from 1520 to 1526, provided insight into how this New World material was produced:

> These balls are made from the juice of a certain vine that climbs the trees like the hops climb the fences; this juice, when boiled becomes hardened and turned into a mass and is able to be shaped

"Moon-vine" and *Calonyction* are synonyms for *Ipomoea alba*.[10]

Modern Techniques of Making Rubber
In our ethnographic study of modern indigenous rubber production in Zacualpa, Chiapas, Mexico, we found that the combination of *C. elastica* and *I. alba* for rubber production is still a part of contemporary knowledge in the area, although it

134 Diagonal channels are cut into the *Castilla elastica* tree. With this method, many parallel diagonal incisions are made to flow into the center channel, greatly increasing the volume of latex collected.

However, they had not made rubber with this method for at least 30 years, until they demonstrated the technique for us in June 1997.

The Guillén brothers first cut a vertical channel into the bark of the tree (fig. 132), using a tool specifically designed for this purpose (fig. 133). This tool consists of a curved metal blade attached to a wooden handle. Fausto Guillén maintained that this tool probably had a pre-Columbian counterpart made of wood or bone as the bark and wood of *C. elastica* are soft enough to incise using a cutting tool made of either of these materials. The Guillen brothers then cut diagonal channels into the tree, to direct the flow of latex into the central channel (fig. 134). The latex runs quickly from these channels and is collected in a bucket at the base of the tree (fig. 135). After 10 to 15 minutes, the latex stops flowing. It is then strained into another container to remove any insects or plant matter present in the collection bucket (fig. 136). Luis Guillén asserted that rubber collection should take place before 11 a.m., as the flow of latex is at its peak during the morning. He also said that the volume of latex is greatest in March or April, at the end of the dry season. Our observations confirmed this: we collected latex in March and late June, and found that the latex flow was considerably greater earlier in the year.

After the latex is collected, the *I. alba* can be prepared for mixing. Luis and his brothers cut a 16-ft (5-m) length of *I. alba* vine, strip the leaves

is practiced infrequently. Zacualpa was the site of a large *C. elastica* research plantation in the early 1900s and is home to many of these trees today. In Zacualpa, we worked with the Guillén family, who live on the former plantation lands, to learn traditional rubber-processing techniques. The older men of the family, Luis and Fausto Guillén, recalled making large solid balls in their childhood by mixing *C. elastica* and *I. alba.*

135 The latex is funneled into a bucket placed at the bottom of the tree. Osvaldo Guillén-Sanchez holds a curved piece of metal that is hammered into the trees to guide the collected latex into the bucket.

136 Fausto Guillén and Osvaldo Guillén-Sanchez filter the latex with a metal kitchen sieve to remove debris.

137 *(right)* After stripping the *Ipomoea alba* vine of its leaves and flowers, Luis Guillén wraps the vine into a coil. He then softens it by beating it on a rock with a pipe.

138 *(above)* Luis Guillén squeezes liquid from the *Ipomoea alba* vine directly into the latex. He used approximately 25 fl. oz (750 ml) of latex and 2 fl. oz (50 ml) of *Ipomoea alba* in this demonstration.

139 *(above right)* The latex-*Ipomoea alba* mixture solidifies into a workable mass that can be formed into any shape. The latex began to solidify in the shape of the container approximately 10 minutes after mixing with the *Ipomoea alba*.

and flowers, and wrap the vine into a coil. After beating and crushing the coiled vine on a rock (fig. 137), they squeeze the juice of the *I. alba* vine directly into the bucket of latex (fig. 138). The Guillén brothers used approximately 2 fl. oz (50 ml) of the *I. alba* liquid mixed with 25 fl. oz (750 ml) of *C. elastica* latex in their demonstration for us. They then stirred the mixture for 10 minutes, causing the latex to coagulate into a solid, elastic mass of rubber (fig. 139). After the latex coagulates, it can be shaped into any desired form. We easily shaped the resulting rubber into a ball approximately 5.5 in (14 cm) in diameter (fig. 140). The rubber hardens fully after several minutes and cannot then be reshaped.

Our laboratory research has shown that by using the juice of *I. alba*, the ancient Mesoamericans were able to alter the mechanical properties of natural latex and produce a rubber with double the elasticity of unprocessed latex.[11] *Ipomoea alba* achieves this effect through two complementary mechanisms. It adds sulfur-containing molecules capable of cross-linking the latex chains, creating a more elastic and tougher

material. At the same time, it purifies the latex, removing certain proteins that inhibit elastic behavior and would deter cross-linking, even if sulfur-containing molecules were present.[12] Sulfur is the element used to cross-link natural rubber in the modern vulcanization process.

Rubber Artifacts in the Archaeological Record

Rubber artifacts are unusual in the archaeological record, but archaeologists have recovered over a hundred examples from ancient Mesoamerican contexts. The oldest archaeological rubber artifacts are 12 solid rubber balls recovered at the site of El Manatí in the modern state of Veracruz, Mexico. These balls range from 5 to 12 in (13 cm to 30 cm) in diameter. The two oldest Manatí balls date to 1600 B.C., on the basis of radiocarbon determinations of associated material.[13] This is the earliest known date for the use of solid rubber. Latex in its liquid state was probably used far earlier than 1600 B.C., for the medicinal purposes discussed below.

Apart from the Manatí balls, rubber artifacts were also dredged from the Sacred Cenote at Chichén Itzá, Yucatán, Mexico, in the 20th century. The Cenote rubber artifacts date to between A.D. 850 and 1550 on the basis of stylistic attributes of associated artifacts.[14] The range of artifacts recovered suggests numerous applications of this material, including small rubber balls, hollow and solid rubber human figurines and body parts, and a stone tool hafted with a rubber band. The stone tool is particularly interesting as it utilizes a thick rubber band to secure a stone blade to a wooden handle. This ingenious use of rubber both binds and secures the blade to the handle and provides a means of absorbing shock during use.

Among the most common of the Cenote artifacts were wooden tool handles coated with rubber and small rubber balls embedded in a copal matrix used as wicks in ceremonial incense burners (see cat. 2–4). These wicks were manufactured using four distinct techniques. Wicks containing rubber and copal could be made by coating a solid copal sphere with rubber, or by wrapping strips of rubber around a solid copal core. The two other wick types were made solely from rubber: one by winding strips of rubber into a ball and the other by shaping solid rubber into a sphere.

Medicinal and Religious Uses of Rubber

It is clear from both the archaeological evidence, such as that from the Cenote, and documentary sources, that latex and rubber were materials of great significance to ancient Mesoamerican peoples. Latex was highly prized for its healing powers. Fray Bernardino de Sahagún, who chronicled the daily lives and practices of the Aztecs in the early 16th century, catalogued many uses of rubber in the *Florentine Codex*. His most detailed accounts relate to its medicinal applications. Ear aches, dry nostrils, hoarseness, and lip sores could all be alleviated with drops of liquid rubber. More serious ailments such as the "spitting of blood" could be remedied by drinking a mixture of chocolate, liquid rubber, small chilis, and water. Suppositories made in part of rubber were used to cure female fertility problems, male urinary difficulties, and colic.[15]

According to native texts, Aztec gods and the priests or other individuals who impersonated them painted themselves with liquid rubber. Tlaloc, Teteo innan, Tzapotlan tenan, Ciuapipiltin, Opochtli, Xipe totec, and their impersonators, had rubber painted on their arms and faces or wore rubber-painted paper crowns. Many of these gods were water-related deities and used rubber for its water-resistant properties.[16] Opochtli, the god of water folk, is depicted entirely coated with rubber.[17]

Although Sahagún never explicitly writes that ancient Mesoamericans coated items with rubber, there are accounts of Mesoamericans sealing bags with rubber to carry water. Also, South American people reportedly waterproofed cloth with latex from the *Hevea brasiliensis* tree. Like the gods, the Aztec people frequently painted themselves with rubber and wore rubber-painted paper crowns in ritual ceremonies. Rubber-coated papers and other rubber items were often burned during ceremonies, producing a dense, sweet-smelling black smoke.

Sahagún also mentions several mechanically intensive uses of rubber, including "very precious" rubber-soled sandals,[18] rubber hammers, and rubber-tipped drumsticks for playing the two-toned drum. Such items have not yet been found in the archaeological record. While many of the uses of rubber that Sahagún reports utilize unprocessed liquid latex, rubber for items such as sandals, hammers, drum sticks, and balls needed to be processed with *I. alba* to give it the necessary elasticity, strength, and toughness.[19]

Unprocessed latex and rubber artifacts produced using *I. alba* occupied a singular and exclusive niche in the Mesoamerican material world. We do not yet know how Mesoamerican peoples discovered that liquid extracted from

I. alba mixed with *C. elastica* latex produced a rubbery material suitable for balls and other items, but we do know that they were familiar with morning glory: the plant appears in iconography at least from the Classic Period. At least two species (*Rivea corymbosa* and *Ipomoea violacea*) contain d-lysergic acid amide and d-isolysergic amide (closely related to the hallucinogenic drug LSD) and were ingested by priests to produce altered states of consciousness in divinatory rituals and healing.

Regardless of how the ancient Mesoamerican peoples came to understand the effect of morning glory on latex, their ingenious and successful experiments in materials processing were prerequisite to the emergence of the Mesoamerican ballgame, which became a focal and integrating element in ancient ritual, religious, and political life.

140 Luis Guillén and Michael Tarkanian show a ball that they made by mixing *Ipomoea alba* with *Castilla elastica* latex.

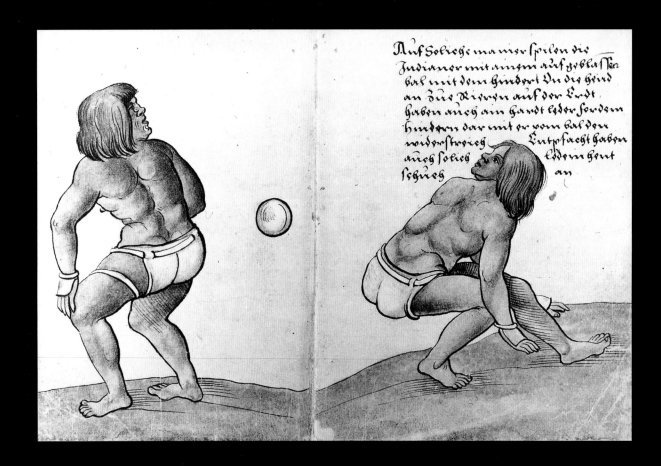

Auf solliche manier spilen die
Judianer mit ainem auffgeblassnen
bal mit dem Hindert vnd die Hend
an die Niewen auff der Erdt
haben auch ain Handt leder forden
hindten dar mit er vom halben
widerstraich   Entpfacht haben
auch sollich   Lodem heut
schuech   an

TED J.J. LEYENAAR

10 THE MODERN BALLGAMES OF SINALOA: A SURVIVAL OF THE AZTEC ULLAMALIZTLI

*U*llamaliztli was the rubber ballgame played by the Aztecs and other Nahuatl-speaking peoples in Mexico at the time of the Spanish Conquest. The name is a combination of two words: *ullama*, which means the playing of a game with a ball, and *ulli*, rubber. The Colonial sources document that at the time of the arrival of the Spanish in Central Mexico in the 16th century, indigenous peoples played a type of ballgame in which the players deflected the ball with their hips and buttocks.[1] The essential garment for these hip ballplayers consisted of a *maxtlatl* (loincloth), leather hipguards, and wide leather bands around the buttocks. The game could, however, also be played using the arms and elbows to deflect the ball, with a stick, or with a *manopla* (a handstone) used to bat the ball.[2] In ceremonies before and after the game players wore a variety of accessories decorating their uniforms.

Elaborate ceremonies surrounding the games and distinct uniforms developed early in the history of the sport (see Bradley and Scott). Thousands of surviving works of art depicting the ballgame from the Formative Period to the Early Colonial Era (1500 B.C.–A.D. 1530) attest to its preeminence in Mesoamerican life.

During the Classic Period (A.D. 300–900), the cultural context of the ballgame appears to have been largely religious, hence the widespread use of the term "ritual ballgame." By the Late Postclassic, however, a secular, recreational aspect to the ballgame is documented in the early Colonial sources.[3] The Spaniards regarded this secular aspect of the game as separate from its religious function. So, when Hernán Cortés—

the Spanish conqueror of Mexico—returned to Spain in 1528, he took with him ballplayers who gave a demonstration at the court of Charles V (fig. 141 and frontispiece).

The rubber ballgame survived throughout the entire Colonial Period (1521–1821), and afterward. During investigations conducted in the 1970s, I was able to document two types of ballgames, known as *ulama de brazo* (or *de antebrazo*) and *ulama de cadera*, in the northwestern Mexican state of Sinaloa.[4] Decades later, I witnessed a third form of the surviving ballgame called *ulama de palo* (or *de mazo*). These three modern ballgames, all known by the Aztec name *ulama*, provide a fascinating glimpse into the ancient past. What follows is a description of the Sinaloa games and players, and their roots in the games of pre-Hispanic Mesoamerica.

Ulama de Brazo

The game in which the arm is used to keep the ball in play is called *ulama de brazo*, or arm-*ulama*. Arm-*ulama* is played in the northern part of Sinaloa, from Culiacán, the state capital, to Río Sinaloa. In the little towns of Mocorito and Guamúchil it is a popular game, especially in the dry season when work on the land takes up less time. It is played on a field, called a *taste* (fig. 142), a corruption of *tlachtli*, the Nahuatl word for ballcourt.

When a game is to be played, the *taste* is marked off by thick lines drawn with the sandal or shoe. The court must be completely flat so that the ball will bounce properly. The *taste* is 330 ft (100 m) long but only 4.5 ft (1.40 m) wide. In the middle of the court a dividing line called

141 Drawing by Christoph Weiditz (1528) showing Central Mexican ballplayers performing at the court of Charles V.

143 *(opposite, left)* Playing
the *por abajo* position,
Mocorito 1971.

144 *(opposite, right)*
Playing the *por arriba*
position, Mocorito 1971.

analco is drawn, giving each team a field of 165 by
4.5 ft (50 by 1.40 m). The back line is called *chivo*,
and at both this line and the *analco* an umpire is
stationed who is called *juez* or *veedor*. The game
is played with a solid rubber ball weighing about
18 oz (500 g). To prevent the ball from losing its
round shape when not in use it is kept in a
wooden mold.[5]

Games are played between two teams
consisting of one, two, or three players per side.
A three-man team is the most popular. The
players have a name corresponding with their
number and position on the court. When there
is only one man to a side, both players are called
mano. With two men to a side the first player,
the one closest to the *analco*, is called *topador*,
meaning hitter, and the second player *chivero*,
after the back-line. When three play against
three, the first player is called *topador*, the second
segundo golpe (second hitter), and the third
chivero. The players wear a *rodillera* (knee
protector) to protect their knee from scraping
against the ground when playing *por abajo*, or
low over the ground (fig. 143). *Por arriba*, or
jumping high into the air, is the other way of
playing (fig. 144). The ball is hit with the forearm
near the elbow, which is wrapped with a *faja*,
a cotton tape at least 10 ft (3 m) long and 1.1 in
(3 cm) wide.

The first phase of the game starts with the
pegua, meaning "to begin," in Nahuatl, during
which a toss determines which team will serve.
The *topador* serves the ball with his hand, and a
member of the opposing team returns it with the
wrapped part of his forearm. From then on, only
the forearm is used, except during a service.
When the ball is returned it must always cross
the *analco*, but need not stay within the side-
lines. If the ball comes to a stop on the *pegua*
side, the other team takes the service, which is
now called *male*. The *malero*, or server, can be
any of the three players but is often the *topador*.
The *malero* now serves the ball with the forearm,
first holding it with his left hand against the
taped part of his right forearm.

For the service, which can be played *por abajo*
or *por arriba*, the ball must always bounce within
the *taste* and in front of the *analco*. During

rallys—to use a tennis term—it is fascinating
to see players jumping high into the air or
dropping into an almost prone position when
playing *por abajo*. Points are called *rayas* (lines),
from the marks made on the ground to keep
score, and they are scored in one of the following
ways:

When the ball is received in the wrong way
(fig. 145), that is, on an unwrapped part of the
arm, with a straight arm or with some other
part of the body, the *male* (service side) gets a
point when the fault is made by the other side;
if the *male* team makes the fault, the service
goes to the other team and the score remains
the same.

When a served ball is not returned but passes
the *chivo* within the width of the *taste*, the
service side gets a point. The ball is then said
to be *chiviada*. This situation illustrates the
function of the narrowness of the court. If at
service, the ball is not received but goes off-
side before the *chivo*, the *male* is repeated
until a good serve is made, the receiving and
returning of the ball not being affected by
the width of the *taste*.

The service side receives a point if the ball
is not returned beyond the *analco*, whether
inside or outside the *taste*; in other words,
in this instance the players are not limited
to the width of the court.[6]

Points are counted in a curious manner; for
example from one the score progresses straight
to three, skipping two. A game ends when a team
with seven *rayas* (points) gains two more points
clear of the other side. These winning points are
not counted as eight or nine, but are called *se
van* ("they are at the point of") and *ganan*
("they win").

The most interesting aspect of the game lies in
the possibilities for both upward and downward
fluctuation of the score. As a result, a game can
seem endless, especially when the two teams are
well matched. There are several phases during
the match at which a team has a critical, movable

142 A *taste* for arm-*ulama*
at the start of the game.

veedor	7 meters		juez			veedor
chivero	segundo golpe	topador	topador	segundo golpe	chivero	
chivo		analco				chivo

score and losing one or two points will cause it to return to zero. These critical, movable phases during the match are called *urre*, derived from the Nahuatl word *ollin*, meaning "movement." For arm-*ulama* these critical phases of the game occur when the points of three, five, and seven are scored. These are called *urre tres*, *urre cinco*, and *urre siete*. This fluctuation of the score is also characteristic of the other two *ulamas* in Sinaloa.

145 Receiving the ball in the wrong way in the *por abajo* position, Guamúchil 1969.

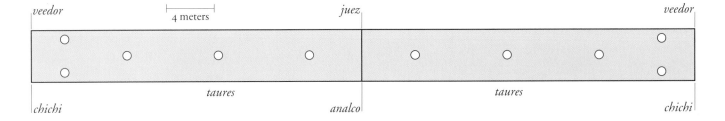

veedor   juez   veedor

4 meters

taures   taures

chichi   analco   chichi

146 A *taste* for hip-*ulama* at the start of the game.

Ulama de Cadera

Ulama de cadera (hip-*ulama*) is played in southern Sinaloa and south of Mazatlán. As with arm-*ulama*, it is played on a *taste*, a field about 215 ft (65 m) by about 13 ft (4 m) (fig. 146). The *taste* is paced off for the game and the lines are drawn with the sandal or shoe, which gives a certain variation of the dimensions.

The center line is called *analco*, the base line *chichi*. At *analco* and *chichi* there is an umpire called *juez* or *veedor*. A team consists of at least five players, called *taures*, derived from Nahuatl word *tlaulle* ("the owners of something made of rubber"). Their outfit, called a *fajado*, consists of a *gamuza de venado* (deerskin loincloth) held in place by a *faja de algodón* (cotton belt). Sometimes a player adds a second piece of leather on his playing hip for extra protection (fig. 147).

147 Gregorio from El Habal in a ballplayer's outfit, with an extra hip pad, El Chilillo 1974.

Each player also wears a *chimali*, a leather belt placed low around the buttocks. *Chimalli* is also a Nahuatl word meaning "shield," or "protection"—an accurate description. It keeps the buttocks protected when a player slides over the ground to return a low ball and is the most important part of the hip ballplayer's uniform.

The solid rubber ball for hip-*ulama* weighs about 6.6 lb (3 kg) and is kept in a mold made of wood or cement to prevent it from losing its shape when not in use (fig. 148). The ball can be played *por arriba* (fig. 149) or *por abajo* (fig. 150). Watching the players is a fascinating spectacle. The player propels the ball with the hip; the hand is used only for serving. The first team to get eight *rayas* is the winner. When one of the team has one, four, or five *rayas*, the ball is served high in the air. The *golpe por arriba*, as this high service is called, can be performed by any of the five players of the team, but it is considered better to have a separate service player, the *golpeador*, for this particular serve. When the leading team has two, three, six, or seven points, the serve is low over the ground. This low serve is called *male por abajo*. This serve, too, can be made by a separate player, called *malero*, if the umpire of the *analco* does not make it. Thus, there can be seven players on each side when use is made of a special *golpeador* and *malero*, but due to the shortage of hip-*ulama* players a team consists mostly of five players. Just as in arm-*ulama*, points are called *rayas* and we also find the *urre*-phases. Those occur when one team with two or three points loses the next one; it is then said to be an *urre* of two to three, or *urre tres* (three). If the team loses the next *raya* its score returns to zero. *Urre* also occur when a team has six or seven points. Losing the next *raya* the players speak then of *urre* of six to seven or *urre siete* (seven). If a team gains four consecutive points, the other team loses all their *rayas*. Table 4 sets out the fluctuations in the score during a typical game played by teams designated A and B (U = *urre*).

When one team accumulates eight points or, to be more accurate, reaches the eighth position, the game is over. In this version of the ballgame, points are scored as follows: when a player sustains two hits on the body it constitutes a fault; other body faults include receiving the ball in places other than the leather-covered hip; or landing on the ball when playing *por abajo*. All of these give the opponent a point. If the ball passes over *de chichi* (end line) but is still within the lines during a rally or on service *por arriba*, the other side gets a point. If a served ball does not cross the *analco*, also called the *pelota muerta* (dead-ball), the opponents get a point.

A fault in returning the service *por abajo* in which the player's foot, buttock, or some other part of the body touches the *analco* or goes beyond it, also costs a point. This is called *guala*. Because the score can go up or down for so many reasons, it can take a very long time to win a game. In the games observed during fieldwork in the 1970s, neither side scored higher than three *rayas*, repeatedly returning to zero after the *urre tres* phase. The longest match of the last century is recorded for Don Germán Tirado de La Palma. In 1930, his team vanquished the team of Puerto de Las Canoas only after seven consecutive days of play. Such epic matches, however, are a thing of the past.

Ulama de Palo

A third game which I did not observe during my original investigations in the 1970s was one called *ulama de palo*, in which a wooden instrument called a *palo* functioned as a kind of racket or bat (fig. 151). Surprisingly, this game, which I had been informed had not been played since the 1950s, experienced a successful revival around 1980. The bat or *palo* weighs between 11 and 15 lb (5 and 7 kg). The *taste* measures 395 ft (120 m) long by 6.6 ft (2 m) wide, and the solid rubber

A – B	A – B	A – B	
1 – 0	1 – 0	0 – 3	
2 – 0	0 – 1	1 – U3	
3 – 0	0 – 2	2 – 0	
4 – 0	1 – U3		
4 – 1	2 – 0		
4 – 2			
4 – 3	1 – U3		
0 – 4	0 – 3		

A – B	A – B	A – B	A – B
2 – 0	3 – 0	3 – 0	3 – 0
U3 – 1	U3 – 1	U3 – 1	U5 – 1
0 – 2	3 – 0	0 – 2	4 – 0

A – B	A – B	A – B	A – B
4 – 0	4 – 0	6 – 0	U7 – 1
5 – 0	5 – 0	U7 – 1	5 – 2
4 – 1	6 – 0	5 – 2	4 – 3
7 – 0	U7 – 1	5 – 3	5 – U3
	7 – 0	0 – 4	6 – 0

A – B	A – B	A – B	A – B
6 – 1	7 – U3	6 – U3	6 – U3
U7 – 2	8 – 0	7 – 0	2 – 0
6 – 3		8 – 0	8 – 1
0 – 4			

Table 4 Fluctuations in the score in a typical game of hip-*ulama* between teams A and B.

148 Cement mold with solid rubber ball, Gregorio and his family, El Habal 1974.

The survival of terms such as *taste*, *taures*, *analco*, *pegua*, and *urre*, and, especially, *ulama*, the name of the game itself, points to a pre-Spanish origin. And of course, the material from which the ball is made, *ulli* (rubber), was unknown outside the New World until European contact.

As previously mentioned, the game took on a distinctly recreational function in the Late Postclassic (A.D. 1200–1519). Thus, it must have been played by many who did not belong to the nobility. The disintegration of the indigenous priestly class and the almost total destruction by the Spaniards of the visible expressions of native religion—the ballcourts too were demolished—did not mean the immediate loss of the game. In the 16th century it must certainly still have been played everywhere in the central highlands and other Mesoamerican regions—albeit with some modifications since the courts themselves quickly fell into ruin. In central Mesoamerica the game lost favor because the Spanish priests saw it as a survival of heathen practices and so suppressed it. In northwestern Mexico, however, rubber ballgames have continued uninterrupted, perhaps because the Spanish did not colonize this peripheral region on a large scale. We may also assume that the religious function of the game was more important in central than in northwestern Mexico.

149 Manuel playing the *por arriba* position, El Habal 1970.

ball weighs 18 to 21 oz (500 to 600 g). As in *ulama de brazo* one can play one to one, two to two, and three to three. The *rayas* are scored in the same way as in *ulama de brazo*, resulting in similar fluctuations in the score. *Ulama de palo* is as fascinating as the other two *ulamas*, so it is fortunate that it has been revived and is no longer just an artifact of the past.

Considerations and Conclusions

It will be evident from the foregoing that the three *ulamas* played in northern and southern Sinaloa have a very special character. Although none of the 16th-century sources describes all of the facets of the game, it is clear from archaeological evidence that several kinds of rubber ballgames were also performed at the time of the arrival of the Spaniards.

The use of the lower arm and hip in games in Sinaloa today is a clear indication of the survival and perpetuation of the pre-Hispanic game. None of the ballgames popular in Spain at that time can be seen as a possible precursor.

150 Kike playing the *por abajo* position, El Chilillo 1974.

In Sinaloa, Mexico, a prototype of the rubber ballgame has survived in a form without the use of a court with earthen or stone walls. The players' equipment, especially that of the hip-*ulama* ballplayer and the protective padding of the arm-*ulama* ballplayer, have their roots in the distant pre-Columbian past. The method of counting *rayas* points in the same direction.[7] The similarity between the posture of the hip-*ulama* ballplayer of the Nayarit model-ballcourt (fig. 152) dating from the Late Formative Period and that of the Sinaloan player in 1974 points to an extraordinary continuity in the way of playing.

All of these elements attest that *ulama*, in the three forms played today, can be seen as the survival of the Aztec ballgame *ullamaliztli*. That the Mesoamerican ballgame has survived and flourished for more than 3,000 years earns it the distinction of being one of humanity's great cultural expressions.

151 Ballplayer 'Chevo Rojo' showing the 'mazo', Culiacán 1990.

152 Detail of a model of a ballcourt. The hip-ballgames depicted on the ballcourt models from ancient West Mexico are very similar to the modern game of *ulama* played in Sinaloa. Model of a ballcourt; Late Formative Period, Ixtlán del Río, 300 B.C.–A.D. 200; Western Mexico, Nayarit; *pottery*; 5.5 × 8 × 13 in (14 × 20.3 × 33 cm); Los Angeles County Museum of Art (cat. 30).

E. MICHAEL WHITTINGTON

11 EVERYTHING OLD IS NEW AGAIN: THE ENDURING LEGACY OF THE ANCIENT GAMES

Some three thousand years ago—the dawn of Mesoamerican civilization—teams of players devised a game played with a rubber ball. Although the type of game varied from place to place, all shared two uniquely Mesoamerican innovations: team participation, as opposed to individual competition, and a ball made of rubber. The significance of this wondrous material cannot be overstated. When Europeans first saw bouncing rubber balls they were amazed. Ultimately, rubber would be one of the New World materials that would transform the Old. How did ancient people learn that milky plant juices could be transformed into a bouncing ball? That discovery is shrouded in mystery, but there is no mystery to the result. It led to a game—one which would become fundamentally intertwined with ancient Mesoamerican life and thought.

The ancient Mesoamerican ballgame was a phenomenon, inspiring the creation of countless works of art immortalizing those who played it. In examining this phenomenon, the parallels between those ancient competitions and their modern counterparts are irresistibly fascinating. Certainly, it can be argued that without a bouncing ball many sports as we now know them would not exist. Moreover, the modern concept of teams may itself ultimately owe its influence to Mesoamerica. But there are other, less obvious, parallels which point to the central position of games in both ancient and modern life.

Ancient games of the Old and New Worlds were played in unique structures. In Mesoamerica these were the ballcourts, usually I-shaped masonry structures with a central playing alley and sloped or straight-sided walls

against which the ball would be banked to keep it in play. The courts were situated within an architectural complex, an arrangement that was not accidental. Mesoamerican public buildings—pyramids, temples, and palaces—were both tangible examples of the divine rights of the ruling elites and cosmograms, symbolic representations of the universe. Thus did the Classic Maya perceive the main ballcourt at the site of Copán in Honduras as a chasm into the earth, a symbolic portal into the supernatural Underworld (fig. 153). The Copán ballcourt is also a stage for the magnificent hieroglyphic stairway that rises in the background. Among the events in the stairway's carved text are the histories of conquest by and of Copán kings.[1]

Symbolic relationships such as these were certainly understood by the architects of Chicago's Soldier Field (fig. 154), which was built to resemble a hippodrome—the oval stadium for chariot races in ancient Greece and Rome. Situated high above the spectators in Chicago are replicas of Classical temples. The selection of Classical orders for modern public buildings is deliberate. Libraries, government offices, state memorials, and museums, routinely draw upon this ancient architectural style to evoke feelings of permanence, and even of authority, upon those crossing their thresholds. The message to the spectators is undeniable: you are here as witnesses to a monumental spectacle.

Such a spectacle is indeed unfolding in the historic photograph taken during the 1926 Army-Navy football game. It shows two modern warrior classes—whose disdain for one another is legendary—playing a ballgame. As did their

153 Modern Sinaloan *ulama* players in the ballcourt at Copán, Honduras. The relationship of the ballcourt and the adjacent ceremonial architecture can clearly be seen.

154 The Army-Navy football game at Soldier's Field, Chicago, 1926. This modern stadium was designed to evoke the games and contests of Classical antiquity.

ancient Maya counterparts, the Army and Navy use a ballgame instead of a battle to annually diffuse their rivalries.

This notion of sport as a component of, or perhaps even a substitute for, war is a very Mesoamerican one, especially among the Late Classic Period Maya (A.D. 700–900). Images of war captives and warriors prepared for battle are portrayed on sculptural decoration on ballcourts throughout the Maya region of southern Mesoamerica.[2] Many of these depict the ruling

elite outfitted as ballplayers, suggesting that the games were the final, and very public, spectacle of war between cities. After a battle was won, a ballgame would have been played, with the victor and loser predetermined by the battle's outcome. Sacrifice of those defeated in the battle and ballgame would then have followed. Such spectacularly gruesome scenes of warrior/ballplayer sacrifice are depicted on the ballcourt reliefs at the sites of El Tajín in Veracruz and Chichén Itzá in Yucatán.

155 The mascots for the Army and Navy football teams meet before the game, 1923.

One of the more direct parallels between the ancient games and their modern manifestations —at least in the United States—is the widespread use of animal imagery. As the use of Classical orders for buildings conveys a political message, the behavior of particular animal species— cunning, ferocity, and stealth, to name just a few—are qualities humans often admire and seek to emulate.

Again, the annual competition between our modern warriors demonstrates this. A photograph from the 1923 Army-Navy football game shows the teams' mascots—a goat and a mule—facing one another before the game (fig. 155). The choice of each animal as a symbol is deliberate. In its early history, the army used mules to transport supplies and, according to popular lore, it was this creature's stubborn determination in difficult situations that caused it to be admired and, ultimately, to be elevated to a symbol. The Navy goat relates to a late 19th-century episode in which a pet goat kept on board a seagoing vessel was so beloved by the sailors that after the creature's death it became the symbol for the elite naval academy.[3]

Many modern sports teams choose fearsome predatory beasts and raptors as symbols. What is even more fascinating are the fans who transform themselves into the wild beasts exemplified by their favorite team (fig. 156). In the parlance of Western psychology, this is known as deindividuation—the process of relinquishing one's individual identity to that of the group.[4] Thus, when a fan of the Carolina Panthers paints his face with the team's blue color and feline markings, he has signaled that he is participating in a collective activity of more significance than anything he can accomplish as an individual. Painting one's face is a dramatic example of this type of individual surrender to the group. In many cultures face painting accompanies major ritual rites of passage, as well as warfare. The football fan is relinquishing his control to that of the group, a difficult thing for modern Westerners to do, so steeped as they are in popular culture which idealizes the individual. It was precisely this development of team, rather than individual, initiative that made the Mesoamerican ballgames unique.

A range of animals are associated with the ancient Mesoamerican games. The player's equipment—yokes, *palmas*, and *hachas* (see Scott)—incorporates imagery of jaguars, peccaries, deer, monkeys, coyotes, eagles (fig. 157), parrots, turkeys, and reptiles. A *palma* from the Philadelphia Museum of Art (fig. 158) takes the form of a crocodile, a fierce predator which is equally at home in the watery and terrestrial realms. Other creatures may have more clearly defined roles within the ballgame. Parrot imagery, for example, is commonly associated with the ballgame. Late Classic sculptures of these birds were used delineate the courts of Xochicalco (cat. 35) and Copán into specific zones. An *hacha* from the Maya Highlands of Guatemala, now in the St. Louis Art Museum (cat. 98), depicts a ballplayer wearing an elaborate parrot helmet. Such motifs may relate to an episode from the *Popol Vuh*—the great Maya

156 A Carolina Panthers fan with feline face paint. Modern sports teams (and their fans) and ancient warriors and ballplayers frequently incorporate symbols of powerful predators.

157 Harpy eagle *hacha*; Middle Classic Period, Veracruz, A.D. 400–600; Mexico, Gulf Coast; *stone*; 7.5 × 7 × 10.5 in (19.1 × 17.8 × 26.7 cm); Fine Arts Museums of San Francisco (cat. 65). Mesoamerica's largest raptor, these birds were associated with human sacrifice.

158 Crocodile *palma*;
Late Classic Period,
Veracruz, A.D. 600–900;
Mexico, Gulf Coast; *stone*;
26 × 9 × 5 in
(66 × 22.9 × 13 cm);
Philadelphia Museum
of Art (cat. 70).

159 *(below right)* Maya
painted ceramic vessels
illustrate ballplayers in
standardized poses. This
player kneels on one knee
to prepare to return the
ball to his opponent.
Cylinder vessel with
ballplayer; Late Classic
Period, Maya,
A.D. 700–900; Mexico,
Northern Yucatán; *pottery*;
6.7 × 6 in (17.5 × 15.3 cm);
The Bowers Museum
of Cultural Art (cat. 109).

160 *(below)* Carolina
Panthers linebacker Kevin
Greene. Many of the
postures and gestures
of modern, professional
football players are also
standardized to convey
specific emotion and
information to the
spectators.

creation epic—in which the ballplayers
Xbalanque and Hunahpu shoot out the teeth
of a boastful parrot with their blowguns.[5]
Maya ballplayers are often shown wearing
elaborate deer, jaguar, or vulture headdresses,
which have been interpreted as attributes of gods
and supernaturals attired as ballplayers.[6] It may
also be possible that wearing these headdresses—
such as the bird and deer examples depicted on
the Pearlman Handball Vase (cat. 107)—could
serve to distinguish the players of one team
from another.

The theatrical and symbolic postures and
gestures of ancient and modern athletes are
remarkably consistent. Late Classic Maya
ballplayers are often depicted in a kneeling
posture with their arms extended (fig. 159).
Although the precise rules governing the Maya
game are unknown, this pose is commonly
depicted on works of art. It may have been part
of the standard defense used by a player to deflect
the solid rubber ball from his body and return
it to his opponent. This stance, meaning "play
ball," would have been as widely understood
as that of a modern football referee when he
raises his arms to indicate a touchdown has been
scored. Modern professional football players in
the United States have developed a variety of
postures and gestures, not all of them as heroic
as that of Carolina Panthers linebacker Kevin
Greene, who has just tackled the opposition
quarterback, preventing him from scoring
(fig. 160). Stripped of his protective helmet,

which he holds in his outstretched arm, he kneels to receive the adulation of the crowd. It is a noble and theatrical gesture, worthy of an ancient gladiator bowing before Caesar in the colosseum.

Warfare and contact sports have traditionally been viewed as exclusively male domains. Ancient female warriors may be the stuff of legend, but several types of Formative Period (1500–100 B.C.) figurines do appear to depict female ballplayers.[7] This identification is based on the presence of standard ballgame padded yokes, belts, kneepads, and the like worn by these figurines, combined with their prominent breasts (fig. 161). Whether these figurines depict females *and* ballplayers is a topic of dispute. Gillett Griffin (see catalogue entries on Xochipala in this volume) posits that female ballplayers are a fundamentally un-Mesoamerican concept. But Jane Day's essay on performances in the court is a compelling argument that women may have dressed as ballplayers in their roles as actors in mythic pageants staged in the ballcourt. In our own society, the views regarding women's participation in a variety of public and private areas have changed radically over the past few decades. Women serving in the military, even in combat roles, or playing football (fig. 162), no longer raise eyebrows.

Mesoamerica's ancient ballgame and modern professional and collegiate sports do exhibit striking parallels. Our modern societies elevate our most talented athletes to the status of heroes and heroines. We heap upon them great financial and personal rewards. Some competitors use their sports careers as stepping-stones to positions of even greater power and celebrity in politics and the entertainment industry. The combination of athletics and politics is not new, of course. Many Classic Period monuments depict rulers attired in the costume of a ballplayer. Late Classic Maya rulers commonly took the name of ballplayer (*Ah Pitzlawal*) as one of their official titles.[8]

The above described activities are not the only ones linking the ancient games with the modern. Musical accompaniment—the equivalent of half-time shows—must have been a feature of major games. Caches of ritually interred miniature musical instruments recovered from Tenochtitlan's principal ballcourt (see Matos Moctezuma) confirm the close association of the ballgame and music. Betting also took place. The intense gambling that accompanied the Aztec games was described by the Spanish chronicler Durán in the 16th century.[9] That wagering on the outcome of sporting events is enjoyed with gusto in our own time does not need to be elaborated here. Elevating the status and rewarding those who excel at competition is, after all, understandable. This very human characteristic is the greatest thread linking the ancient Mesoamerican ballgames with our modern world.

162 Danielle Hopkins, a professional football player who plays with the Nashville Dream.

161 Standing female ballplayer with maize sprout helmet; Early Formative Period, Xochipala, 1000–800 B.C.; Western Mexico, Guerrero; *pottery*; h. 7 in (17.8 cm); Snite Museum of Art, University of Notre Dame (cat. 26).

CATALOGUE

Unless otherwise noted,
catalogue entries are by
E. Michael Whittington.

Also contributing:
Gillett G. Griffin GGG
Douglas E. Bradley DEB

RUBBER

1 RUBBER BALL
Formative Period, Olmec
1200–600 B.C.
Mexico, Veracruz,
El Manatí
rubber
3.4 × 10.6 in (8.6 × 27 cm)
Museo Nacional de
Antropología, Mexico
City.
10-357501

One of the few rubber balls to have been recovered archaeologically, this ancient, misshapen ball comes from the site of El Manatí. Rubber is a fragile, organic material, and its remarkable preservation was due to the waterlogged condition at the site. Mesoamerican rubber was not vulcanized in the modern sense, so centuries of burial have deformed the ball's original spherical shape.

For many Mesoamerican peoples, rubber was sacred and a gift worthy of offering to the gods. This group of three bowls (2–4) was discovered during explorations of Chichén Itzá's Sacred Cenote, into which they had been tossed as offerings. The Cenote was a large sinkhole that was a focal point for Maya religious activity. Many types of offerings, including ceramics, textiles, gold, jade, and even people, were thrown into it as gifts to the gods. Each bowl contains a conglomeration of copal incense, rubber, shell and jade ornaments, and pigment. As the charred surface of each attests, this mixture was burned before the bowls were thrown into the Cenote. Both copal and rubber are obtained from tree sap. To the ancient Maya, these substances were analogous to human blood—the most sacred of all gifts to offer to the gods.

2 TRIPOD BOWL WITH
COPAL AND RUBBER
OFFERINGS *(left)*
Late Postclassic Period,
Maya A.D. 1350–1539
Mexico, Yucatán,
Chichén Itzá
pottery, pigments, copal,
rubber
dia. 6.5 in (16.5 cm)
Peabody Museum of
Archaeology and
Ethnology, Harvard
University. Peabody
Museum Expedition.
07-7-20/c4544

3 TRIPOD BOWL WITH
COPAL AND RUBBER
OFFERINGS
Late Postclassic Period,
Maya A.D. 1350–1539
Mexico, Yucatán,
Chichén Itzá
pottery, pigments, copal,
rubber, jade, shell
dia. 6.3 in (16 cm)
Peabody Museum of
Archaeology and
Ethnology, Harvard
University. Peabody
Museum Expedition.
07-7-20/c4562

4 DEER VESSEL WITH
COPAL AND RUBBER
OFFERINGS
Late Postclassic Period,
Maya A.D. 1350–1539
Mexico, Yucatán,
Chichén Itzá
*pottery, pigments, copal,
rubber*
4.3 × 6.5 in (11 × 16.5 cm)
Peabody Museum of
Archaeology and
Ethnology, Harvard
University. Peabody
Museum Expedition.
07-7-20/c4541

5 BALL RATTLE WITH
FEATHER MOTIF
Formative Period, Olmec
1000–500 B.C.
Mexico
pottery
dia. 3 in (7.6 cm)
Denver Art Museum.
Gift of Robert and
Marianne Huber.
1988.0159

6 BALLGAME BALL RATTLE
Late Formative Period
300 B.C.–A.D. 200
Central Mexico
*pottery with orange and
red slip*
dia. 3.5 in (9 cm)
The Field Museum.
94563

7 BALLGAME BALL RATTLE
Early Formative Period,
Xochipala 1300–1000 B.C.
Western Mexico, Guerrero
pottery
dia. 2.5 in (6.4 cm)
Snite Museum of Art,
University of Notre Dame.
Gift of Constance Kamens.
86.40

Rattles depicting rubber balls are fairly common
from the Formative Period. They were probably
one of several types of percussion instruments
played as accompaniment during the ballgames.

ORIGINS

Ceramic figurines depicting individuals dressed as rulers and ballplayers occur at the Early Formative sites of Tlapacoya in Central Mexico and San Lorenzo on the Gulf Coast. They are among the very earliest representations of ballplayers. This figurine wears a protective belt around his waist and padded bands on his arms and legs. His small face mask and round mirror pendant are prominent emblems of rulership.

8 RULER BALLPLAYER
WEARING BICHROME
MASK
Early Formative Period,
Olmec, Pilli-type
1500–1300 B.C.
Central Mexico, Tlapacoya
pottery with cream slip
h. 8.3 in (21 cm)
Snite Museum of Art,
University of Notre Dame.
Purchase funds provided
by the General
Endowment in honor
of Rev. Edmund P. Joyce,
C.S.C.
87.06

This elaborately dressed ballplayer extends his arms in a posture typical of Mesoamerican rulership. He wears an *hacha* on the front of his padded ballgame belt and a headdress with circular appliqués that may symbolize kernels of maize (corn).

9 RULER BALLPLAYER
WITH EXTENDED ARMS
Early Formative Period,
Olmec, Pilli-type
1500–1300 B.C.
Central Mexico, Tlatilco
pottery
h. 6.8 in (17.1 cm)
Snite Museum of Art,
University of Notre Dame.
Purchase funds provided
by Mr. and Mrs. Vincent
Carney.
89.25

Jade and other green-colored stones were the most precious materials in Mesoamerica Finely carved figurines and ornaments of these lustrous materials are a hallmark of the Olmec culture. These two figurines depict standing ballplayers with their arms folded across their chests—a symbol of political authority. One ballplayer (10) wears a mask, a padded waist protector, and protective helmet. The incised emblems on his headband may relate to fertility. The other player (11) is of more robust proportions. The helmets of both ballplayers are reminiscent of the headgear seen on the famous Olmec monumental heads.

10 STANDING MASKED
RULER BALLPLAYER
Middle Formative Period,
Olmec 1100–300 B.C.
Mexico, Veracruz/Tabasco
serpentine
h. 3.3 in (8.3 cm)
Snite Museum of Art,
University of Notre Dame.
Purchase funds provided
by The Martin Foundation
and Mr. and Mrs. Don
Franko, in honor of Rev.
James F. Flanigan, C.S.C.
87.54

11 MALE BALLPLAYER
WITH HELMET *(opposite)*
Middle Formative Period,
Olmec 1100–300 B.C.
Mexico, Gulf Coast,
Veracruz/Tabasco
jade
h. 3.5 in (8.9 cm)
Snite Museum of Art,
University of Notre Dame.
Purchase funds provided
by May Walter.
88.2.1

This *yuguito* is a stone model of a ballplayer's kneepad. Its imagery of the Corn (Maize) God emphasizes the connection between the ballgame and fertility. This god can be identified by the corn kernel in the center of his forehead and the two dots, symbolizing rooting and sprouting corn, flanking the mouth. The central trough below the deity's downturned mouth symbolizes the mutilation of his tongue during personal sacrifice. On the back is a T-shaped emblem that contains an image of a deity with the extended arms gesture of rulership. This *yuguito* may be a trophy, since it is too narrow and deep to accept a ballplayer's leg or knee. DEB

12 *YUGUITO* (KNEEPAD)
Early–Middle Formative
Period, Olmec
1500–300 B.C.
Pacific Slope of Mexico/
Guatemala
basalt
h. 6 in (15.2 cm)
Snite Museum of Art,
University of Notre Dame.
Purchase funds provided
by Mr. Michael G.
Browning (N.D. '68).
88.14

13 *YUGUITO* (KNEEPAD)
WITH TWISTED HUMAN FACE
Formative Period, Olmec
900–600 B.C.
Mexico, Veracruz
granite
5.1 × 5.1 in (13 × 13 cm)
The Art Museum, Princeton
University. Museum
Purchase, gift of Wallace S.
Whittaker Foundation, in
memory of Wallace S.
Whittaker, Yale Class of 1914.
Y1983-17

The ballgame was brutal, with the player continually lunging
to hit the ball with his hip, most often landing on his right knee.
If that knee were personified as a human head, by the end of the
game the face would be battered and look like this *yuguito*: one
eye missing, the other swollen shut, and the tongue split. GGG

14 BALLGAME YOKE
Formative Period, Olmec
c. 600 B.C.
Mexico, Veracruz, Río
Pesquero
greenstone
4.5 × 13 × 15.6 in
(11.5 × 33 × 39.5 cm)
The Art Museum,
Princeton University.
Gift of Gillett G. Griffin.
Y1991-70

Only a few Olmec stone yokes are known. Their design is simple and elegant. This one is the single recorded example from the great cache of stone objects from Río Pesquero. The hip protectors worn by ballplayers were probably made of wood or some lighter material, but by the end of the Olmec civilization trophy yokes were carved in stone to celebrate great games, great teams, or a great player. These may have been wrapped in bundles and kept as a remembrance or as a symbol of prowess and power. GGG

The twisted face on this *hacha (right)* probably depicts a veteran ballplayer, battered from the rigors of the sport. GGG

15 TWISTED FACE HACHA
(right)
Late Formative Period,
Veracruz 200 B.C–A.D. 500
Mexico, Gulf Coast
stone
h. 7.5 in (19 cm)
The Art Museum,
Princeton University.
Gift of Miles Lourie.
Y1984-5

Seated with his hands resting on drawn-up knees, this figurine wears the buttocks belt that characterizes Tlatilco Culture and other non-Olmec Formative Period ballplayers. This belt held the buttocks together to create a solid mass with which to hit the ball. On the top of this ballplayer's helmet is a banded corn (maize) sprout, a borrowing of Olmec fertility symbolism. Tlatilco ballplayer figurines depict ordinary individuals, sanctified by corn, who played a different type of ballgame from that of the rulers of their Olmec neighbors. DEB

16 SEATED BALLPLAYER
WITH MAIZE SPROUT
HELMET
Early Formative Period,
Tlatilco 1350–1250 B.C.
Central Mexico, Tlapacoya
pottery, white paint
h. 5.8 in (14.6 cm)
Snite Museum of Art,
University of Notre Dame.
Purchase funds provided
by The Martin
Foundation.
89.21

Tlatilco female ballplayers have prominent breasts and hourglass torsos. They wear the buttocks belt and other equipment also worn by their male counterparts.

17 STANDING FEMALE BALLPLAYER WITH BUTTOCKS BELT
Early Formative Period, Tlatilco 1300–1000 B.C.
Central Tlapacoya, Mexico
pottery with cream slip, black paint
h. 5.1 in (13 cm)
Snite Museum of Art, University of Notre Dame. The Snite Museum of Art Humana Endowment.

Olmec male and female figurines from Central Mexico are commonly painted with cream and white slips. The female ballplayers have additional paint applied to indicate protective body equipment—a loincloth with small panels to cover the groin and upper thighs. Such figurines may indicate that the earliest female ballplayers competed in a version of the game in which the ball was hit using the waist or hips. DEB

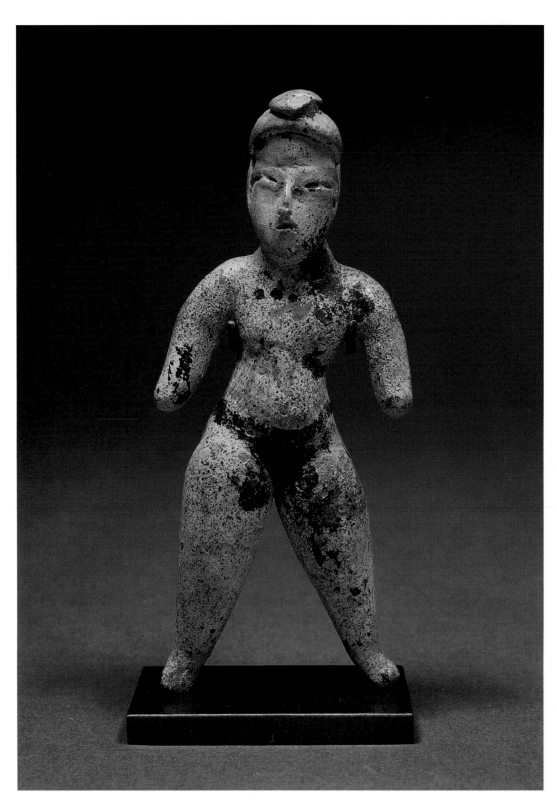

18 FEMALE BALLPLAYER WITH PAINTED EQUIPMENT
Early Formative Period, Olmec, Pilli-type
1500–1300 B.C.
Central Mexico, Tlapacoya
pottery with cream slip, black paint
h. 5.1 in (13 cm)
Snite Museum of Art, University of Notre Dame. The Snite Museum of Art Humana Endowment.

A widespread
Mesoamerican deity
known as the Old God
is represented as a
ballplayer in both
Olmec and Tlatilco
cultures. The Old God
appears as a wrinkled
or stooped old man with
a goatee, a sagittal hair
crest, a humpback, and
chest deformation. His
ballgame equipment
usually consists of the
buttocks belt alone, but
he may also hold a ball.
In this example, the
buttocks belt has a
pendant strap over the
side of each thigh and
an open triangular
device over each
buttock—features
designed to cushion the
impact of the ball and
protect the skin from
abrasion. DEB

19 STANDING HUMPBACK
OLD GOD BALLPLAYER
Early Formative Period,
Tlatilco 1300–1000 B.C.
Puebla, Mexico
pottery with cream slip
h. 6.8 in (17.2 cm)
Snite Museum of Art,
University of Notre Dame.
Purchase funds provided
by Mr. and Mrs. Judd
Leighton.
90.12.22

20 STANDING MALE
BALLPLAYER WITH PADDED
BELT AND KNEEPAD
Middle Formative Period,
Chalcatzingo
1100–300 B.C.
Mexico, Morelos,
Chalcatzingo
slipped earthenware
h. 4.4 in (11.2 cm)
Snite Museum of Art,
University of Notre Dame.
On loan from Mr. and
Mrs. August Uribe.
L91.73.003

This seated figurine is holding a ball in his outstretched hands. Attached to the front of his protective belt is an *hacha* in the form of a bird's head.

21 SEATED MALE
BALLPLAYER HOLDING
A BALL
Late Formative Period,
Ticoman 400–0 B.C.
Central Mexico, Tlatilco
slipped earthenware
h. 3.75 in (9.5 cm)
Snite Museum of Art,
University of Notre Dame.
On loan from Mr. and
Mrs. August Uribe.
L91.73.004

Figurines depicting ballplayers from tombs at El Opeño, Michoacán, dated to around 1500 B.C., are some of the earliest figurines in Mesoamerica. Although there are fragments of clay figurines of Olmec ballplayers from San Lorenzo, Veracruz—the Olmec heartland—the acidic soil destroys the surfaces and, often, the objects themselves. But in the highland states of Guerrero, Puebla, Mexico, and Morelos, figurines of ballplayers have survived in good condition. These reflect what ballplayers wore, and in some cases depict ballplayers in action. But they may also represent several different games during the Formative Period. Xochipala has become a generic designation for a type of figurine (22–27) from an area along the central Balsas River, about halfway between Mexico City and Acapulco, Guerrero. Some Xochipala figures are considered to be very early, while the tradition continued in more debased forms into later times. Pure Olmec vessels and figurines have been found in the same region. GGG

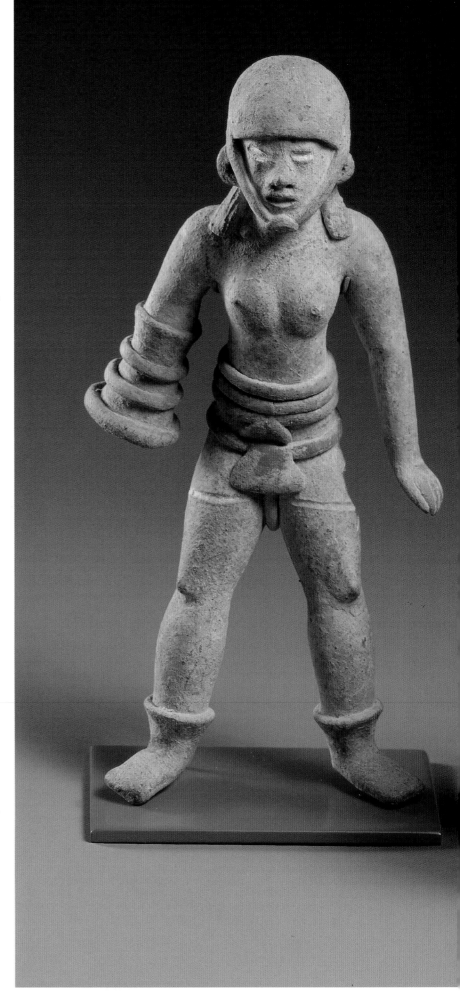

22 STANDING BALLPLAYER
FIGURINE
Formative Period,
Xochipala 1200–900 B.C.
Mexico, Guerrero
*pottery with traces of red
and black pigment*
6.4 × 3.4 × 2 in
(16.3 × 8.5 × 5 cm)
The Art Museum,
Princeton University.
Lent anonymously.
L1971.305

23 KNEELING BALLPLAYER
FIGURINE
Formative Period,
Xochipala 1200–900 B.C.
Mexico, Guerrero
*pottery with traces of red
and black pigment*
4.7 × 3.9 × 2 in
(12 × 10 × 5 cm)
The Art Museum,
Princeton University.
Lent anonymously.
L1971.306

A few scholars have viewed some of these early ceramic figurines as depicting female ballplayers. Formative Period figurines are often sexually enigmatic, their fleshiness read as either male or female. Although this figure *(left)* has been interpreted by some as female, in the context of ancient Mesoamerican society the question of the presence of female ballplayers, and their role in the game, is still debated. GGG

24 FEMALE BALLPLAYER
FIGURINE *(left)*
Formative Period,
Xochipala 1200–900 B.C.
Mexico, Guerrero
pottery, traces of red pigment
6.5 × 2 × 1.3 in
(16.3 × 5.4 × 3.4 cm)
The Art Museum,
Princeton University.
Lent Anonymously.
L1999.57

25 STANDING BALLPLAYER
FIGURINE *(right)*
Formative Period,
Xochipala 1000–800 B.C.
Western Mexico, Guerrero
pottery
4.75 × 2 × 1 in
(11.1 × 5.1 × 2.3 cm)
Denver Art Museum.
1988.0129

Prominent breasts
and an hourglass torso
demonstrate the
femininity of this
figurine, while the
buttocks belt, groin
protector, chaps, and
boots reveal she is a
ballplayer of the hip
ballgame. The groin
protector was a leather
or cloth pad that
covered the pubic
region and was held in
place by the buttocks
belt. It appears only
on Xochipala female
ballplayers. The remains
of a *manopla*, an
implement used to
hit the ball, are present
on the right wrist and
thigh. Her helmet is
topped by a banded
corn sprout. DEB

26 STANDING FEMALE
BALLPLAYER WITH MAIZE
SPROUT HELMET
Early Formative Period,
Xochipala 1000–800 B.C.
Western Mexico, Guerrero
pottery
h. 7 in (17.8 cm)
Snite Museum of Art,
University of Notre Dame.
Purchase funds provided
by the Friends of the Snite
Museum of Art.
87.53

Drawing one's own blood as an act of religious piety has a long history in Mesoamerica. Olmec and other Formative Period cultures used jade and stone perforators to pierce the skin. The blood was then collected and burned with incense as an offering to the gods. The tiny figure on the handle of this stone implement may be one of the earliest depictions of an ancient Mesoamerican ballplayer. GGG

27 BLOODLETTING PERFORATOR WITH BALLPLAYER FIGURE
Formative Period, Xochipala 1500–1000 B.C.
Mexico, Guerrero
stone and white pigment
h. 8.5 in (21.7 cm)
The Art Museum, Princeton University.
Museum purchase, Fowler McCormick, Class of 1921, Fund.
Y1987-27

BALLCOURTS AND ARCHITECTURE

28 BALLCOURT PENDANT
Middle Formative Period,
Mezcala 800–500 B.C.
Western Mexico, Guerrero
stone
2.6 × 1.6 in (6.5 × 4 cm)
The Art Museum, Princeton
University. Gift of Spencer
Throckmorton.
Y1992-7

This is one of a series of small greenstone ballcourt pendants that are known; they were possibly worn by the members of a single ball team. GGG

Ceramic models of ballcourts from ancient West Mexico depict playing fields, ballplayers, and spectators (29–30). They are a unique record of the games played in that region from around 300 B.C. to A.D. 250. The models portray a sport similar to the Aztec *ullamaliztli*, a game played by hitting the ball with the hips. A type of hip-ballgame is still played in the West Mexican state of Sinaloa. Fewer than ten complete models of ballcourts have survived.

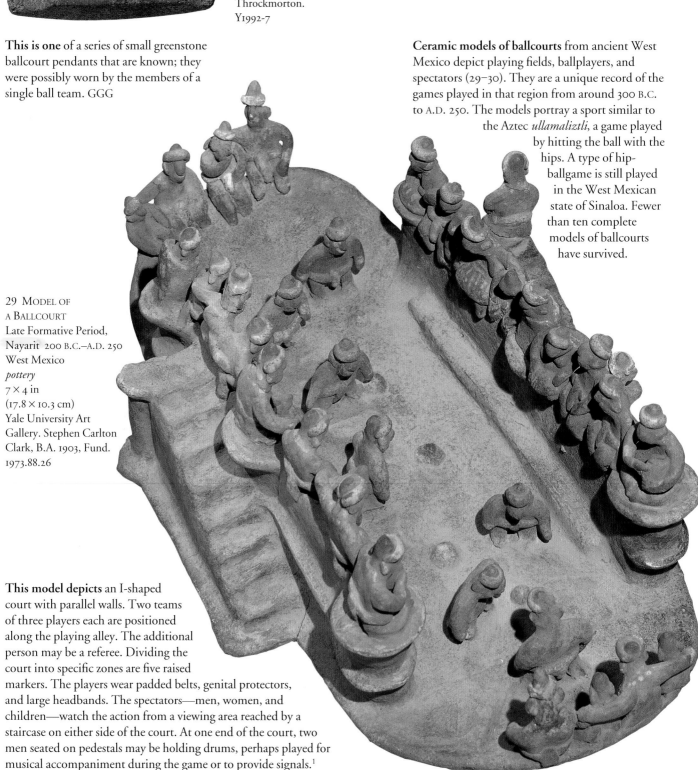

29 MODEL OF
A BALLCOURT
Late Formative Period,
Nayarit 200 B.C.–A.D. 250
West Mexico
pottery
7 × 4 in
(17.8 × 10.3 cm)
Yale University Art
Gallery. Stephen Carlton
Clark, B.A. 1903, Fund.
1973.88.26

This model depicts an I-shaped court with parallel walls. Two teams of three players each are positioned along the playing alley. The additional person may be a referee. Dividing the court into specific zones are five raised markers. The players wear padded belts, genital protectors, and large headbands. The spectators—men, women, and children—watch the action from a viewing area reached by a staircase on either side of the court. At one end of the court, two men seated on pedestals may be holding drums, perhaps played for musical accompaniment during the game or to provide signals.[1]

30 MODEL OF
A BALLCOURT
Late Formative Period,
Ixtlán del Río
300 B.C.–A.D. 200
Western Mexico, Nayarit
pottery
5.5 × 8 × 13 in
(14 × 20.3 × 33 cm)
Los Angeles County
Museum of Art.
The Proctor Stafford
Collection, Museum
Purchase with funds
provided by Mr. and
Mrs. Allan C. Batch.
M86.296.34

Although a less elaborate structure than the Yale model (29) and unfortunately
incomplete, this model also depicts an I-shaped ballcourt. Four players and a
referee occupy the playing alley, which has three raised markers dividing it into
zones. One player slides on the surface of the court to deflect the oversize rubber
ball with his hip. Given such rough and tumble action, the padded cloth
uniforms and genital protectors worn by the players were very practical.
Male spectators crowd the walls and end zone. Jane Day has observed that
a number of finely woven textiles are draped over the end of one wall.[2]
These could be special costumes removed prior to actual play, or the valuable
prize awarded to the winner of the game.

31 BALLCOURT VESSEL
Late Classic Period, Maya
A.D. 600–800
Guatemala Highlands,
Kaminaljuyú
*pottery, traces of red
hematite*
10.5 × 6.5 in (26 × 16 cm)
Kislak Foundation.
84.2.0.5

This extraordinary vessel is in the form of an I-shaped ballcourt. The truncated playing alley is formed from slightly tapering walls that dramatically rise above the alley and terminate with tenoned animal heads. This type of decorative architectural treatment to the sloped ballcourt walls is well known from Late Classic ballcourts such as that at Copán in Honduras. The date of the manufacture of this vessel has been the subject of some dispute. Earlier attribution placed it in the Late Formative Period at roughly 500 to 100 B.C. On the basis of architectural evidence from Guatemala (see Taladoire, this volume), however, it has now been assigned a later date. The vessel may have served as a divination device. It has a spout at one end and holes in the court: liquid poured into the spout would completely fill the I-shaped court, turning it into a mirror-like surface. Throughout Mesoamerican history, mirrors were believed to be portals to other realms. This belief, in combination with the Maya notion that ballcourts were artificial openings into the Underworld, would have made this vessel a powerful instrument for a Maya shaman.

32 PECTORAL WITH
INCISED BALLCOURT
Late Classic Period,
Veracruz A.D. 700–900
Mexico, Gulf Coast
black stone
3.5 × 1.9 in (8.8 × 4.9 cm)
The Art Museum,
Princeton University.
Gift of Malcolm Lloyd,
Class of 1894.
Y1932-3

This vessel is a blend of elements from different regions. Its form and the slab tripod supports in particular are direct copies of Teotihuacan styles from Central Mexico. The ballplayers in the press-molded scene are dressed in Maya-style ballgame gear. The differences in their costumes suggest they belong to opposing teams. Issuing from the players' mouths are scrolls, a convention to indicate speech or singing more common at Teotihuacan than in southern Mesoamerica. The players flank the profile of a ballcourt with the rubber ball above.

33 TRIPOD VESSEL WITH
BALLPLAYERS AND BALLCOURT
Middle Classic Period, Maya
A.D. 400–700
Guatemala, Tiquisate
black pottery, red pigment
5.9 × 5.4 in (14.9 × 13.7 cm)
Denver Art Museum.
Gift of Larry Ottis, M.D.
1984.0616

34 TRIPOD VESSEL WITH
BALLPLAYERS AND
BALLCOURT MARKER
Middle Classic Period,
Maya A.D. 400–700
Guatemala, Tiquisate
gray pottery
7 × 8 in (17.8 × 20.3 cm)
Denver Art Museum.
Museum Purchase.
1971.0417

Differences in the costumes of the players also distinguish the opposing teams on this vessel. Above the profile of the stepped ballcourt is the rubber ball with a skeletal head inside. Ballgame balls with human heads are known from Late Classic Maya painted ceramic vessels as well as the ballcourt reliefs from Chichén Itzá. Such depictions refer to an episode in the *Popol Vuh* in which the head of the Hero Twin Hunahpu was used instead of the rubber ball. Flanking the ballcourt are Teotihuacan-style serpent-head ballcourt markers.

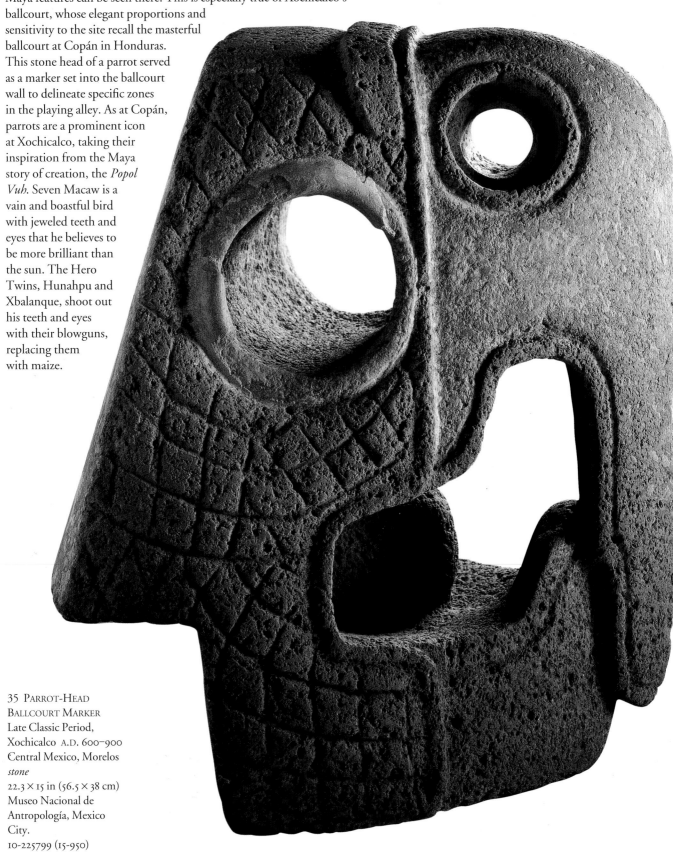

Xochicalco, a site in the Central Mexican state of Morelos, had prolonged contact with the Maya region of southern Mesoamerica. As a result, numerous Maya features can be seen there. This is especially true of Xochicalco's ballcourt, whose elegant proportions and sensitivity to the site recall the masterful ballcourt at Copán in Honduras. This stone head of a parrot served as a marker set into the ballcourt wall to delineate specific zones in the playing alley. As at Copán, parrots are a prominent icon at Xochicalco, taking their inspiration from the Maya story of creation, the *Popol Vuh*. Seven Macaw is a vain and boastful bird with jeweled teeth and eyes that he believes to be more brilliant than the sun. The Hero Twins, Hunahpu and Xbalanque, shoot out his teeth and eyes with their blowguns, replacing them with maize.

35 PARROT-HEAD
BALLCOURT MARKER
Late Classic Period,
Xochicalco A.D. 600–900
Central Mexico, Morelos
stone
22.3 × 15 in (56.5 × 38 cm)
Museo Nacional de
Antropología, Mexico
City.
10-225799 (15-950)

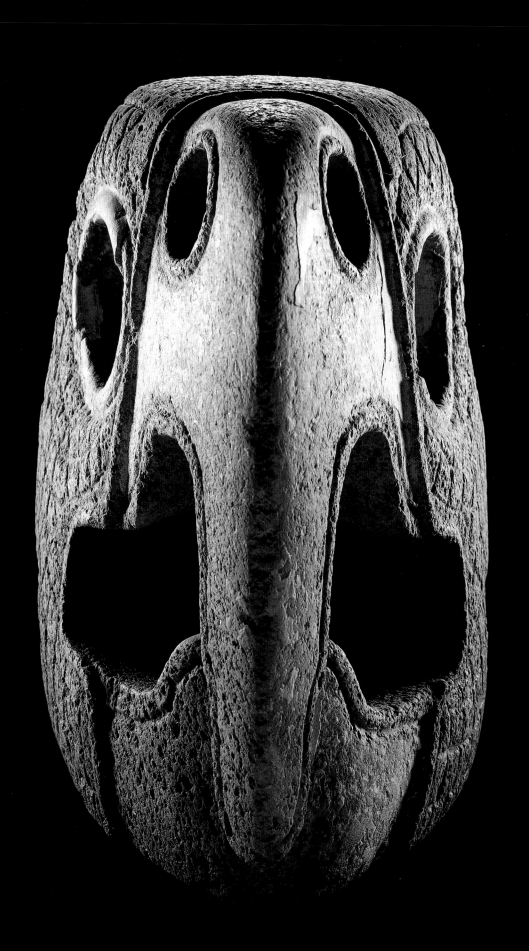

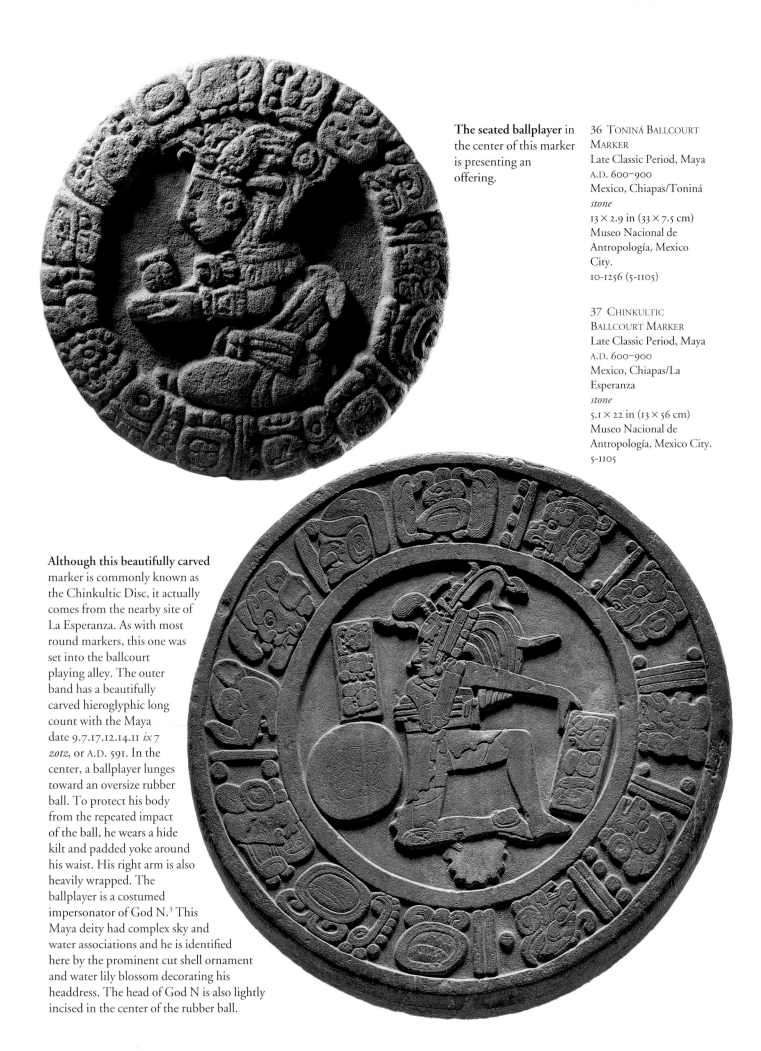

The seated ballplayer in the center of this marker is presenting an offering.

36 Toniná Ballcourt Marker
Late Classic Period, Maya
A.D. 600–900
Mexico, Chiapas/Toniná
stone
13 × 2.9 in (33 × 7.5 cm)
Museo Nacional de Antropología, Mexico City.
10-1256 (5-1105)

37 Chinkultic Ballcourt Marker
Late Classic Period, Maya
A.D. 600–900
Mexico, Chiapas/La Esperanza
stone
5.1 × 22 in (13 × 56 cm)
Museo Nacional de Antropología, Mexico City.
5-1105

Although this beautifully carved marker is commonly known as the Chinkultic Disc, it actually comes from the nearby site of La Esperanza. As with most round markers, this one was set into the ballcourt playing alley. The outer band has a beautifully carved hieroglyphic long count with the Maya date 9.7.17.12.14.11 *ix* 7 *zotz*, or A.D. 591. In the center, a ballplayer lunges toward an oversize rubber ball. To protect his body from the repeated impact of the ball, he wears a hide kilt and padded yoke around his waist. His right arm is also heavily wrapped. The ballplayer is a costumed impersonator of God N.[3] This Maya deity had complex sky and water associations and he is identified here by the prominent cut shell ornament and water lily blossom decorating his headdress. The head of God N is also lightly incised in the center of the rubber ball.

Round ballcourt markers such as this one were "planted" so that the top was level with the playing alley surface. A combination of exposure to the elements and perhaps decades of trampling by the players' feet have eroded many of the details and rendered the hieroglyphic text illegible. The dynamism of the composition survives, however. Against a stepped ballcourt wall two players elaborately outfitted in padded yokes and plumed headdresses lunge toward a rubber ball.

38 BALLCOURT MARKER
Late Classic Period, Maya
A.D. 700–900
Belize, Lubaantún
stone
dia. 22.4 in (57 cm)
Peabody Museum of Archaeology and Ethnology, Harvard University. Peabody Museum Expedition. 15-73-20 / C7615

39 HERO TWIN
BALLCOURT MARKER
Late Classic Period, Maya
A.D. 550–850
Mexico, Chiapas
stone
23 × 24 in (59.8 × 61 cm)
North Carolina Museum
of Art. Gift of Mr. and
Mrs. Gordon Hanes.
82.14

The outer band of this ballcourt marker has scrolls pointing to
each of the four cardinal directions. These are separated by *caban*
glyphs, symbols of the earth. Squatting in the very center is the
Hero Twin, Hunahpu, identified by his Sun God headdress.
He holds a rubber ball in his left hand and the decapitated head
of the Jester God in his upraised right hand.

Perhaps either a ballcourt marker or part of a sculptural frieze decorating the walls of the court, this panel features the undulating body of a feathered serpent.

40 FEATHERED SERPENT
BALLCOURT MARKER
Early Classic Period,
Veracruz A.D. 200–600
Mexico, Gulf Coast
stone
36 × 14 × 5 in
(91.4 × 35.6 × 12.7 cm)
Denver Museum of Nature
and Science. Crane
American Indian
Collection.
AC.11385

THE GAMES AND THEIR PLAYERS

Both of these vessels (41–42) incorporate a ballplayer effigy. Monte Albán ballplayers wear U-shaped yokes tied around the waist with cords. Many have *hachas* mounted on the yokes, and some wear kneepads. Wrapped forearms or arm guards indicate that a hip and arm combination game was being played. DEB

41 Resting Ballplayer
Vessel
Late Formative Period,
Zapotec, Monte Albán II
200 B.C.–A.D. 200
Southern Mexico, Oaxaca
pottery
h. 5.6 in (14.3 cm)
Snite Museum of Art,
University of Notre Dame.
The Snite Museum of Art
Humana Endowment

42 BALLPLAYER VESSEL
Late Formative Period,
Zapotec, Monte Albán II
200 B.C.–A.D. 200
Southern Mexico, Oaxaca
pottery
5 × 3.25 in (12.5 × 9.5 cm)
The Saint Louis Art
Museum. Gift of Morton
D. May.
171:1979

In **ancient West Mexico**, ceramic sculptures depicting husbands and wives were placed in tombs as memorial offerings to provide comfort and companionship for the deceased. These couples are the embodiment of their society's notions of gender. Women usually offer serving vessels, symbolic of their stewardship of hearth and home. Men often hold the instruments of war—clubs or *atlatl* darts. This man grips a ball, identifying him as a ballplayer. Ballplayers must have enjoyed elevated status in ancient West Mexican societies, and such depictions might be compared to retired military officers in our own culture who still wear their uniforms on special occasions.[4]

43 MATRIMONIAL COUPLE
(left)
Late Formative Period,
Ixtlán del Río
200 B.C.–A.D. 250
West Mexico
pottery, slip, paint
(male) 17.2 × 11.5 × 11.3 in
(43.8 × 29.2 × 28.6 cm)
(female) 17.3 × 10 × 9.7 in
(44 × 25.3 × 24.2 cm)
Hudson Museum,
University of Maine.
William P. Palmer III
Collection.
(male) HM 4125
(female) HM 4126

This ballplayer *(right)*
clutches the ball in the
crook of his arm as if
about to serve to his
opponents.

44 STANDING BALLPLAYER
(right)
Late Formative Period, El
Arenal 200 B.C.–A.D. 250
West Mexico, Jalisco
pottery, slip, paint
16.1 × 9.5 × 4.9 in
(41 × 24 × 12.5 cm)
Hudson Museum,
University of Maine.
William P. Palmer III
Collection.
HM 3826

Although West Mexican ballcourt models depict a game in which the players deflected the ball with their hips and waists, many single figures depict players holding the rubber ball. Obviously, at some point during the game, players held the ball to serve or were perhaps allowed to catch it with their hands.

45 CROUCHING BALLPLAYER
Late Formative Period
300 B.C.–A.D. 200
Western Mexico, Jalisco
pottery with red slip
7.1 × 6.5 × 6.5 in
(18.1 × 16.5 × 16.5 cm)
Mint Museum of Art.
Gift of Dr. and Mrs. Francis
Robicsek.
1974.51.3

Clutching the rubber ball in his hands, this player wears a loincloth tied at the rear with an elaborate sash and protective headgear with a chin strap and a horn-like projection in front. Single- and double-horned helmets are often seen on West Mexican warrior figures and are usually interpreted as emblems of supernatural status. Like his warrior counterparts doing battle in the Underworld, the horn on this player may signify that the ballgame he was playing was not of this world.

46 STANDING BALLPLAYER
Late Formative Period,
Colima 200 B.C.–A.D. 250
West Mexico
pottery with brown slip
17.1 × 6.9 in
(43.5 × 17.5 cm)
Hudson Museum,
University of Maine.
William P. Palmer III
Collection.
HM 512

Waist protectors, popularly called yokes, were made of leather, wood, cloth, or stone. Some version of this piece of equipment was worn throughout Mesoamerica. This pottery vessel depicts a simple, yet effective type of yoke.

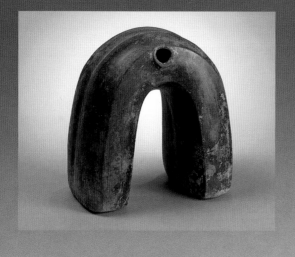

47 YOKE-FORM VESSEL
Late Formative Period,
Colima 200 B.C.–A.D. 300
West Mexico
pottery
5.5 × 10 × 10.8 in
(14.5 × 25 × 27.5 cm)
The Saint Louis Art
Museum. Gift of Morton
D. May.
175:1980

Many single figurines depicting ballplayers may originally have been part of dynamic, group scenes. Purportedly found together, this group includes figurines of two different styles. The first group of players can be identified by their padded yokes, *hachas*, and headgear; one figurine holds a staff. The other group are strange-looking, pot-bellied individuals, one of whom holds what may be a rubber ball. Their wrinkled bodies suggest they may depict the Old God, a widespread Mesoamerican deity who is often associated with the ballgame.

**48 BALLPLAYER FIGURINE
GROUP**
Late Formative Period,
Colima 200 B.C.–A.D. 300
Mexico, West Coast
pottery
1.5 × 1 × 0.3 in
(3.8 × 2.5 × 0.6 cm) (average)
San Antonio Museum of Art.
Bequest of Elizabeth Huth
Coates.
97.1.6 a–n

The wrinkled face of the Old God is
seen on the mask of this ballplayer,
who wears a buttocks belt and holds
the ball in his hand behind his back.
Hanging down his back is a woven
bag often carried by the Colima
depictions of this deity. The twisted
posture may depict preparation for
a serve. Dangling from his neck
is a toad, probably *Bufo marinus*,
a species that subdues its prey by
spraying it with hallucinogenic
poisons. DEB

**49 OLD GOD BALLPLAYER
WHISTLE** *(above)*
Late Formative Period,
Colima 250 B.C.–A.D. 250
West Mexico
pottery
h. 4.3 in (10.8 cm)
Snite Museum of Art,
University of Notre Dame.
Gift of Mr. and Mrs. Herbert
L. Lucas.
88.39

MEXICO'S GULF COAST

Two major themes of ancient Mexican art are represented in this powerful and evocative sculpture—duality and the ritual ballgame. The bent shoulder and wrinkled face of the Old Fire God on the left side contrast sharply with the erect shoulder and smooth face of the youthful human on the right. Both are united as a ritual ballplayer. Dualities such as this reflected the fundamental dichotomies of existence for ancient Mesoamericans—life and death, youth and age, supernatural and mortal. This ballplayer wears the quintessential Classic Period gear: a U-shaped yoke, an *hacha*, a protective mitt on his right hand, and ankle bands. The *hacha* itself also incorporates the duality theme, depicting a youthful dog on the right, and an old dog on the left. On top of the mitt is a rope that encircles the neck and is knotted at the back. This may refer to partial strangulation of sacrificial victims to render them unconscious before heart extraction or decapitation. DEB

50 OLD FIRE GOD/
HUMAN BALLPLAYER *(left)*
Early Classic Period,
Veracruz A.D. 250–400
Mexico, Gulf Coast
stone
h. 12 in (30.5 cm)
Snite Museum of Art,
University of Notre Dame.
Purchase funds provided
by the family of John S.
Marten and Mr. and Mrs.
Al Nathe.
89.12

51 BALLPLAYER FIGURINE
(right)
Middle Classic Period,
Huastec A.D. 400–600
Mexico, Veracruz
pottery
h. 5 in (12.7 cm)
Los Angeles County
Museum of Art. Gift of
the Art Museum Council
in honor of the museum's
twenty-fifth anniversary.
M90.168.25

The ornate facial paint of this standing ballplayer indicates that gearing up for the game involved more than just getting dressed. He wears a U-shaped yoke and a knee protector (*yuguito*) in the form of a human face, and padded leg and wrist guards, which would have protected him during play. A circular pendant and ear ornaments complete his costume.

52 FIGURINE OF
A BALLPLAYER
Late Classic Period,
Veracruz A.D. 700–900
Mexico, Gulf Coast,
Nopiloa area
pottery with white and black paint
8.4 × 20.5 × 4.5 in
(21.3 × 52 × 11.5 cm)
American Museum
of Natural History.
30.3 / 1287

This extraordinary ballplayer figurine is wearing a mask representing a supernatural being—a composite of several creatures. The antennae clearly relate to snails and mollusks. The face itself is toad-like, with flanges next to the eyes that may be depicting the parotid glands of *Bufo marinus*—a toad whose bodily secretions contain a powerful hallucinogen. Earth monster and hallucinogenic imagery are frequently associated with the Veracruz and Maya ballgames, no doubt related to the concept of ballcourts as portals into a supernatural realm. The player's stance resembles the *por abajo* position of contemporary Sinaloan players as they slide on their knees to return the ball with their hips and waists. His yoke is much like the many surviving examples from Veracruz and shows how these would have been worn.

53 Reclining Ballplayer with Earth Monster Mask
Late Classic Period, Veracruz
A.D. 700–900
Mexico, Gulf Coast
pottery
5 × 10 × 6.8 in
(12.7 × 25.4 × 17.2 cm)
San Antonio Museum of Art.
Bequest of Elizabeth Huth Coates.
97.1.13

Whether women actually played the ballgame is still a controversial question. Many Late Classic and Postclassic figurines (54–59) from Mexico's Gulf Coast depict individuals with prominent breasts wearing ballgame equipment, such as yokes, and padding on the knees and legs. Since numerous Formative Period figurines also depict similar individuals, it would seem reasonable that women indeed played the game—perhaps in all-female teams—or participated in some yet to be understood ceremony enacted on the ballcourt.

54 FEMALE BALLPLAYER
Late Classic Period,
Huastec A.D. 800–1000
Mexico, Gulf Coast
pottery
8 × 3.5 × 1.5 in
(20.3 × 8.9 × 3.8 cm)
Denver Art Museum.
Museum Purchase with
Marion Hendrie Fund.
1972.0399

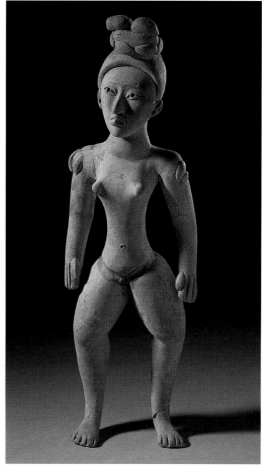

55 FEMALE BALLPLAYER
FIGURINE *(far left)*
Postclassic Period, Huastec
A.D. 1100–1400
Mexico, Gulf Coast
pottery
11.3 × 4.5 × 3.5 in
(28.6 × 11.4 × 8.9 cm)
Denver Art Museum.
Gift of Mr. William T.
Lee.
1985.0642

56 FEMALE BALLPLAYER
FIGURINE *(left)*
Postclassic Period, Huastec
A.D. 1100–1400
Mexico, Gulf Coast
pottery
11.5 × 4.5 × 2 in
(29.2 × 11.4 × 5.1 cm)
Denver Art Museum.
Museum Purchase.
1969.0277

57 FEMALE BALLPLAYER
FIGURE *(far left)*
Late Classic Period,
Huastec A.D. 700–900
Mexico, Gulf Coast
pottery
h. 12 in (30.5 cm)
New Orleans Museum
of Art. Gift of Richard
McCarthy, Jr.
97.639

58 FEMALE(?) BALLPLAYER
FIGURINE *(left)*
Middle/Late Classic
Period, Huastec
A.D. 400–800
Mexico, Veracruz
pottery
11.8 × 4 × 1.5 in
(29.8 × 10.2 × 3.8 cm)
Los Angeles County
Museum of Art. Gift of the
Art Museum Council in
honor of the museum's
twenty-fifth anniversary.
M90.168.47

Six ceramic figurines—four male and two female—two removable masks, and a throne make up this group. There may have been a seventh figurine as only one of the masks fits a figure. The eyes are closed on all six figures, as well as on the two masks, suggesting the players are dead and the scene is taking place in the Underworld. All the male figures wear wide yoke-like belts, protective bands on their arms, and elaborate jewelry consisting of nose rings, ear ornaments, and bead necklaces. Two of the standing figures hold balls in their upraised right hands. The seated figure probably also once held a ball, but the hand is broken off from the upraised right arm. The fourth male holds a handstone (*manopla*) in his left hand and what may be an *atlatl* (a type of spearthrower) in his right. The heads of both females (seated on the throne and extreme right) are rudimentary, as the full head masks were meant to cover them. The masking suggests performance. Perhaps the two masked women played specific parts in a mythic drama (see Day, this volume).

59 UNDERWORLD
BALLGAME SCENE
Late Classic Period,
Oaxaca A.D. 700–900
Mexico, Isthmus of
Tehuantepec
pottery
8.25 × 4.5 × 3.5 in
(21 × 11.5 × 8.9 cm)
tallest figure
Denver Art Museum.
Anonymous Gift.
1981.319

60 YOKE AND *HACHA*
VESSEL *(right)*
Late Classic Period,
Veracruz A.D. 700–900
Mexico, Gulf Coast
pottery
5.1 × 8.7 × 7.1 in
(13 × 22 × 18 cm)
American Museum
of Natural History.
30.3/2363

61 TROPHY-HEAD *HACHA*
(far right)
Late Classic Period,
Veracruz A.D. 700–900
Mexico, Gulf Coast
stone
h. 9.3 in (23.5 cm)
American Museum
of Natural History.
30.3/2364

This pottery vessel *(above left)*
superbly illustrates how ballgame
yokes and *hachas* would have been
worn together. *Hachas* are notched,
allowing them to be secured to the
front or side of the yoke. In this
example the *hacha* is in the form of
a trophy head. The round projections
on the top of the yoke may have
allowed the player to fasten it on
with lashing for a more secure fit.

Also in the form of a human trophy head, this stone
hacha (above right) is identical to the miniature
pottery version attached to the yoke (60). According
to museum records, both are reported to have come
from the same tomb near Cerro de las Mesas in
Central Veracruz. Such trophy heads were no
doubt taken from unfortunate war captives.
Scenes of human decapitation in association with
the ballgame are well known from Mexico's Gulf
Coast. The large ring in front of the mouth may
represent a rope threaded through the nose to hang
the head for display. The victim's hair is dressed
in a basketweave, or mat, pattern.

Much too tiny to have been worn by actual players, this miniature yoke *(below left)* and *hacha (below)* may have been part of the costuming for a pottery or stone ballplayer figure. The *hacha's* wrinkled face possibly identifies this character as the Old God. Incised into the front of the yoke is the face of an earth monster.

62 MINIATURE *HACHA*
(above)
Late Classic Period,
Veracruz A.D. 700–900
Mexico, Gulf Coast
stone
h. 3.8 in (9.5 cm)
Yale University Art
Gallery. Gift of Mr. and
Mrs. Allan Wardwell.
1989.83.1

63 MINIATURE YOKE *(left)*
Late Classic Period,
Veracruz A.D. 700–900
Mexico, Gulf Coast
stone
1.8 × 3.8 × 4 in
(4.4 × 9.5 × 10.2 cm)
Yale University Art
Gallery. Gift of Mr. and
Mrs. Allan Wardwell.
1989.83.2

A variety of birds provided the inspiration for ancient Mexican Gulf Coast *hachas* (64–67). Parrots and macaws—easily identified by the rings encircling the eyes—have a special association with the ballgame. In the *Popol Vuh*, it was the ballplaying Hero Twins, Hunahpu and Xbalanque, who shot Seven Macaw with blowguns. Eagles are identified by their sharp downturned beaks, and feather crests. They are Mesoamerica's fiercest raptor and are associated with warfare and human sacrifice. Turkeys were domesticated throughout the Americas, but their symbolism in connection with the ballgame is unclear.

64 MACAW *HACHA*
Late Classic Period,
Veracruz A.D. 600–900
Mexico, Gulf Coast
stone
h. 16.8 in (42.5 cm)
Philadelphia Museum
of Art. The Louise and
Walter Arensberg
Collection.
1950-134-382

The prominent crest and hooked beak identify this bird as a harpy eagle. Flesh-eating birds are frequently depicted in the ballgame reliefs at El Tajín, sometimes gorging themselves on the sacrificed victims.

65 HARPY EAGLE *HACHA*
Middle Classic Period,
Veracruz A.D. 400–600
Mexico, Gulf Coast
stone
7.5 × 7 × 10.5 in
(19.1 × 17.8 × 26.7 cm)
Fine Arts Museums
of San Francisco,
Gift of Elizabeth and
Lewis K. Land.
1986.67.1

66 Turkey *Hacha*
Middle Classic Period,
Veracruz A.D. 400–700
Mexico, Gulf Coast
stone
6.3 × 5.1 × 4.4 in
(15.8 × 13 × 11.4 cm)
Worcester Art Museum.
Museum Purchase.
1942.3

This *hacha* depicts a
ballplayer wearing an
elaborate parrot-head
helmet *(right)*. The
player's face can be
seen inside the parrot's
mouth. On the outside
of the helmet another
ballplayer is depicted,
wearing a bird mask.

67 *Hacha* of a
Ballplayer Wearing
a Parrot Helmet *(right)*
Late Classic Period,
Veracruz A.D. 700–900
Mexico, Gulf Coast
stone
h. 14 in (35.4 cm)
Peabody Museum of
Archaeology and
Ethnology, Harvard
University. Peabody
Museum Purchase.
28-1-20 C10413

68 DEER *HACHA*
Late Classic Period,
Veracruz A.D. 600–900
Mexico, Gulf Coast
stone
9.5 × 6 × 2 in
(24.1 × 15.2 × 5.1 cm)
Denver Museum of
Nature and Science.
Crane American Indian
Collection.
AC.8360

This *hacha* has the profile head of a young male deer. Deer were the largest game animals in Mesoamerica and were valued for their meat and hides. They also had spiritual importance and a special relationship with the ballgame. On Classic Maya ceramic vessels, deer are *uayob* (animal companion spirits) and served as the consort of the Moon Goddess. Maya ballplayers commonly wear deer headdresses as part of their uniforms, probably to honor the Hero Twin Xbalanque, whose name means Jaguar-Deer. The Aztec deity Xochipilli— god of music, dance, and flowers, and patron of the ballgame—is sometimes shown wearing a deerskin apron marked with calendar signs.

Human and feline characteristics merge into a fantastic, probably supernatural, being in this *hacha (right)*. The eyes and mouth were once inlaid with shell or stone.

69 HUMAN-FELINE *HACHA (right)*
Middle Classic Period, Veracruz
A.D. 550–650
Mexico, Gulf Coast
greenstone
5.5 × 3.9 × 3.1 in
(13 × 9.8 × 7.9 cm)
Mint Museum of Art. Museum
Purchase. Robicsek Fund and
Exchange Funds from the Gift
of Harry and Mary Dalton.
1999.53

Palmas **were worn on top** of the front portion of the ballplayer's yoke. This example takes the form of a formidable crocodile which appears to be diving into the earth itself. Saurians—lizards, crocodiles, alligators, and composites of such creatures—appear frequently in Mesoamerican art. The remains of crocodiles and alligators have also been discovered in tombs in the Maya region and as ceremonial offerings from the Aztec Templo Mayor. In the *Popol Vuh*, the crocodile Zipacna was the son of Seven Macaw, a boastful bird defeated by the Hero Twins. Zipacna was responsible for the deaths of 400 youths who tried to kill him; their souls rose in the night sky to form the stars of the Pleiades.

70 CROCODILE *PALMA*
Late Classic Period, Veracruz
A.D. 600–900
Mexico, Gulf Coast
stone
26 × 9 × 5 in (66 × 22.9 × 13 cm)
Philadelphia Museum of Art.
The Louise and Walter
Arensberg Collection.
1950-134-216

The antics of monkeys and apes often mirror human behavior. In Mesoamerica, monkeys were calendar signs and could symbolize sexually inappropriate behavior. This monkey-head *hacha (right)*, however, probably refers to 1 Howler Monkey and 1 Spider Monkey, the half-brothers of the Hero Twins of the *Popol Vuh*.

71 MONKEY-HEAD *HACHA*
Late Classic Period, Veracruz
A.D. 700–900
Mexico, Gulf Coast
stone
10.75 × 8.5 × 1.5 in
(27.5 × 21.5 × 4 cm)
Peabody Museum of
Archaeology and Ethnology,
Harvard University. Gift of
the Museum of Comparative
Zoology, Harvard University.
80-25-20 /22914

This small *palma* takes the form of a temple platform on top of which two coyotes engage in a human-like embrace. Coyotes and humans wearing coyote masks are commonly depicted in Veracruz ballgame sculpture, often in association with rituals of human sacrifice.

72 *PALMA* WITH
TWO COYOTES
Late Classic Period,
Veracruz A.D. 700–900
Mexico, Gulf Coast
stone
8.7 × 4.6 × 4.3 in
(22 × 11.8 × 11 cm)
American Museum
of Natural History.
30.0 /6205

The leaping dolphin on the ballplayer's helmet distinguishes this *hacha* as one of the finest examples of ancient Veracruz sculpture. The sunken areas along the spine of the dolphin and face of the ballplayer at one time probably held stone or shell inlay.

73 *HACHA* OF A
BALLPLAYER WEARING
A DOLPHIN HELMET
Late Classic Period,
Veracruz A.D. 700–900
Mexico, Gulf Coast
stone
10.6 × 9.1 in (27 × 23 cm)
Museo Nacional de
Antropología, Mexico
City.
10-2647 (4-1066)

Representations of a bloated, potbellied supernatural, commonly called the Fat God, are known throughout Mesoamerica. The full meaning of these depictions is unclear, but the deity may have been a clown-like performer and dancer. This *hacha* may depict someone impersonating this deity, who perhaps performed during the ballgame.

74 FAT GOD *HACHA*
Early Classic Period,
Veracruz A.D. 200–400
Mexico, Gulf Coast
stone
h. 6.1 in (15.5 cm)
The Saint Louis Art
Museum. Gift of Morton
D. May.
377:1978

The scroll motifs on this *hacha* suggest its origin was the vicinity of El Tajín, a major center for the ballgame in Veracruz.

75 HUMAN-HEAD *HACHA*
Late Classic Period,
Veracruz A.D. 600–900
Mexico, Gulf Coast
stone
18.5 × 5.5 × 8.5 in
(47 × 14 × 21.6 cm)
Philadelphia Museum
of Art. The Louise and
Walter Arensberg
Collection.
1950-134-336

76 *HACHA* WITH HUMAN
FACE
Late Classic Period,
Veracruz A.D. 700–900
Mexico, Gulf Coast
stone
16.4 × 5.5 × 9.6 in
(41.6 × 14 × 24.5 cm)
Cleveland Museum of Art,
Gift of Mr. and Mrs. James
C. Gruener.
1990.240

77 HUMAN-HEAD
HACHA (left)
Late Classic Period,
Veracruz A.D. 700–900
Mexico, Gulf Coast
stone
15.9 × 2.6 × 8.3 in
(37.8 × 6.6 × 21.1 cm)
Yale University Art
Gallery. Gift of Peggy
and Richard Danziger
LLB 1963
1986.134.5

78 *HACHA*
Late Classic Period, Veracruz
A.D. 700–900
Mexico, Gulf Coast
stone, pigment
7.5 × 5.4 × 0.8 in (19.1 × 13.7 × 1.9 cm)
Denver Art Museum.
Gift of Mr. and Mrs. Edward M. Strauss.
1985.395

Intertwined motifs symbolic of weaving and political authority cover this *palma.* In Mesoamerica, finely woven rush mats were restricted to the nobility and works of art depict rulers sitting on mats. Among the Maya, rulers were called the *Ah Pop,* or "He of the Mat."

79 *PALMA* WITH MAT SYMBOLS
Late Classic Period, Veracruz A.D. 700–900
Mexico, Gulf Coast
stone
h. 20.1 in (51.1 cm)
Metropolitan Museum of Art. The Michael C. Rockefeller Memorial Collection, Bequest of Nelson A. Rockefeller, 1979.
1979.206.425

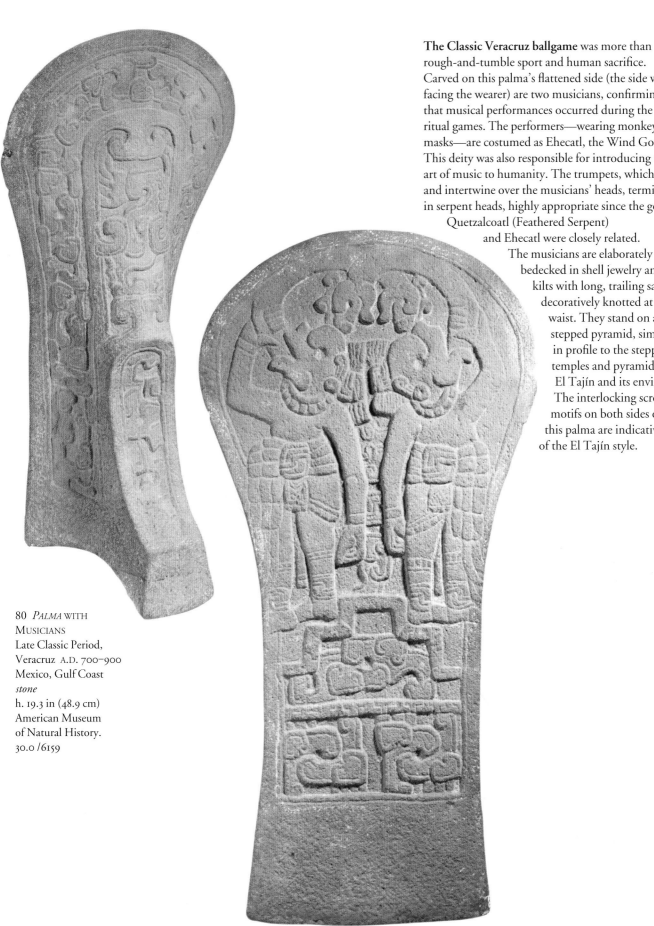

The Classic Veracruz ballgame was more than rough-and-tumble sport and human sacrifice. Carved on this palma's flattened side (the side worn facing the wearer) are two musicians, confirming that musical performances occurred during the ritual games. The performers—wearing monkey-like masks—are costumed as Ehecatl, the Wind God. This deity was also responsible for introducing the art of music to humanity. The trumpets, which arch and intertwine over the musicians' heads, terminate in serpent heads, highly appropriate since the gods Quetzalcoatl (Feathered Serpent) and Ehecatl were closely related.

The musicians are elaborately bedecked in shell jewelry and kilts with long, trailing sashes decoratively knotted at the waist. They stand on a stepped pyramid, similar in profile to the stepped temples and pyramids of El Tajín and its environs. The interlocking scroll motifs on both sides of this palma are indicative of the El Tajín style.

80 *PALMA* WITH
MUSICIANS
Late Classic Period,
Veracruz A.D. 700–900
Mexico, Gulf Coast
stone
h. 19.3 in (48.9 cm)
American Museum
of Natural History.
30.0 /6159

81 BALLGAME YOKE
Late Classic Period,
Veracruz A.D. 600–900
Mexico, Gulf Coast
greenstone
4.3 × 13 × 15.8 in
(11 × 33 × 40 cm)
The Saint Louis
Art Museum.
Gift of Morton D. May.
356:1978

Denizens of the Underworld were a popular subject matter on Classic Veracruz yokes. The toothed, scaly creature on this yoke is a crocodile or alligator. As on many yokes and *palmas*, the recessed portions would have been filled with inlay. Sections of the original, fragile shell inlay have been preserved on the sides of this yoke.

82 YOKE WITH REPTILIAN
MOTIF
Late Classic Period,
Veracruz A.D. 700–900
Mexico, Gulf Coast
stone, red pigment, shell
16.5 × 14 × 14 in
(41.9 × 35.6 × 35.6 cm)
San Antonio Museum
of Art. Bequest of
Elizabeth Huth Coates.
97.1.12

Closed yokes are rarer than the open type, and scholars debate whether such yokes would have actually been worn. This yoke is carved with images of four male figures dressed in ballgame gear. Ornate speech scrolls issue from their mouths. The two full figures along each side and on the bottom appear to be swimming. Many Mesoamerican cultures believed that the terrestrial world and the Underworld were separated by water and so the figures on this yoke may depict sacrificed ballplayers swimming through this watery realm.

83 CLOSED YOKE WITH
SWIMMING FIGURES
Late Classic Period, Veracruz
A.D. 600–900
Mexico, Gulf Coast
stone
20 × 15.8 in (51 × 40 cm)
Fine Arts Museums of San
Francisco. Land Collection.
T#92.166.38

84 CLOSED YOKE WITH SCROLL MOTIFS *(right)*
Late Classic Period, Veracruz A.D. 700–900
Mexico, Gulf Coast
stone
h. 19 in (48.3 cm)
Metropolitan Museum of Art. The Michael
G. Rockefeller Memorial Collection, Bequest
of Nelson A. Rockefeller, 1979.
1979.206.445

85 EARTH MONSTER
YOKE *(below)*
Late Classic Period,
Veracruz A.D. 700–900
Mexico, Gulf Coast
diorite
14.5 × 17.3 in
(36.8 × 43.5 cm)
Los Angeles County
Museum of Art.
Gift of Constance
McCormick.
M81.253.1

The central image of this
exquisitely carved yoke *(below)* is
a supernatural saurian—a creature
combining the features of reptiles and
amphibians. The deeply set eyes of this earth
monster (as they are commonly called) dominate the
U-shaped curved portion. Between the eyes, a human head
emerges from the creature's mouth. The ends of the yoke
have three-dimensional human heads. Slight differences
in their facial features and relief-carved headdresses indicate
these are two separate individuals, perhaps Xbalanque and
Hunahpu, the Hero Twins of the *Popol Vuh*.

This yoke has the deeply carved scroll work commonly seen on El Tajín-style sculpture. Dominating the curved front of the yoke is a human face, whose inset eyes probably once held stone inlay. The five plume-like elements on its headdress (see top view, *opposite below*) identify this individual as the Pulque God.[5] Pulque, an alcoholic beverage made from the agave, or maguey, plant, played an important role in ritual ballgame ceremonies at El Tajín. Stylized representations of agave and large vessels filled with pulque abound in the ballcourt reliefs at El Tajín. Its consumption may well have been important in human sacrifice ceremonies.

86 PULQUE GOD BALLGAME YOKE
Late Classic Period, Veracruz
A.D. 700–900
Mexico, Gulf Coast
stone
16 × 15 × 5 in (40.6 × 38.1 × 12.7 cm)
Cleveland Museum of Art,
Purchase from the J.H. Wade Fund.
1943.662

EL TAJÍN SOUTH
BALLCOURT PANEL 1

The right portion
of this panel shows a
skeletal being wearing
the Pulque God
headdress rising from
a large vessel.

The body of this unusually fine yoke is composed
of three human heads. Each is bedecked in a
headdress and large earspools—the trappings of the
Mesoamerican elite class. However, their swollen
eyes and dangling tongues speak of the brutality
that the ritual ballgame inflicted upon the players.
Severe injuries, either from the impact of the solid
rubber ball or the zeal of the opposing team, must
have been commonplace. GGG

According to archaeologist S. Jeffrey K. Wilkerson, this yoke was originally carved in earth monster form and then elaborated with scroll motifs several centuries later.[6] From the mouth of the earth monster, a human face emerges. This individual wears earspools and a nose ornament and has a forked tongue. Two rattlesnakes are carved on the yoke top. At the ends of the yoke human heads are carved in deep relief. Each wears a fancy scroll headdress with feathers and shell jewelry. The eyes, along with other roughly carved recesses, once held inlay. Each of the tongues protrudes slightly, suggesting these may be decapitated heads, collected and displayed as trophy heads after ritual sacrifice at the end of the ballgame.

88 EARTH MONSTER BALLGAME YOKE
Late Classic Period, Veracruz
A.D. 700–900
Mexico, Gulf Coast
stone
16.5 × 14.8 in (42 × 37.5 cm)
American Museum of
Natural History.
30.2 /3408

Ballplayers throughout Mesoamerica carried handstones (*manoplas*) as part of their standard-issue gear. The rules concerning the use of this piece of equipment are unknown, but presumably handstones were used to hit the ball, returning it to the opposing team. This example depicts the head of a ballplayer. He wears a helmet and a mask that covers the mouth and nose. This buccal mask with its "false beard" can also be seen on the Metropolitan Museum of Art plaque (90).

89 BALLPLAYER HANDSTONE (*MANOPLA*)
Late Classic Period, Veracruz A.D. 700–900
Mexico, Gulf Coast
stone, pigment
12 × 11 × 1.3 in (30.5 × 27.9 × 3.2 cm)
Mint Museum of Art. Gift of Dr. and
Mrs. Francis Robicsek.
1998.132.1

This plaque, with its profile of a ballplayer, is among the most beautiful of ancient Veracruz sculptures. The ballplayer wears a buccal mask (covering the mouth and nose) and a false beard. His jewelry consists of a shell or jade necklace and round earspools with curved, dangling pendants, much like the ones worn by Tajín-style figures. A piece of jade, believed to help in the journey to the Underworld, is placed beneath his nose. He wears a netted cap, held in place with a knotted sash. This plaque is generally believed to be a backing for a hematite mirror which might have been worn as a pendant. Similar mirrors are represented in the El Tajín reliefs.

90 BALLPLAYER PLAQUE
Late Classic Period,
Veracruz A.D. 700–900
Mexico, Gulf Coast
stone
dia. 6 in (15.2 cm)
Metropolitan Museum
of Art. Museum Purchase,
1900.
00.5.91

This pair of pendants of incised conch shell illustrate variations on the theme of Quetzalcoatl, the Feathered Serpent. The rough incising on one of the pendants *(below)* and haphazard and incomplete drilling suggest it was unfinished. Nonetheless, it presents a powerful image of a ballplayer. Attached to his ballgame yoke is a human skull *hacha*. His tasseled headdress is very similar to the type worn by the Pulque God in Classic Veracruz sculpture, and this may be a later version of that deity. He stands on top of two intertwined feathered serpents. The other pendant *(right)* is much more finely finished, with skillful incision and well-placed perforations and holes along the top for suspension. The imagery is complex and is crowded into every available space. Writhing over the entire composition are the bodies of two feathered serpents. In the upper register a warrior/ballplayer holds a captive by the hair in preparation for decapitation. The body of a previous victim lies beneath his upraised foot.

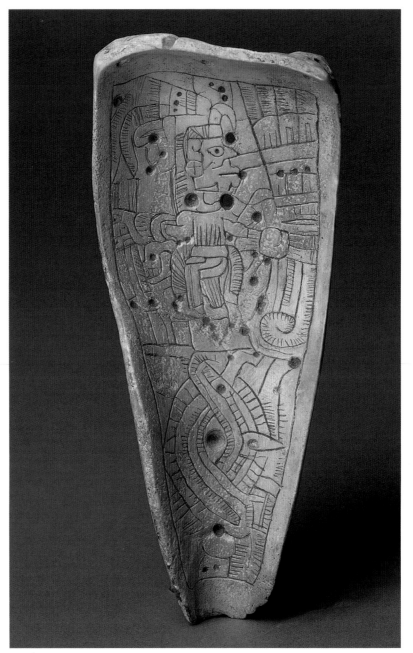

91 Pair of Pendants
Postclassic Period, Huastec
A.D. 1100–1400
Mexico, Gulf Coast
shell
6.8 × 3.5 in (17.1 × 8.9 cm)
Denver Art Museum.
Gift of Mr. Robert J.
Stroessner.
1992-0016 *(left)*

6.8 × 3.5 in (17.1 × 8.9 cm)
On Loan to the Denver
Art Museum.
496-1989-1 *(right)*

These conch shell bracelets are remarkable for their narrative content and exquisite carving. Taking advantage of the conch's natural spiral structure, they would have gently gripped the wearer's arm. The figures are outlined and perforated, creating a three-dimensional effect, while details are incised and filled with white pigment. Although there are minor variations between the two bracelets, the story they tell is essentially the same. Emerging from the mouth of an ornate feathered serpent is a female seated on a throne. Standing before her is a male dressed in a deer headdress, ballgame yoke, and *palma*, and holding spears and a spearthrower. He wears cylindrical ear plugs and an oval pendant on his chest. He is both warrior and ballplayer. Although there is no exact correlation between these bracelets and the earlier El Tajín ballcourt reliefs—none of which depict warrior/ballplayers in attendance on female elites— they belong stylistically to the Tajín tradition. The meaning of the event depicted here may be astronomical. In the mythology of Central Mexico, a region with prolonged Gulf Coast contact, Quetzalcoatl (Feathered Serpent) was born from a deer shot by Mixcoatl, god of the Milky Way and the hunt.[7]

92 PAIR OF BRACELETS
Postclassic Period, Huastec
A.D. 900–1000
Mexico, Gulf Coast
shell, white pigment
each 3 × 4.6 in
(7.8 × 11.7 cm)
Denver Museum of
Nature and Science.
Crane American Indian
Collection.
AC.9205 a–b

Today, even though well marked, the site of Las Higueras is bypassed by most tourists driving from Xalapa to the coast. Those who do stop will find a dismal-looking mound completely surrounded by modern development. During the Middle and Late Classic periods, however, the situation was very different. Although not as large as its northerly neighbor El Tajín, Las Higueras had elite structures decorated with elaborately painted frescos. Sadly, these exist only in fragments today. They depict the typical Gulf Coast preoccupation with the ballgame and its players.

93 MURAL FRAGMENT
WITH BALLPLAYERS
Early Classic Period,
Veracruz, Las Higueras
A.D. 300–500
Mexico, Gulf Coast
plaster, paint
22.8 × 38 in (58 × 96.6 cm)
Museo de Antropología,
Universidad Veracruzana.
4875

94 MURAL FRAGMENT
WITH BALLPLAYERS
Early Classic Period,
Veracruz, Las Higueras
A.D. 300–500
Mexico, Gulf Coast
plaster, paint
22.8 × 38 in (58 × 96.6 cm)
Museo de Antropología,
Universidad Veracruzana.
4892

The scene on this bowl depicts the Hero Twins, from the *Popol Vuh*, dressed in ballgame gear as they defeat the Lords of the Underworld in Xibalba. The bowl is evidence that the ballgame and heroic themes were pan-Mesoamerican, from the Maya world to the Gulf Coast of Veracruz. GGG

95 BOWL WITH BALLGAME
SCENE
Late Classic Period,
Veracruz A.D. 600–900
Mexico, Gulf Coast
pottery
4.1 × 6.2 in (10.3 × 15.7 cm)
The Art Museum,
Princeton University.
Lent Anonymously.
L1989.16

GAMES AND PLAYERS
OF THE MAYA REGION

96 MONKEY YOKE VESSEL
(*left*)
Early Classic Period, Maya
A.D. 100–400
Guatemala
black pottery
6.3 × 6.5 × 9.5 in
(15.9 × 16.5 × 24.1 cm)
Denver Art Museum.
Museum Purchase with
funds provided by Walt
Disney Imagineering.
1991.0641

Howler and spider monkeys are native to southern
Mesoamerica. This handstone *(right)* depicts a
howler monkey seated upright with his tail arching
away from the body. The tail forms the loop handle,
which would have been hidden by the player's
hand. The pattern of wear on the handle suggests
its owner was right-handed, and that the top of
the monkey's head was the hitting surface. DEB

97 HOWLER MONKEY
HANDSTONE (*MANOPLA*)
Early Classic Period, Maya
A.D. 250–400
Guatemala, Kaminaljuyú
stone, red pigment
h. 7 in (17.8 cm)
Snite Museum of Art,
University of Notre Dame.
Rev. Anthony J. Lauck,
C.S.C. and Mr. and Mrs.
J. Moore McDonough
Endowments.
96.37

This *hacha* depicts a ballplayer wearing a macaw-serpent helmet. The beak of the bird is in front of the ballplayer's face, its eye is just above his head. The long body of a serpent arches over the front of the *hacha*, terminating in a scroll-eyed head. The site of Cotzumalhuapa on Guatemala's Pacific Coast is something of a puzzle to scholars. The people themselves were not Maya, despite their proximity to that region. Ballgame imagery and scenes of human sacrifice predominate in Cotzumalhuapa art. The sculpture has an affinity with Classic Veracruz styles and may demonstrate contact between the two regions.[8]

98 *HACHA* OF A BALLPLAYER WEARING A MACAW-SERPENT HELMET
Middle Classic Period, A.D. 400–700
Guatemala, Pacific Coast, Cotzumalhuapa
basalt, traces of red cinnabar
13.4 × 9.9 × 1.4 in (34 × 25 × 3.5 cm)
The Saint Louis Art Museum. Gift of Morton D. May.
256:1978

The ancient Maya created one of Mesoamerica's great figurine traditions. A variety of male, female, real, and supernatural subjects were depicted in delicately hand-built or mold-made forms. Figurines were produced all over the Maya region, but three areas are especially noteworthy: the Petén, Tabasco, and Jaina Island (99–106). Jaina figurines have received the most attention from scholars and especially collectors and art museums, since they are among the most evocative and expressive works in all of ancient America. Jaina, a tiny island in the Bay of Campeche, was an extensive necropolis during the Late Classic Period. It is believed that it served as an honored burial place for much of the neighboring Yucatán Peninsula. Its location to the west of the Maya region would have been symbolically important, since west was closely linked with death.[9] Given the prominence of the ballgame among the Maya, it is not surprising that representations of ballplayers constitute a major category of figurines. Maya ballplayer figurines occur in a variety of active and static postures. Some appear to be sitting for a formal portrait; others are dynamically posed, as if caught in a freeze-frame instant replay.

This ballplayer has his protective waist yoke casually draped over his shoulder. Unlike the stone yokes of Veracruz, Maya yokes were padded, and made of perishable materials such as wood or leather. This figure also wears an elaborately wrapped turban.

99 STANDING BALLPLAYER
WITH YOKE
Late Classic Period, Maya
A.D. 700–900
Mexico, Campeche,
Jaina Island
pottery
9 × 3 × 2.8 in
(22.9 × 7.6 × 7 cm)
Denver Art Museum.
Gift of William I. Lee.
1986.0617

The proud stance and expressive face of this ballplayer clearly communicate that in antiquity, as today, winning was everything. He wears an elaborately tied turban, earspools, and a magnificent double-strand jade necklace. Attached to his waist yoke is a bird-head *hacha*.

100 BALLPLAYER WEARING
A YOKE AND *HACHA*
Late Classic Period, Maya
A.D. 600–800
Mexico, Campeche,
Jaina Island
pottery
h. 7.25 in (18.4 cm)
Yale University Art
Gallery. Stephen Carlton
Clark, B.A. 1903, Fund.
1973.88.13

101 SEATED BALLPLAYER
Late Classic Period, Maya
A.D. 600–900
Mexico, Campeche,
Jaina Island
pottery
6 × 9 in (15.2 × 22.9 cm)
Private Collection.

Although seated in a cross-legged position, this ballplayer is fully alert. He gives the
impression that he is performing the ancient equivalent of "warming the bench," just waiting
to spring into action. His gear is among the most elaborate of any Jaina ballplayer figurine.
Two spectacular jade bead necklaces are combined with a third necklace of crescent-shaped
objects, perhaps jaguar claws. He has several layers of padding wrapped around his waist,
underneath which he wears a protective hide kilt, similar to the type represented on Maya
painted ceramic vessels (see 108), as well as protective padding on both wrists. In his right hand
he holds a handstone, or *manopla*, with which to hit the solid rubber ball.

A dwarf ballplayer holds an oversize rubber ball, much as Atlas shouldered the weight of the earth. Representations of dwarves are common in Mesoamerican art. The ancient Maya believed dwarves to be the children of the Chacs—the rain gods. Dwarves also appear as attendants to the king in a monument at Yaxchilán depicting a ballgame.[10]

102 DWARF BALLPLAYER
Late Classic Period, Maya A.D. 700–900
Mexico, Tabasco(?)
pottery, traces of blue pigment
4.5 × 3.5 in (11.4 × 8.8 cm)
Mint Museum of Art. Museum Purchase:
Exchange Funds from the Gift of Harry
and Mary Dalton.
2000.54

Doubling as a whistle, with the mouthpiece at the base, this ballplayer figurine wears a thickly padded yoke held in place with a belt and tied sash. Whistles were common burial offerings in Jaina tombs. Many scholars believe that whistles and ocarinas were used in funeral services to call the souls of the dead. Musical performances were a prominent feature of the Mesoamerican ballgame.

103 STANDING BALLPLAYER WHISTLE
Late Classic Period, Maya
A.D. 600–800
Mexico, Campeche, Jaina Island
pottery, traces of blue pigment
6 × 2.8 × 3 in
(15.2 × 7 × 7.6 cm)
Mint Museum of Art. Lent by Dr. and Mrs. Francis Robicsek.
L1997.48.1

The legs and feet of this ballplayer figurine are disproportionately reduced in size and detail, as the artist focussed all his attention on the player's upper torso and equipment. He is outfitted with round knee pads and a padded yoke around his waist and has a large jade pendant around his neck and oversize jade earspools. His distinguishing feature is the dramatic bird headdress. Painted scenes on Late Classic Maya ceramic vessels show opposing ball teams wearing towering bird and deer headdresses.

104 BALLPLAYER WEARING
A BIRD HEADDRESS
Late Classic Period, Maya
A.D. 600–900
Mexico, Campeche,
Jaina Island
pottery, post-fired blue paint
7.8 × 3.6 in (19.7 × 9.2 cm)
Mint Museum of Art.
Gift of Dr. and Mrs.
Francis Robicsek.
1984.237.15

Although fragmentary, this ballplayer figurine still conveys the excitement that must have accompanied the sight of these superb athletes engaged in competition. He wears a towering deer headdress—a class of headgear favored by ballplayers and hunters. In the crook of his right arm he holds the rubber ball, implying that he is ready to serve. Unlike the heavy padding worn by other Jaina ballplayers, this player has a rather skimpy waist belt and loincloth. This suggests a variety of appropriate costume for ballplayers and also that some of the more elaborate gear may have had strictly ritual significance.

105 BALLPLAYER WEARING
A DEER HEADDRESS
Late Classic Period, Maya
A.D. 700–900
Mexico, Campeche,
Jaina Island
pottery with blue pigment
9.8 × 3 × 3.9 in
(25 × 7.5 × 10 cm)
Hudson Museum,
University of Maine.
William P. Palmer III
Collection.
HM 646

An elite ballplayer, in all his regal attire, is portrayed in this splendid large Jaina figure. The dignity and elegant stance of this individual bespeak his importance. His spectacular bird headdress appears to depict one of the many aquatic species common to the marshy area of the Bay of Campeche, where Jaina Island is located. Late Classic Maya ballplayers wore their heavily padded yokes up under their arms rather than around their hips, as was the custom elsewhere in Mesoamerica. This player's waist padding is exaggerated, perhaps in accordance with his stature as a member of the nobility. The curious three-flanged feature on the front of the yoke is a belt and sash tied over the layers of padding to keep everything in place. His loincloth appears to be looped through the yoke, terminating in a fringed panel. He wears a single-strand jade bead necklace, wrist guards, and anklets. This figure's facial features are so individualized that it may be a portrait of the person whose burial it accompanied. GGG

106 BALLPLAYER WITH
THREE-PART YOKE AND BIRD
HEADDRESS
Late Classic Period, Maya
A.D. 650–850
Mexico, Campeche,
Jaina Island
pottery, polychrome
13.5 × 7 in (34.2 × 17.8 cm)
The Art Museum, Princeton
University. Museum
Purchase, Fowler
McCormick, Class of 1921,
Fund, in honor of Gillett
G. Griffin on his seventieth
birthday.
1998-36

Two elaborately outfitted players are captured in mid-volley in this extraordinary ballgame scene—the ancient equivalent of a freeze-frame instant replay. Using his well-padded mid-section, the player on the right has just returned the solid rubber ball to his opponent. To the right of the first player is a large, round feathered shield mounted on a staff, probably a movable ballcourt marker. To present this entire scene—ballcourt, players, and pyramid in the background—the painter of this vase opened up the perspective like a book. The viewer is looking down the length of the playing alley. The small horizontal structures behind each player are the sloped walls of the ballcourt. Both the rim text and secondary blocks of text on this vessel consist of repeated and reversed signs and numbers in a thoroughly irregular order; the result is a meaningless jumble.[11]

107 CYLINDER VESSEL WITH BALLPLAYERS
(THE PEARLMAN HANDBALL VASE)
Late Classic Period, Maya A.D. 700–900
Mexico, Southern Campeche
pottery with cream and brown slip, black paint
h. 8.5 in (21.6 cm)
Chrysler Museum of Art. Gift of Edwin
Pearlman and Museum Purchase.
86.409

108 CYLINDER VESSEL
WITH BALLGAME SCENE
Late Classic Period, Maya
A.D. 600–800
Mexico, Campeche
*pottery with cream, brown
and orange slips, black
paint*
8.25 × 6.25 in
(21 × 15.8 cm)
National Museum of
the American Indian,
Smithsonian Institution.
24 /6503

One of the more complex ballgame events depicted on a Maya painted ceramic vessel, this scene consists of a group of five ballplayers and a musician. The scene is divided by the rubber ball, above which is a hunchback standing on a platform. The presence of a hunchback is an indication that this game is being played not on earth, but in the Maya Underworld of Xibalba. To the right of the rubber ball, a player is kneeling on one knee, one of the standard positions for play. He is distinguished by his trophy-head headdress and the slightly different markings on his deerhide kilt. This player was also the vessel's patron, and his name and royal titles are listed in the L-shaped text block above his head. On either side of him are the four other players; they wear deer headdresses, and *k'in* (sun) signs decorate their long kilts. Standing apart from this action is a musician blowing a conch shell trumpet. The horizontal band of text just under the rim is a nonsensical jumble of pseudoglyphs, painted by a talented, but illiterate, artist.

109 CYLINDER VESSEL
WITH BALLPLAYER
Late Classic Period, Maya
A.D. 700–900
Mexico, Northern Yucatán
pottery
6.7 × 6 in (17.5 × 15.3 cm)
The Bowers Museum of
Cultural Art. Foundation
Acquisition Fund
Purchase.
F74.9.2

This player is kneeling in the Classic Maya "play ball" stance.

The ballplayers on this vessel are less elaborately outfitted than most Maya ballplayers. They wear simple padded yokes around their waists and long kilts. The "derby hat" worn by one player is unusual. This type of headgear is more commonly associated with hunters than ballplayers and may identify this individual as the Hero Twin Hunahpu (hunter). He also has an improvised, but practical, kneepad secured around his left knee. Unfortunately, the text on this vessel is nonsensical, consisting of a meaningless jumble of real and fanciful glyphs.

110 CYLINDER VESSEL WITH BALLPLAYERS
Late Classic Period, Maya
A.D. 700–900
Guatemala, Northern Petén Region
pottery
7.5 × 4.8 in (19 × 12.1 cm)
New Orleans Museum of Art. Museum purchase, Ella West Freeman Foundation Matching Fund.
68.16

This beautifully carved blackware vessel belongs to a style called Chocholá, produced in northern Yucatán, southwest of Mérida.[12] The panel depicts an elaborately attired ballplayer in a kneeling playing posture. He has just returned the solid rubber ball which is bouncing off the stepped walls of the ballcourt. Two persons stand to the side of the ballcourt watching the action. The seated individual is a dwarf, implying that this ballgame is taking place in the Underworld.

111 Kneeling
Ballplayer Vessel
Late Classic Period, Maya
A.D. 700–900
Mexico, Northern Yucatán
black pottery
7.1 × 6 in (18 × 15 cm)
Cleveland Museum of Art,
Gift of Mr. and Mrs. James
C. Gruener.
1990.180

112 PANEL WITH HERO
TWIN BALLPLAYER
Late Classic Period, Maya
A.D. 600–800
Guatemala, Usumacinta
River Region
limestone
10.9 × 15 × 0.8 in
(27.6 × 38.1 × 2 cm)
National Museum of
the American Indian,
Smithsonian Institution.
24/0457

These two panels, 112 and 113, are from an unidentified Maya city called Site Q, located somewhere along the Usumacinta River. More than a dozen or so Site Q panels are known to exist in museum and private collections around the world. The majority contain only hieroglyphic inscriptions, while others have images of richly attired ballplayers. The ballgame scenes are paired panels, and they seem to depict the Hero Twins playing ball with various Lords of the Underworld. Originally, the panels may have formed the risers of a staircase or decorated the sloping walls of a ballcourt.

The Hero Twin Xbalanque, the great ballplayer of the *Popol Vuh,* is depicted on this panel *(left).* He is kneeling, ready to use his padded midsection to deflect the large rubber ball at the lower right portion of the panel. Befitting his mythic status, he is elaborately costumed. The base of his magnificently plumed headdress is the head of the Sun God. At its top, maize foliage emerges from an *ahau* sign—a day name and a title meaning "lord." The lower glyph in the vertical column translates as *pitzal,* or "play ball."[13] In the center of the rubber ball is the date 9 *ahau.* The number nine, especially when paired with the *ahau* sign, is associated with the Hero Twins.[14] This panel's pair, depicting God L in his *muan* bird headdress, is in a private collection *(right* in the reconstructed drawing above). Maya deities were assigned letter names by the German scholar Paul Schellhas in the late 19th century.

RECONSTRUCTION OF TWO BALLGAME PANELS
a *(left)* Panel from the National Museum of the American Indian, Smithsonian Institution (112).
b *(right)* Panel from a private collection.

The reconstruction of these two panels shows Xbalanque (panel a; 112) playing ball with God L, the Lord of the Underworld (panel b).

Reconstruction of
two ballgame panels
a *(left)* Panel from a
private collection.
b *(right)* Panel from the
Kislak Foundation (113).

The reconstruction of
these two panels shows
Xbalanque (panel a)
playing ball with God N
(panel b; 113).

The crocodile jaw headdress with its cut shell nose ornament identifies this ballplayer as God N. He is kneeling and leaning toward the rubber ball, which appears in the paired panel in the drawing opposite. Two hieroglyphs are incised on the left middle side of the panel. The lower glyph is *pitzal*, or "play ball."

113 PANEL WITH GOD N
BALLPLAYER
Late Classic Period, Maya
A.D. 600–800
Guatemala, Usumacinta
River Region
limestone
10.9 × 15 × 0.8 in
(27.6 × 38.1 × 2 cm)
Kislak Foundation, Inc.
95.15.00

THE AZTEC GAMES

This stone version of a rubber ball was originally placed near the great ballcourt in the center of the Aztec capital Tenochtitlan. It was excavated by Leopoldo Batres in the year 1900.

114 BALL ON A PEDESTAL
Late Postclassic Period,
Aztec A.D. 1325–1520
Central Mexico,
Tenochtitlan
stone
2.8 × 23.6 in (7 × 60 cm)
Museo Nacional
de Antropología,
Mexico City.
10-349499

Stone rings (115–116), through which the rubber ball was passed in order to score points, began to appear in ballcourts during the Late Classic Period. They became a standard feature of ballcourt architecture thereafter. The interior diameter of the rings varied, indicating the rubber balls were not of uniform size.

The flower form of this ballcourt ring refers to Xochipilli—the Aztec god of flowers, music, and dance, and patron of the ballgame. Representations of this deity frequently show his body covered with flowers.

115 FLOWER BALLCOURT RING
Late Postclassic Period, Aztec
A.D. 1400–1520
Central Mexico
sandstone
35 × 7 in (89 × 17 cm)
Philadelphia Museum
of Art. The Louise and
Walter Arensberg Collection.
1950-134-372

A monkey clutches the rim of this ballcourt ring. The inner rim of the ring is a solar symbol, whose rays are partially obscured beneath the monkey's body. The imagery may symbolize a solar eclipse.

116 BALLCOURT RING WITH SOLAR MONKEY
Late Postclassic Period, Aztec A.D. 1400–1520
Central Mexico
sandstone
27 × 5.8 in (68.5 × 14.6 cm)
Philadelphia Museum of Art. The Louise and Walter Arensberg Collection.
1950-134-225

Xochipilli, which means "flower prince" in Nahuatl, was the Aztec god of flowers, dance, and music. He was also the god of games and the patron deity of the ballgame.

117 SEATED FIGURE OF
XOCHIPILLI
Late Postclassic Period
A.D. 1325–1521
Central Mexico,
Tenochtitlan
stone
38 × 14 in (95.5 × 35.5 cm)
Museo Nacional
de Antropología,
Mexico City.
10-222236 (11-4386)

The following group of four offerings (118–121) is from the Great Ballcourt of Tenochtitlan—the Aztec capital city. Today Tenochtitlan is buried beneath modern Mexico City, and most of the Great Ballcourt is covered by the Metropolitan Cathedral. The small portions of the ballcourt that have been excavated have yielded groups of objects ritually buried as offerings.

118 BALLCOURT OFFERING ONE
Late Postclassic Period, Aztec A.D. 1400–1520
Central Mexico, Tenochtitlan/Templo Mayor
shell, rubber
pieces range in size from 1.4 × 0.7 × 0.1 in (3.5 × 1.7 × 0.1 cm) to 1.8 × 3 in (4.5 × 7.5 cm)
Museo del Templo Mayor.
10-264339, 10-265337, 10-265336, 9981

This offering consists of a miniature rubber ball and three tiny shell carvings in the form of a flower and a human femur and hand.

Various items were included in this offering. The two standing, slightly flared square objects are miniature braziers for burning incense. Two types of small pots were also included, along with greenstone beads, ornaments, and pendants. The most intriguing pieces are the miniature musical instruments—four eagle-head whistles, four flutes, and two drums (*teponaztli*)—which illustrate the close association between music and the ballgame.

119 BALLCOURT
OFFERING TWO
Late Postclassic Period,
Aztec A.D. 1400–1520
Central Mexico,
Tenochtitlan/Templo
Mayor
pottery, greenstone, flint
pieces range in size from
0.2 × 1.3 in (0.4 × 3.4 cm) to
10.1 × 3 × 0.6 in (25.6 × 7.6
× 1.4 cm)
Museo del Templo Mayor.
10-604233, 10-604234,
10-604232, 10-604231,
10-265339, 10-265340,
10-265338, 10-604225,
10-604226, 10-604224,
10-604223, 10-604227,
10-604228, 10-604229,
10-604230, 10-604219,
10-604220, 10-604221,
10-604222, 10-604432,
10-604236, 10-604235,
10-604237, 10-604434,
10-604238, 10-604437,
10-604438, 10-265341,
10-265342, 10-265333,
10-265330, 10-265332,
10-265329, 10-265328,
10-265326, 10-265327,
10-265325, 10-265331,
10-265334

A miniature rubber ball, a flint knife, and five shell ornaments depicting a flower, human hands, and femurs make up this offering. The dismembered parts, along with the flint blade, may refer to the sacrificial aspects of the ballgame.

120 BALLCOURT OFFERING FOUR
Late Postclassic Period,
Aztec A.D. 1400–1520
Central Mexico,
Tenochtitlan/Templo
Mayor
shell, flint, rubber
pieces range in size from
1.2 × 0.7 × 0.1 in
(3.1 × 1.7 × 0.1 cm) to
5.5 × 1.9 × 0.5 in
(14 × 4.9 × 1.2 cm)
Museo del Templo Mayor.
10-265349, 10-265352,
10-265353. 1/2, 10-265353
2/2, 10-265354. 1/2,
10-265354 2/2, 10-265335

This elaborate offering deposit includes objects carved in stone and obsidian. It includes two miniature I-shaped ballcourts and a variety of models of percussion instruments, from wooden drums to turtle shells. The most striking objects, however, are the balls: one of dark obsidian, the other of light alabaster. Duality and the pairing of opposites are common threads in Mesoamerican thought and art.

121 BALLCOURT
OFFERING GROUP
Late Postclassic Period,
Aztec A.D. 1325–1521
Central Mexico,
Tenochtitlan/Templo
Mayor
stone
pieces range in size from
0.8 × 1.4 in (2 × 3.5 cm) to
2 × 14.2 in (5 × 36 cm)
Museo Nacional
de Antropología,
Mexico City.
10-222324, 10-222327,
10-222326, 10-222325,
10-222320, 10-222321,
10-222318, 10-222317,
10-222322

DEATH AND RESURRECTION

Death and resurrection are paramount themes of the Mesoamerican ballgame. It is the great drama of human sacrifice depicted on ballcourt reliefs and numerous portable objects that fuels our imagination. For Mesoamerican peoples, human sacrifice was a contractual agreement with the gods, in which the gift of creation was constantly repaid with blood—humanity's most precious offering. The ballgame-playing Hero Twins of the *Popol Vuh* are sacrificed and reborn, thus becoming the model for human interaction with the supernatural. Most assuredly, not every ancient ballgame was accompanied by human sacrifice. This practice gained momentum among the Late Classic and Early Postclassic Period Maya and Veracruz cultures. For the Maya, there was a relationship between the increased warfare between city-states of the Late Classic Period and ballgames in which human sacrifice was the culminating spectacle. Such ballgames were the aftermath of a battle, played between the victors and their captive opponents. Thus, the game's outcome was already known and the losers were sacrificed. The most common method of sacrifice was decapitation, although heart extraction is also depicted in the El Tajín ballcourt reliefs. Although we may focus on the grisly aspects of death in the ballcourts, to Mesoamerican peoples it was a means to an end, and absolutely necessary for the great cycle of life to continue.

This *palma* depicts a wooden or basketry quiver filled with arrows. The cross-hatching represents the fletched ends of the projectiles. Arrows, spears, and shields are symbols of warfare in Mesoamerican art. Warfare and the ballgame were closely related. Classic Maya and Veracruz works of art illustrate human sacrifice as the culmination of the ballgame, the victims of which were almost certainly war captives.

122 QUIVER AND ARROWS
PALMA
Late Classic Period,
Veracruz A.D. 700–900
Mexico, Gulf Coast
stone
26.3 × 8.3 × 4.8 in
(66.4 × 21 × 12.1 cm)
Los Angeles County
Museum of Art. Gift of
Constance McCormick
Fearing.
AC1993.217.20

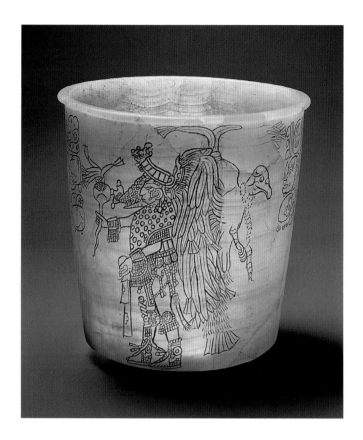

Carved from translucent alabaster, this extraordinary vessel is incised with fantastically costumed human figures and hieroglyphic texts. The scene is replete with war imagery and the text refers to the dual roles of the nobility as warriors and ballplayers. The figure on the left *(below)* is Yax Pac, the ruler of Copán from A.D. 763 to 820.[15] Yax Pac wears a mask, an elaborate feathered headdress and backrack, and a pectoral of jade mosaic. Jade ornaments also decorate his knees, ankles, and wrists. Around his waist is a padded ballgame belt and apron. The goggle eyes on the belt symbolize Tlaloc, the central Mexican rain god, and were an emblem of warfare among the Late Classic Maya. His anklets also have Tlaloc masks. The hieroglyphic text to the left refers to Yax Pac: it begins with a calendar date and the last glyph in the middle line is Yax Pac's name. The third line reads, "he danced with his *sahal* [lesser lord] at the ballcourt [*ta pitzil*]." To the right in this scene, the *sahal* is seen in X-ray fashion inside the enormous peccary mask. He is further outfitted in a padded jaguar vest, anklets with Tlaloc masks, and a headdress with an enormous plumed train. Many of the train's feathers appear to be from the vulture tethered into this assemblage. In the text block to the left of this figure, the emblem glyph for the city of Copán is the middle glyph in the first line. The final line of text names this *sahal* and states that he too participated (danced?) at the ballcourt. Both Yax Pac and his *sahal* carry bizarre staffs that resemble giant human eyeballs with dangling optic nerves. This narrative scene demonstrates that ballcourts were multi-purpose public spaces, and that war rituals must have been one of the activities conducted in them.[16]

123 VESSEL WITH YAX PAC AS
WARRIOR BALLPLAYER
Late Classic Period, Maya A.D. 600–900
Honduras, Copán
alabaster, cinnabar
5.9 × 6.1 in (15.1 × 15.4 cm)
The Art Museum, Princeton University.
Lent Anonymously.
L1998-73

Stripped of all his trappings of rank, the aristocratic war captive depicted in this figurine has none of the elaborate gear or accessories usually seen on Maya ballplayers. Instead, he wears the simple loincloth of a prisoner of war. The only indication that he is about to play the ballgame is the small ball he holds in his right hand. The marks on his bruised and swollen face and the sash draped over his left arm convey that he has undergone bloodletting rituals in preparation for his sacrifice. For the Maya nobility, bloodletting—drawing one's own blood to be burned with incense as an offering to the gods—was a deeply spiritual act.[17]

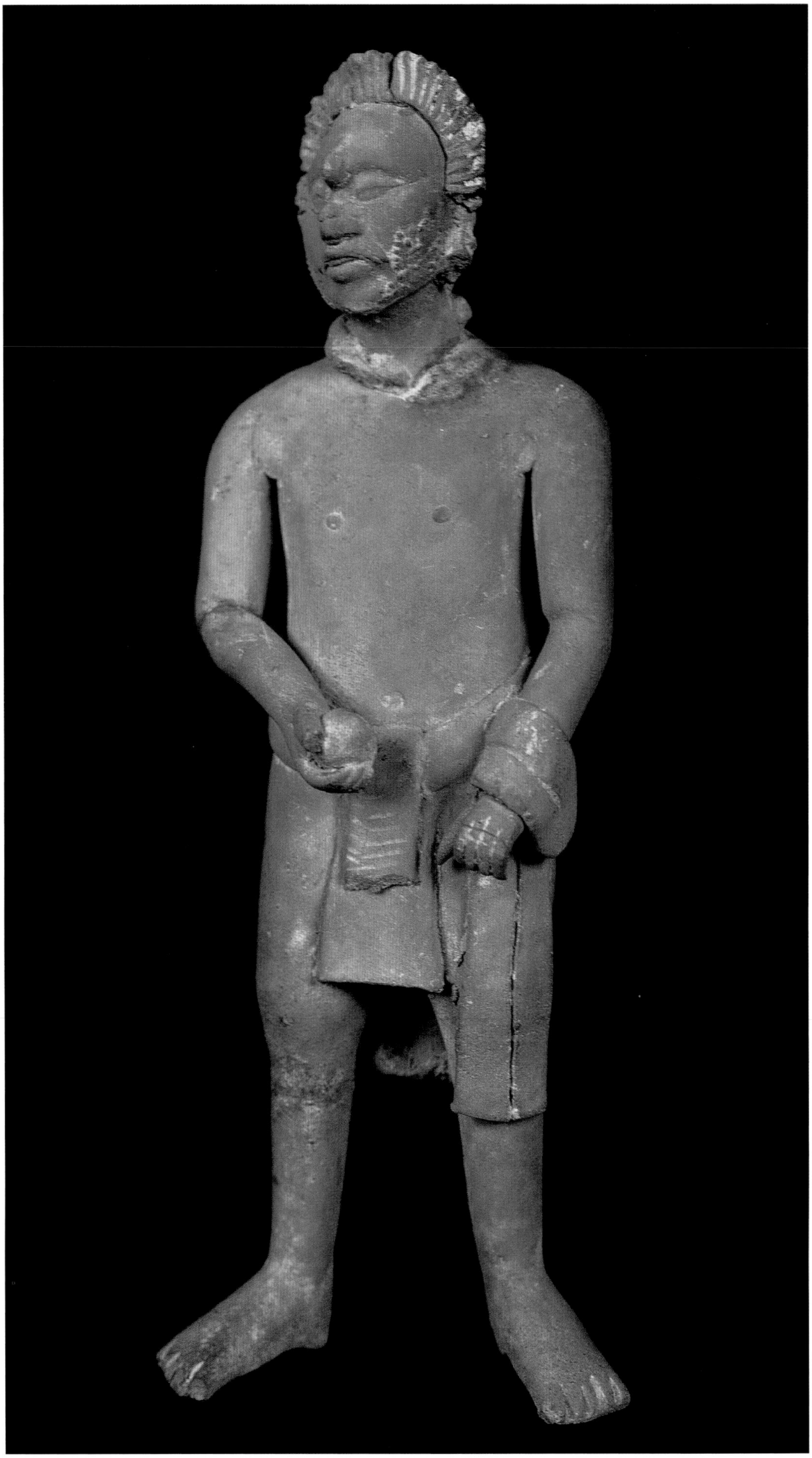

124 WAR CAPTIVE
BALLPLAYER
Late Classic Period, Maya
A.D. 700–900
Mexico, Campeche,
Jaina Island
pottery
h. 9.3 in (23.7 cm)
New Orleans Museum
of Art. Museum Purchase,
Women's Volunteer
Committee Fund.
74.211

125 Tripod Plate with
Kneeling Ballplayer
Late Classic Period, Maya
A.D. 600–900
Guatemala, Northern
Petén Region
*pottery with red, cream,
and black slips*
3 × 15.3 in (7.6 × 38.7 cm)
Mint Museum of Art.
Gift of Dr. and Mrs.
Francis Robicsek.
1979.23.1

A kneeling ballplayer is about to hit the rubber ball
with his elbow. The three knots on his headdress
and the paper strips pulled through his earlobes
refer to human sacrifice.[18]

126 SKULL *HACHA*
Late Classic Period,
Veracruz A.D. 700–900
Mexico, Gulf Coast
stone
10.8 × 7.5 × 6.5 in
(27.3 × 19.1 × 16.5 cm)
Los Angeles County
Museum of Art. Gift of
Constance McCormick
Fearing.
AC1996.146.37

The ballplayer on the front of this whistle *(right)* wears a skeletal mask, a reference to the sacrificial aspects of the ballgame. In his right hand he holds the severed head of a sacrificial victim.

127 SKELETAL BALLPLAYER
WHISTLE *(right)*
Late Classic Period, Maya
A.D. 700–900
Mexico
pottery
5.1 × 3.1 in (13 × 7.9 cm)
Denver Art Museum.
Anonymous Gift.
1983.0408

Ceramics from Guatemala's Escuintla region are a blend of Maya and Central Mexican elements. The form of this straight-sided vessel with slab feet is distinctly Teotihuacan. The press-molded decapitation scene is one that is elaborated at later sites such as Chichén Itzá and El Aparicio. It shows a squatting ballplayer holding the head of a just-decapitated victim. Blood spouting from the neck of the victim has turned into serpents.

128 TRIPOD VESSEL WITH BALLGAME
SACRIFICE SCENE
Middle Classic Period, Maya
A.D. 400–700
Guatemala, Tiquisate
pottery
7.6 × 5.4 in (19.4 × 13.7 cm)
Denver Art Museum. Anonymous Gift.
1980.0237

The victim awaiting sacrifice on this *hacha* is arched backwards over a solid form. Throughout Mesoamerica, this was the posture assumed by victims awaiting heart extraction. In the hands of a skilled priest using razor-sharp obsidian blades, removal of the heart could be accomplished very quickly. Below the victim are a double row of scrolls and possibly the face of a raptorial bird. Eagles and vultures are prominently depicted in the ballgame art of Veracruz, often in scenes involving human sacrifice.

129 *HACHA* OF A SACRIFICIAL VICTIM
Middle Classic Period, Veracruz
A.D. 400–700
Mexico, Gulf Coast
stone
h. 9.6 in (24.5 cm)
The Saint Louis Art Museum.
Gift of Morton D. May.
366:1978

Two complementary and complex scenes unfold on the front and back of this extraordinary *palma*. On the front *(left)* is a ballplayer wearing a coyote mask, standing on a small temple platform, and surrounded by scrolls and swirls typical of the sculptural style of El Tajín and nearby sites. From his head sprouts a stylized maguey (agave) plant, source of the intoxicating beverage pulque. A very similar scene unfolds in a ballcourt panel (South Ballcourt 3, *opposite*) from El Tajín, showing a coyote-masked individual sprouting maguey and kneeling atop a small temple. On the reverse side of this *palma* is a complete narrative carved in much shallower relief. The action centers on the sacrificial scene in the center. The victim, supine on a small platform, is about to have his chest ripped open and his heart removed by a knife-wielding executioner. The maguey sprouting from the executioner's head suggests that he, too, is of supernatural status. Below are humans wearing coyote masks, and deer and additional coyotes stand above. Swooping down from the top of the *palma* is a human costumed as a bat. This scene and corollary narratives from El Tajín illustrate that human sacrifices were elaborate pageants in which key players were costumed as deities and supernaturals.

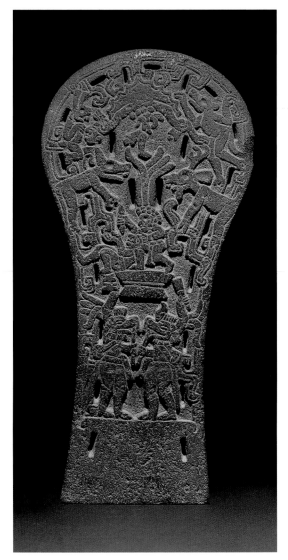

The relief carving on this
ballcourt panel shows a
human atop a temple
platform wearing a coyote
mask *(center right)*.
A stylized maguey plant
sprouts from his head.
To the far right, a skeletal
deity rises from a pulque
vessel.

130 *PALMA* WITH COYOTE
BALLPLAYER AND SACRIFICE
SCENE *(left)*
Late Classic Period,
Veracruz A.D. 700–900
Mexico, Gulf Coast,
El Tajín region
stone
19.4 × 9.3 × 4.5 in
(49.2 × 23.5 × 11.4 cm)
Cleveland Museum of Art,
Purchase from the
J.H. Wade Fund.
1973.3

This *palma* is in the form of a serrated sacrificial knife blade upon which living Death—with a skeletal head and a body from which the heart has been removed—is stretched out. Death wears the triangular leather loincloth with a broad front panel, knee bands, and feet protectors commonly found on ritual ballplayers from 1300 B.C. onward. In his right hand he holds a knife identical to the one upon which he is displayed. His left hand holds the severed head of a ballplayer. The removal of the heart or decapitation of a losing team member after a ballgame was a ceremonial event. Life was not cheap, but regarded as a person's most valuable treasure and therefore worthy of offering to the gods. The concept of Death as a living being is very common in Mesoamerican art. It emphasizes a powerful duality—life and death—faced by everyone, then and now. Rarely is that duality captured with the power and eloquence seen here. DEB

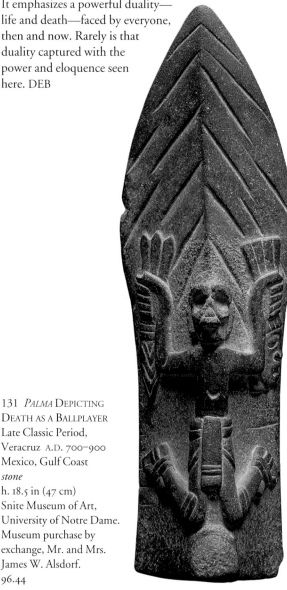

131 *PALMA* DEPICTING DEATH AS A BALLPLAYER
Late Classic Period,
Veracruz A.D. 700–900
Mexico, Gulf Coast
stone
h. 18.5 in (47 cm)
Snite Museum of Art,
University of Notre Dame.
Museum purchase by
exchange, Mr. and Mrs.
James W. Alsdorf.
96.44

These two panels (132 and 133) are from a set of four from the ballcourt at El Aparicio, a site in Veracruz near El Tajín. Mirror images of one another, each depicts a decapitated ballplayer seated on a stepped temple platform. He wears a ballgame yoke around his waist, complete with a fan-shaped *palma* at the front. In one hand he carries a *manopla*, or handstone, with which to bat the solid rubber ball. But the most dramatic part of the composition is the severed neck of both players, from which the spurting blood is transformed into serpents. Snakes are among the most frequently depicted creatures in Mesoamerican art and their representations convey a diverse set of meanings. In this dramatic example they symbolize fertility and the regenerative power of human blood.

132 Monument with
Decapitated Ballplayer *(left)*
Late Classic Period, Veracruz
A.D. 700–900
Mexico, Gulf Coast, El Aparicio
stone
49.3 × 21 × 9 in
(125 × 53.3 × 23 cm)
Museo de Antropología,
Universidad Veracruzana.
44PJ-337

133 Monument with
Decapitated Ballplayer *(below)*
Late Classic Period, Veracruz
A.D. 700–900
Mexico, Gulf Coast, El Aparicio
stone
49.3 × 21 × 9 in
(125 × 53.3 × 23 cm)
Museo Nacional de Antropología,
Mexico City.
10-136579

For the peoples of Mesoamerica maize (corn) was more than the staff of life. This plant—with its young, green shoots appearing in the spring and stalks withering away after the tender ears had been harvested—was a metaphor for life, death, and the promise of resurrection. For the ancient Maya, the Maize God was the personification of youthful vigor, and he is usually portrayed as a handsome young man. The Maize God was closely associated with the ballgame—Hun Hunahpu, the father of the ballplaying Hero Twins, was resurrected as this deity.

Two ears of maize, the base of their stalks emerging from a temple platform, form this beautifully carved *palma.* The maize ears are swollen with ripeness; they are at the perfect moment for harvest. *Palmas* with this type of imagery may have been worn by costumed impersonators of the Maize God.

134 Maize *Palma*
Late Classic Period,
Veracruz A.D. 700–900
Mexico, Gulf Coast
stone
18.3 × 7.5 × 5.5 in
(46.4 × 19.1 × 14 cm)
Denver Art Museum.
Gift of Hugh J. Smith.
1953.106

135 PLATE WITH MAIZE GOD
Late Classic Period, Maya
A.D. 600–900
Guatemala, Petén Region/Tikal
pottery with red, black, and
orange slips
4 × 12 in (10.2 × 30.5 cm)
Mint Museum of Art.
Gift of Mr. Andrew A. Lanyi.
1983.172.25

A dancing Maize God fills the center of this plate, the feathered plumes of his costume swirling around him. The roundel form of the composition recalls the circular ballcourt markers of Chinkultic and other Maya sites and serves as a reminder that the resurrection of the Maize God occurred in the center of the ballcourt. The four I-shaped elements are much like the quatrefoils of ballcourt markers pointing to the cardinal directions. Put into the tomb as an offering, this plate may have been placed over the face of the deceased, the center hole drilled as a final act to free the soul. Painted on the inner band are the 20 day signs of the Maya calendar—a clear representation of the unending cycle of death and the hope of rebirth.

Justifiably, this *hacha* is one of the most celebrated sculptures of ancient Maya art.
It depicts a youthful male profile with a prominent nose and slightly open mouth.
Although it is essentially a flat carving, the sensitive modeling of the face gives a
life-like volume to its features. The finesse of this sculpture points to its origin as
Palenque, a Late Classic site celebrated for its exceptionally beautiful carvings.
Like the numerous Veracruz *hachas*, this Maya example also portrays a trophy
head, probably the decapitated head of Hun Hunahpu,[19] the father of the Hero
Twins, Hunahpu and Xbalanque. Hun Hunahpu's decapitated head is buried
in the ballcourt and he is resurrected as the Maize God (see Miller, this volume).

In the center of this plate the Maize God dances. He is dressed in the costume of a ballplayer, signifying that his resurrection has occurred in the ballcourt, the symbolic center of the Maya universe.

137 PLATE WITH MAIZE GOD BALLPLAYER
Late Classic Period, Maya A.D. 600–900
Guatemala, Petén Region
pottery with red, black and orange slips
2.75 × 14 in (7 × 36 cm)
Mint Museum of Art.
Gift of Mr. Andrew A. Lanyi.
1984.217.14

CONTRIBUTORS

DOUGLAS E. BRADLEY is Curator of Arts of the Americas, Africa, and Oceania at the Snite Museum of Art, University of Notre Dame, Notre Dame, Indiana.

JANE STEVENSON DAY, Ph.D., is Emerita Chief Curator and Curator of Latin American Archaeology at the Denver Museum of Nature and Science, Denver, Colorado.

GILLETT G. GRIFFIN is Emeritus Curator of Pre-Columbian and Primitive Art at The Art Museum, Princeton University, New Jersey.

DOROTHY HOSLER, Ph.D., is Professor of Archaeology and Ancient Technology in the Department of Materials Science and Engineering, Massachusetts Institute of Technology, Cambridge, Massachusetts.

TED J.J. LEYENAAR, Ph.D., is Honorary Curator, Latin American Department at the Rijksmuseum voor Volkenkunde, Leiden, the Netherlands.

MARY MILLER, Ph.D., is Master of Saybrook College/Vincent Scully Professor of the History of Art at Yale University, New Haven, Connecticut.

EDUARDO MATOS MOCTEZUMA, Ph.D., is Director of the Museo del Templo Mayor, Mexico City, Mexico.

LAURA FILLOY NADAL, M.A. is a Senior Conservator at the Museo Nacional de Antropología, Mexico City, Mexico.

JOHN F. SCOTT, Ph.D., is Professor of Art History at the University of Florida, Gainesville.

ERIC TALADOIRE, Ph.D., is Professor of Pre-Columbian Archaeology at the Université de Paris, Paris, France.

MICHAEL J. TARKANIAN is a Research Affiliate, Center for Materials Research in Archaeology and Ethnology, Department of Materials Science and Engineering, Massachusetts Institute of Technology, Cambridge, Massachusetts.

MARÍA TERESA URIARTE, Ph.D., is Director of the Instituto de Investigaciones Estésticas, Universidad Nacional Autonóma de México, Mexico City, Mexico.

E. MICHAEL WHITTINGTON is Curator of Pre-Columbian and African Art at the Mint Museum of Art, Charlotte, North Carolina.

NOTES

INTRODUCTION, E. MICHAEL WHITTINGTON pp. 16–19
1. Tedlock 1996, p. 64.
2. Sahagún 1961, p. 87.
3. Haury 1992, p. 428.
4. Alegría 1983, p. 29.

1 RUBBER AND RUBBER BALLS IN MESOAMERICA,
LAURA FILLOY NADAL, pp. 20–31
The author would like to thank the altruistic support of
numerous colleagues and friends in the preparation of this
paper. Among them are Frances Berdan (State University
of California at San Bernardino), Miguel Ángel Canseco
(Universidad Nacional Autónoma de México), José Luis
Criales (CT-Scanner de México), Leonardo López Luján
(Instituto Nacional de Antropología e Historia), Juan Manuel
Malpica (INIF/SAGAR), David F. Maynard (State University
of California at San Bernardino), Debra Nagao, Felipe Solís
Olguín (Instituto Nacional de Antropología e Historia),
Eric Taladoire (Université de Paris I-Panthéon-Sorbonne),
and Michael Whittington (Mint Museum of Art).
1. Stern 1966, pp. 4–5.
2. Ortíz and Rodríguez 1994.
3. Filloy 2000.
4. Filloy 1993, and in preparation.
5. Leyenaar and Parsons 1988, p. 95.
6. Casas 1966, p. 23.
7. Casas 1966, p. 23
8. Durán 1971, p. 316.
9. Hernández 1959, p. 388; Valdés and Flores 1976, pp. 76–78.
10. Serier 1992, p. 27.
11. Polhamus 1962, p. 92; Serier 1992, p. 29.
12. Clavijero 1964, book I, chapter II, pp. 20–21.
13. Coran 1994, pp. 340–41.
14. Polhamus 1962, pp. 31–33, 51–59; Le Bras 1969, pp. 9,
22–23; Compagnon 1986, pp. 4–5.
15. Compagnon 1986, p. 5; Valdés and Flores 1986, p. 79.
16. Chapel 1892, p. 158; Valdés and Flores 1986, p. 78;
Martínez 1994, p. 467.
17. Valdés and Flores 1986, pp. 78–81; Martínez 1994, p. 1076.
18. Chapel 1892, p. 92; Valdés and Flores 1976, pp. 71–72.
19. Polhamus 1962, pp. 101–02; Le Bras 1969, p. 33.
20. Rollins 1950, p. 40–42.
21. Compagnon 1986, p. 521.

22. Martínez 1994, pp. 393, 1178.
23. Rollins 1950.
24. Le Bras 1969, p. 41.
25. Bally 1952, pp. 1346–47; Le Bras 1969, pp. 33, 44.
26. Le Bras 1969, p. 45; Hofmann 1989; Mark, Erman, and
Eirich 1994.
27. Dern 1911, pp. 107–08; Polhamus 1962, p. 264.
28. Hosler, Burkett, and Tarkanian 1999.
29. Ochoa 1992, p. 30; Torquemada 1977, v. 4, p. 429.
30. Torquemada 1977, v. 4, p. 429.
31. Martínez 1994.
32. Hosler, Burkett, and Tarkanian 1999; Tarkanian and Hosler
2000, pp. 56–57; Maynard and Berdan 2000.
33. MNA: Museu Etnòlogic 1988, p. 178; MTM: Filloy, 1993,
pp. 43–46; López Luján 1998; Matos Moctezuma, Hinojosa,
and Barrera Rivera 1998, p. 18; Barrera Rivera 1999, p. 37;
SM: Amsden 1936; Haury 1937; Stern 1966, p. 89; Baird 1982;
Kaminitz 1988, p. 144; PUMA: Norman Muller, personal
communication, November 1995; PM: Coggins 1992, pp. 284,
348, 354–56; BM: Eric Taladoire, personal communication,
May 1993; MN: Serier 1992, p. 253.
34. Zyska 1981; Blank 1990; Filloy 1993, 1996, and in preparation.
35. Filloy 1993, pp. 28–48; Filloy in preparation.
36. Ortíz and Rodríguez 1989, p. 36; Ortíz, Rodríguez, and
Schmidt 1988; Ortíz, Rodríguez, and Delgado 1992, pp. 63–64.
37. Ortíz and Rodríguez 1994, p. 86; Ortíz and Rodríguez
2000, p. 79; Tarkanian and Hosler 2000, p. 54.
38. Hill, Blake, and Clark 1998.
39. Ortíz and Rodríguez 1994, pp. 86–87; 2000, p. 89.
40. Thompson 1992; Tozzer 1957, p. 197; Coggins 1992,
pp. 284, 348, 354–56; technical reports of objects 301, 306, 311,
315, 317, 318/83 and 145/82, restored at the Coordinación
Nacional de Restauración del del Patrimonio Cultural del INAH.
41. Solís and Morales 1991, p. 302.
42. Gussinyer 1970, p. 12
43. Technical reports of objects 422, 442/74; 38, 42, 66, 101,
107, 108, 117, 132, 135, 138, 152, 263/82; 269, 273, 277/89;
770/727; B-69 167, B-77 167, B-77 189, B-78 190, B-79 191,
B-80 192, B-81 193, B-97 226, B-145 369, B-161 400, restored
at the Coordinación Nacional de Restauración del Patrimonio
Cultural del INAH.
44. Matos Moctezuma, this volume.
45. Lumbrera 1, OF.4-12 and 1-3, see Matos Moctezuma,
Hinojosa, and Barrera Rivera 1998, pp. 16-17; Barrera Rivera

1999; Barrera Rivera, personal communication, January 2000.
46. López Luján 1998.
47. Filloy and Canseco 1996; Maynard and Berdan 2000.
48. *Codice Mendocino* 1979, pl. 46r.
49. Sahagún 1989, pp. 531, 622.
50. Torquemada 1977, book XIV, chap. XII, p. 342; Fernández de Oviedo 1944, book VI, chap. 2, p. 297; Mártir de Anglería 1944, Decade V, book X, chap. 5, p. 469.
51. Mártir de Anglería 1944, Decade V, book X, chap. 5, p. 469.
52. Further information see Marion 1992, p. 789; Sociedad de Amigos del Museo 1986, p. 40; Oliver Vega 1992, p. 152.
53. Lounsbury 1973, p. 18.
54. Filloy et al. 2000.
55. Taladoire 1981, pp. 505–23, 1994 and 2000; cf. Cohodas 1991, p. 51.
56. Taladoire 1981, pp. 505–23, 1994 and 2000.
57. Pomar 1941, p. 27.
58. Taladoire 1981, pp. 513, 518; Leyenaar and Parsons 1988; Oliver Vega 1992, p. 154; Cortés Ruiz 1992, pp. 170, 228–29.
59. Krickeberg 1966; Gillespie 1991.
60. Sahagún 1989, book 2.
61. Blom 1932, p. 495.
62. Cohodas 1991, p. 253; Leyenaar and Parsons 1988, p. 85.
63. Gillespie 1991, pp. 225–27, 345.
64. Tarkanian 2000.

2 GENDER, POWER, AND FERTILITY IN THE OLMEC RITUAL BALLGAME, DOUGLAS E. BRADLEY, pp. 32–39
1. Mesoamerica is the parts of central and southern Mexico, Guatemala, Belize, Honduras, and El Salvador between the Tropic of Cancer and the 12th parallel.
2. Coe 1965, p. 54, referred to this style of figurine as Tlapacoya ballplayers. He was the first to compare them with ballplayer figurines from later cultures and to conclude that they portrayed ballplayers. At that time, it was impossible for Coe to have known that the Tlapacoya ballplayers were Olmec.
3. Coe and Diehl 1980, p. 23, list the Chicharrus, San Lorenzo A, and San Lorenzo B phases as ranging from 1250 to 900 B.C., radiocarbon; Coe and Diehl did not calibrate the radiocarbon dates to sidereal or star time, the time by which we live, but those dates would be approximately 1500–1100 B.C.
4. Coe and Diehl 1980, p. 268.
5. Niederberger Betton 1987, pp. 279–80.
6. Piña Chan 1955, no. 41.
7. Bradley and Joralemon 1993, pp. 18–20.
8. Ibid., p. 18.
9. Coe 1972, pp. 9–10.
10. Drucker 1959, fig. 22.
11. Joralemon 1974 and Schele and Miller 1986 (chapter 4) remain the most authoritative sources on ritual bloodletting.
12. Joralemon 1976 discusses duality in Olmec religion.
13. Coe and Diehl 1980, p. 343.
14. Bradley and Joralemon 1993, pp. 19–23.

15. Bradley 1997, pp. 15–17.
16. The padded belt on the front of Monument 1 contains vertical bands identical to those on another Olmec Pilli ballplayer from Tlapacoya.
17. Bradley 1997, pp. 17-18, is confusing. These figurines often are referred to as Olmec from Las Bocas, but they are Olmec Pilli type from Tlapacoya. Bradley 2000 contains the complete attribution of Olmec Pilli female ballplayers.
18. Bradley 1997, pp. 22–23.
19. Niederberger Betton 1987, p. 280, reports that 76 per cent of the Pilli figurines at Tlapacoya are male, and the remainder are female. Pilli-type figurines are 65 per cent of all Olmec figurines uncovered in her excavations.
20. Niederberger Betton 1987, p. 427.
21. Robert B. Pickering, personal communication, July 27, 2000.
22. Niederberger Betton 1987, p. 434.
23. Cyphers Guillén and Botas 1994 discuss the Olmec practice of reworking stone sculpture.
24. Bradley and Joralemon 1993, p. 22.
25. Niederberger Betton 1987, pp. 279–80.
26. Bradley and Joralemon 1993, pp. 23–28.

3 UNITY IN DUALITY: THE PRACTICE AND SYMBOLS OF THE MESOAMERICAN BALLGAME, MARÍA TERESA URIARTE, pp. 40–49
The author dedicates this essay to Marina Padilla Lang.
1. Ortíz, Rodríguez, and Delgado 1992.
2. Idem.
3. Seler 1980.
4. Miller and Taube 1993, p. 144.
5. Sahagún 1981. Book 2, p. 239
6. El juego de pelota en Mesoamérica. 1984, p. 13.
7. Idem.
8. Kowalski 1992, pp. 305–33. See also Parsons 1991, p.197; Cohodas 1991, pp. 255, 281.
9. Parsons 1991, p. 197. See also Fox, J. W., 1991, p. 217.
10. Schele and Freidel 1991, p. 291.
11. Dobkin de Rios 1984, p. 126.
12. Eliade 1958.
13. Schultes and Hofmann 1979.
14. Van Bussel 1991.
15. Ibid., pp. 256–57.

4 DRESSED TO KILL: STONE REGALIA OF THE MESOAMERICAN BALLGAME, JOHN F. SCOTT, pp. 50–63
1. Leyenaar and Parsons 1988, pp. 109–10.
2. Scott 1976, 1979, 1991, 1997.
3. Oliveros 1974, fig. 8.
4. Oliveros 1992, p. 47.
5. Schöndube, personal communication 1990; Schöndube and Galván 1978, p. 164.
6. Porter 1953, p. 54.
7. Bernal and Seuffert 1970, p. 7.

8. First proposed by Lothrop 1923 and expanded by Ekholm 1949, 1973.
9. Ortiz, Rodríguez, and Delgado 1992, p. 61.
10. Ibid., p. 63.
11. Ibid.
12. Gillett Griffin, personal communication 1992.
13. Oliveros 1974, fig. 17, object #13.
14. Scott 1964 manuscript.
15. Leyenaar this volume.
16. Bernal and Seuffert 1979.
17. Recinos 1950, p. III.
18. Cuevas de Álvarez 1970 manuscript.
19. Conant and Collins 1991, pp. 307–08.
20. Furst 1974, p. 89.
21. Miller and Taube 1993, p. 167.
22. Génin 1928, p. 523.
23. Scott 1976, fig. 12.
24. Ibid., p. 41.
25. Recinos 1950, p. III.
26. Scott 1976, p. 43.
27. Easby and Scott 1970, no. 139.
28. Scott 1987, no. 53.
29. Medellín 1960, Lám. 110.
30. A similar smooth stone yoke, with perfectly parallel sides and differential polishing—the outer sides smooth, the interior and bottom rough—was found on the property of Guillermo Peñafiel in Olmeaca, in the western mountains of south-central Veracruz (Génin 1928, p. 525). The famous photo reproduced by Génin shows the yoke encircling the head of a carefully arranged, disarticulated skeleton, probably an inventive creation of the farm laborers trying to please Peñafield and his visitor by reassembling bones from a secondary burial. Therefore the position of the yoke cannot be trusted either.
31. Scott 1991, p. 211.
32. Tlaxcala Regional Museum staff, personal communication 1990; illus. Scott 1997, abb. 104.
33. Leyenaar and Parsons 1988, no. 55.
34. Leyenaar 1997, p. 85.
35. Weiant 1943, p. 118.
36. Ibid., pl. 66, no. 4.
37. García Payón 1971, p. 525.
38. García Payón 1947, p. 327.
39. As I stated in Scott 1991, p. 205.
40. Shook and Marquis 1996, p. 8.
41. Ibid., pp. 13–15.
42. Hellmuth 1987, pp. 126–29, identifies the site as Hacienda la Barranquilla in Tiquisate municipality, and says the cache was associated with Esmeraldas pottery diagnostic of the Early Classic (A.D. 300–600).
43. Shook and Marquis 1996, pp. 16–17.
44. Brüggemann 1992, p. 94.
45. Wilkerson 1970, p. 44.
46. Sarro 1995 manuscript, pp. 145–54.

47. Scott 1976, p. 27.
48. Ekholm 1973, p. 48.
49. I am grateful to Lic. Luis Melgarejo Vivanco, then director of the Xalapa Museum of Anthropology, for allowing me to study and photograph the El Zapotal yokes and *hachas* in that museum in 1990. Those on display could not be removed from their cases to be measured and photographed in a controlled environment.
50. Scott 1997, abb. 107.
51. For a photo of both yokes lying side by side after excavation, see Scott 1979, p. 14.
52. Scott 1997, abb. 112–13.
53. Wilkerson 1990, p. 170.
54. Medellín 1960, p. 112.
55. Proskouriakoff 1954, p. 81, first proposed this evolution.
56. Shook and Marquis 1996, p. 66.
57. Ibid., pp. 75–217. Count made by present author.
58. Ibid., pp. 71–72. Those *hachas* from the Aguna site were reported "stacked like tortillas."
59. Easby and Scott 1970, no. 153, illustrate the *palma* in the Museo Nacional de Antropología, Mexico, with hands pressed together in a prayerful position.
60. Wilkerson 1990, p. 171.
61. Ibid., pp. 172–73.
62. Scott 1982, p. 16.
63. Sarro 1995 manuscript, p. 157.
64. Wilkerson 1990, p. 173.
65. Shook and Marquis 1996, p. 219.
66. Ibid., p. 220.

5 PERFORMING ON THE COURT, JANE STEVENSON DAY, pp. 64–77

1. Lahr 1976, p. 199.
2. Taladoire 1994, pp. 6–15.
3. Durán 1971; Sahagún 1981.
4. Pasztory 1972; Stern 1948; Leyenaar and Parsons 1988.
5. Algarin 1992.
6. McNeill 1995.
7. Oliveros 1992.
8. Cyphers 1997, p. 185.
9. Soustelle 1984, p. 38.
10. Day 1998.
11. Ibid.
12. Taube 1993, p. 66
13. Uriarte 1992, p. 113.
14. Day 1998, fig. 23, p. 167.
15. Lahr 1976, pp. 199–201.
16. Schele and Miller 1986.
17. Miller 1986.
18. Brüggemann, 1994; Wilkerson 1991.
19. Koontz 1994.
20. Cook 1994, pp. 60–65.
21. Durán 1971; Sahagún, 1979.

22. Durán 1971, p. 305.
23. Ibid., p. 305.
24. Sahagún 1981.
25. Solis 1992, p. 149.

6 THE MAYA BALLGAME: REBIRTH IN THE COURT OF LIFE
AND DEATH, MARY MILLER, pp. 78–87
1. Sahagún 1961, p. 87.
2. Despite the title of her book—*Varieties of Classic Central
Veracruz Sculpture*—Tatiana Proskouriakoff (1954) recognized
that many ballgame objects had been made and used in Guatemala.
3. Stuart 1987 originally read the title *pits*.
4. Hellmuth 1991; see also Taube 1988 on the hunt.
5. For further consideration of the historical interpretations of
the ballgame, as well as a consideration of the meaning of the
visual representations, see Schele and Miller 1986, chapter 6,
and Miller and Houston 1987.
6. Karl Taube brought the Maya Maize God back to modern
attention after a long period in which the deity was ignored
(Taube 1985).
7. Freidel, Schele, and Parker 1993, p. 367.
8. The large plate over the interred lord of Burial 128 features
a seated scribe and central kill hole (Adams 1971, Smith 1972).
Although Maya scribes are often considered to be exclusively
the "other" twins, Hun Batz and Hun Chuen, half-brothers
to the Hero Twins, the Maize God, their father, is often
represented as a scribe. In other words, the Maya Scribe Twins
have gone into the "family business."

7 THE BALL COURT IN TENOCHTITLAN, EDUARDO MATOS
MOCTEZUMA, pp. 88–95
1. Sahagún 1956.
2. Matos Moctezuma 1992, p. 133–41.
3. Sahagún, op. cit.
4. Sahagún, op. cit.
5. Batres 1902.
6. Matos Moctezuma 1992. Based on Marquina's supposition,
I first thought the game was oriented from north to south.
The excavations demonstrated that the right orientation was
from east to west.
7. Taladoire 2000, pp. 20–27.
8. Marquina 1960.
9. López Arenas 2000.
10. Caso 1978.
11. Seler 1963; Beyer 1965.
12. Turok 2000.
13. Corona Núñez 1992, pp. 83–87.
14. Guevara 2000, pp. 36–41.
15. Sahagún, op. cit.
16. Durán 1967.
17. López Arenas 2000.
18. Garibay 1953, pp. 300–02.

8 THE ARCHITECTURAL BACKGROUND OF THE
PRE-HISPANIC BALLGAME: AN EVOLUTIONARY PERSPECTIVE,
ERIC TALADOIRE, pp. 96–115
1. Filloy Nadal 1993 and this volume.
2. Acosta and Moedano Koer 1946; Blom 1932; Leyenaar 1978;
Quirarte 1977; Smith 1961; Stern 1949; Taladoire 1981.
3. Leyenaar 1997; Leyenaar and Parsons 1988; Scarborough
and Wilcox 1991; van Bussel, van Dongen, and Leyenaar 1991.
4. Boot 1991; Houston 1983; Miller and Houston 1987.
5. García Moll 1977; Graham 1982.
6. Patrois 1999.
7. Baudez 1984.
8. Baquedano, in van Bussel, van Dongen, and Leyenaar 1991.
The story is also well documented in Mireille Simoni Abbat
1976. *Les Aztèques.* Coll. Le temps qui court no. 43. Paris: Seuil.
9. Scarborough, in Scarborough and Wilcox 1991, pp. 129–44
10. Hill, Blake, and Clark 1998.
11. Leyenaar 1978 and this volume.
12 This is of course a mean evaluation, since sometimes several
months pass, while suddenly an article or a book expands our
corpus with data about several courts. See, for instance,
Brambila, Crespo, and Saint-Charles 1993; Cabrero 1989;
Daneels 1990, 1991; Gyarmati 1995; Hirth 1980; Ichon 1991;
Markman 1981; Michelet 1986; Naylor 1985; Quintana
Samayoa 1995; and Roldán 1995a and b.
13. Taladoire 1981.
14. García Cook and Merino Carrión 1998. Lincoln 1987. For
the El Tajín area, there are only 18 registered courts on the site
proper, but close peripheral sites include many more examples,
raising the total to more than 27 (Jimenez Lara 1992).
15. Although the number of small sites with ballcourts is still
few, several examples have been registered in the Basin of
Mexico at Acozac (Ixtapaluca Viejo) (Nicholson 1985),
Petulton and Mosil in the Ocosingo Valley (Becquelin and
Baudez 1979–82, Becquelin and Taladoire 1990), and
Gualterio Abajo in Durango (E. Kelley 1976). Others might
be discovered, but small sites have not been the focus of as
much attention as major sites.
16. Zeitlin 1993.
17. Recent salvage archaeology disclosed the existence of
several ballcourts under colonial buildings in Mexico proper
(Baños Ramos 1990), and of course in the Templo Mayor
precinct, under the Cathedral (Matos Moctezuma et al. 1998).
Related offerings with ballcourt representations have been
documented from the same area (Gussinyer 1974, Taladoire
in press), thus completing our scant data for that part of
Mesoamerica.
18. See other contributions in this volume, and notes 2 and 3.
19. Leyenaar 1978; Stern 1949.
20. Day 1998.
21. Smith 1961.
22. Acosta and Moedano Koer 1946; Satterthwaite 1933;
Quirarte 1977.
23. Pincemin 1993

24. Alegría 1983.
25. The proposed typology has been tested especially in the Maya Lowlands, that is, in southeastern Petén (García Barrios 1992; Roldán 1995a and b), or in Belize (Hammond 1994), but also in Veracruz (Daneels 1990), especially during the El Tajín excavations (Raesfeld 1990, 1992). It had already proved useful in San Luis Potosí, Rio Verde area (Michelet 1986), and we verified its validity for Michoacán, with the results of the recent French project in the Zacapu region (Taladoire 1990).
26. Weigand in Scarborough and Wilcox 1991, pp. 73–86; Weigand 1993.
27. Braniff 1988.
28. Filloy 1993 and this volume.
29. Wyshak et al. 1971.
30. Hill, Blake, and Clark 1998.
31. To the Abaj Takalik ballcourt (Schieber de Lavarreda 1994), one can at least add the El Ujuxte example (Love 1995).
32. To the El Vergel, San Mateo, and Finca Acapulco courts in Chiapas (Agrinier, in Scarborough and Wilcox 1991) can be added six excavated courts in the Maya Lowlands (Nakbé, Cerros (2), Toniná North, Pacbitún, and Colha) (Velasquez 1992; Scarborough et al. 1982; Becquelin and Baudez 1979–82; Healy 1992; Eaton and Kunstler 1980), one in Honduras (Fox, J.G. 1996), maybe Teopantecuanitlan in Guerrero, several in Oaxaca (especially at Monte Albán) or in the Tehuacan Valley, and Capulac Concepción in Puebla (Beristáin Bravo 1983).
33. Taladoire (in press). Type V courts, while generally associated with the ballgame, correspond to a specific area, and a relatively restricted period, that is, the Late Formative and Early Classic. Besides, the known profiles of the few excavated courts differ from other types of profiles, and, of course, their floor plan is quite unusual. This set them apart from the other identified types in most respects. This could be due to the lack of reliable data, but it could also be justified by a different function. Given the existence of several types of ballgames in Mesoamerica, it would be possible the Type V Palangana courts might be representative of another tradition.
34. Daneels 1990; Stresser-Péan 1977.
35. Weigand in Scarborough and Wilcox 1991, pp. 73–86; Braniff 1988.
36. Wilcox in Scarborough and Wilcox 1991, pp. 101–25.
37. Six ballcourts each have been documented at Tula and Xochicalco (López Luján, Cobean, and Mastache 1995), but many others are known in Puebla, the state of Mexico, Morelos, and Oaxaca.
38. On the Gulf Coast, the sites of Cantona and El Tajín, with more than 20 courts each, are only the most prominent examples (García Cook and Merino Carríon 1998; Jimenez Lara 1992; Raesfeld 1990, 1992).
39. Taladoire 1990; Brambila, Crespo, and Saint-Charles 1993.
40. Weigand 1993; Taladoire 1998.
41. Fash and Lane 1983.
42. Van Tuerenhout, in van Bussel, van Dongen, and Leyenaar 1991.

43. Fialko 1986.
44. Healy 1992.
45. Becquelin and Baudez 1979–82; Becquelin and Taladoire 1990.
46. Taladoire 1979c.
47. Taladoire 1975.
48. Ringle and Bey 1992, Johnstone 1994.
49. Van Tuerenhout in van Bussel, van Dongen, and Leyenaar 1991.
50. Hammond 1994.
51. Fash and Lane 1983.
52. Lincoln 1987.
53. García Cook and Merino Carrión 1998.
54. In his analysis of the iconography of the ballcourt markers, Baudez (1984) proposed that they represented the Underworld, where the king had to go to confront the Lords of Death, in order to allow the regeneration of life and vegetation. Kowalski and Fash (1991) confirmed this interpretation and even consider that the complete iconography of the ballcourt, including the tenoned parrot heads would stand for the Underworld. The Copán court would thus be the Underworld itself and not just an entrance.

9 AN ANCIENT TRADITION CONTINUED: MODERN RUBBER PROCESSING IN MEXICO, MICHAEL J. TARKANIAN AND DOROTHY HOSLER, pp. 116–121

The authors thank Professor Sandra Burkett at Amherst College; the Consejo de Arqueología at the Instituto Nacional de Antropologia e Historia (INAH) and Joaquín García-Bárcena, Ma. del Carmen Rodríguez and Ponciano Ortiz; in Chiapas, J. Gasco, F. Guillén, L. Guillén, A. Castaneda, O. Guillén-Sanchez, and M. Escobar-Ortiz; at Harvard University, the staff at the Peabody Museum of Archaeology and Ethnology and the Botany Library; the Undergraduate Research Opportunities Program at MIT.
1. Sahagún 1970, vol. 11, p. 112; Tarkanian 2000.
2. Standley 1920.
3. Olsson-Seffer 1907.
4. Olsson-Seffer 1908.
5. Lloyd 1911.
6. Altamirano and Rose 1905.
7. Benavente 1984, pp. 35–36.
8. Martir 1964, vol. 2, p. 547.
9. Standley 1942, p. 123.
10. Van Ooststroom 1940.
11. Hosler, Burkett, and Tarkanian 1999; Tarkanian and Hosler 2000; Tarkanian 2000.
12. Hosler, Burkett, and Tarkanian 1999; Tarkanian 2000.
13. Rodríguez and Ortiz 1994.
14. Coggins and Ladd 1992. Clemency Coggins, personal communication 1996.
15. Sahagún 1970, vol. 10, pp. 141, 145, 146, 154, 155; Tarkanian 2000.

16. Tarkanian 2000.
17. Sahagún 1970, vol. 1, p. 37.
18. Sahagún 1970, vol. 10, p. 188.
19. Tarkanian 2000.

10 The Modern Ballgames of Sinaloa: A Survival
of the Aztec Ullamaliztli, Ted J.J. Leyenaar, pp. 122–129
1. Gómara 1826; Motolinía 1903.
2. Ibid.
3. Sahagún 1989.
4. Leyenaar 1978.
5. Leyenaar 1978, fig. 57.
6. Leyenaar 1978, pp. 61 ff., for more details.
7. Leyenaar and Parsons 1988, pp. 153 ff.

11 Everything Old is New Again: The Enduring Legacy
of the Ancient Games, E. Michael Whittington,
pp. 130–135
1. Freidel, Schele, and Parker 1993, p. 362.
2. Taladoire and Colsenet 1991, pp. 172–73.
3. Histories of the Army mule and Navy goat were provided
by the public affairs offices of West Point and the United
States Naval Academy.
4. Zimbardo 1969.
5. Tedlock 1996, pp. 78–79.
6. Freidel, Schele, and Parker 1993, p. 350.
7. Bradley 1997.
8. Cohodas 1991, p. 259.
9. Durán 1971.

Catalogue, E. Michael Whittington, pp. 136–265
1. Day 1998, p. 162.
2. Ibid.
3. Cohodas 1991, pp. 260-61.
4. Jane Day, personal communication, 2000.
5. Wilkerson, 1984.
6. Wilkerson 1990, p. 173.
7. Miller and Taube 1993, p. 75
8. Miller 1986, p. 101.
9. Miller 1975, pp. 13–14.
10. Miller and Taube 1993, p. 82
11. Bill Ringle, personal communication, 2000.
12. Grube 1990, p. 320.
13. Friedel, Schele and Parker 1993, p. 338.
14. Schele and Miller 1986
15. Schele and Freidel, 1990, p. 311.
16. I am grateful to Justin Kerr, Matthew Robb, and
Hector Escobedo for their insights on this vessel's text
and iconography.
17. Schele and Miller 1986, p. 256.
18. Reents-Budet 1994, p. 268.
19. Mary Miller, personal communication, 2000.

BIBLIOGRAPHY

Acosta, Jorge R., and Hugo Moedano Koer. 1946. Los Juegos de Pelota. In *México Prehispánico: Culturas, Deidades, Monumentos*, ed. J.A. Vivó, pp. 365–84. Mexico City: Antología de Esta Semana.

Adams, Richard E.W. 1971. *The Ceramics of Altar de Sacrificios*. Peabody Museum Papers, vol. 63:1. Cambridge, MA: Harvard University.

Alegría, Ricardo E. 1983. *Ball Courts and Ceremonial Plazas in the West Indies*. Yale University Publications in Anthropology, no. 79. New Haven: Dept. of Anthropology, Yale University.

Algarin, Miquel. 1992. Mesoamerican Pre-Columbian Pop Culture: The Team. Supplement to catalogue for *Ana Pellicer y Ulama: La Pelota que Rebota* ('Ana Pellicer and Ulama: The Ball that Bounces') on the occasion of the Columbus Quincentenary/The Encounter Between Two Worlds. Lincoln Center Out-Of-Doors Festival (New York: All Area #3, 1992).

Altamirano, Fernando, and Rose. 1905. *El Palo Amarillo*. Mexico City: Instituto Medico Nacional.

Amsden, Charles. 1936. A Prehistoric Rubber Ball. *The Masterkey* 10, no. 1, pp. 7–8.

Arana Alvarez, Raúl M. 1984. El Juego de Pelota de Coatetelco, Morelos. Sociedad Mexicana de Antropología, San Cristobal de Las Casas. *Mesa Redonda*, 17, pp. 191–203.

Baird, Leslie. 1982. The Museum's 1000-Year-Old Rubber Ball. *The Masterkey* 56, no. 4, pp. 142–46.

Bally, W. 1952. Les Plantes à Caoutchouc. *Les Cahiers CIBA 4*, no. 40, pp. 1346–50.

Baños Ramos, Eneida. 1990. Elementos de Juegos de Pelota en la Ciudad de México, D.F. *Mexicon*, vol. 12, 4, pp. 73–75.

Barrera Rivera, José Álvaro. 1999. El Rescate Arqueológico en la Catedral y el Sagrario Metropolitanos de la Ciudad de México. In *Excavaciones en la Catedral y el Sagrario Metropolitanos: Programa de Arqueología Urbana*, ed. Eduardo Matos Moctezuma, pp. 21–50. Mexico City: Instituto Nacional de Antropología e Historia, Colección Obra Diversa.

Batres, Leopoldo. 1902. *Exploraciones Arqueológicas en las Calles de las Escalerillas, Año de 1900*. Mexico.

Baudez, Claude F. 1984. Le Roi, la Balle et le Maïs: Images du Jeu de Balle Maya. *Journal de la Société des Américanistes de Paris* 70, pp. 139–52.

Becquelin, Pierre, and Claude F. Baudez. 1979–82. *Toniná. Une Cité Maya du Chiapas*. Études Mésoaméricaines I(6)I–III. Mexico City: Mission Archéologique et Ethnologique Française au Mexique.

Becquelin, Pierre, and Eric Taladoire. 1990. *Toniná. Une Cité Maya du Chiapas*. Études Mésoaméricaines I(6)IV. Mexico: Centre d'Études Mexicaines et Centre-Américaines.

Benavente, Toribio de. 1984. *Historia de los Indios de la Nueva Espana*. Mexico City: Editorial Porrúa.

Beristáin Bravo, Francisco. 1983. Análisis Arquitectónico del Juego de Pelota en el Área Central de México. *Revista Mexicana de Estudios Antropológicos* 29:1, pp. 211–42.

Bernal, Ignacio. 1968. The Ball Players of Dainzú. *Archaeology* 21, pp. 246–51.

———. 1969. El juego de Pelota Más Antiguo de México. *Artes de México* 119, pp. 28–33.

Bernal, Ignacio, and Andy Seuffert. 1970. Yugos de la Colección del Museo Nacional de Antropología. *Corpus Antiquarum Americanensium IV*.

———. 1979. *The Ball Players of Dainzú: Corpus Antiquarum Americanensium*. Graz, Austria: Akademische Druck u- Verlagsanstalt.

Beyer, Hermann. 1965. Mito y Simbología del México Antiguo. In *Revista Internacional de Arqueología, Etnología, Folklore, Historia, Historia Antigua y Lungüística*, vol. X. Mexico: Sociedad Alemana Mexicanista.

Blank, Sharon. 1990. An Introduction to Plastics and Rubbers in Collections. *Studies in Conservation* 35, no. 2, pp. 53–63.

Blom, Frans. 1932. The Maya Ballgame "Pok-ta-pok," called *Tlachtli* by the Aztecs. In *Middle American Research Series* 4, pp. 487–527. New Orleans: Tulane University, Middle American Papers.

Boot, Eric. 1991. The Maya Ballgame, as Referred to in Hieroglyphic Writing. In *The Mesoamerican Ballgame*, eds. Gerard W. van Bussel, Paul L.F. van Dongen, and Ted J.J. Leyenaar. Leiden: Rijksmuseum voor Volkenkunde.

———. 2000. The Great Ball Court at Chichén Itzá, Yucatán, Mexico. Paper presented at the International Colloquium on "Pre-Columbian and Ethnographic Collections of Latin America," Leiden.

Borhegyi, Stephan F. de. 1969. The Pre-Columbian Ballgame: a Pan-Mesoamerican Tradition. *Proceedings of the 38th International Congress of Americanists, 1968*, Munich, 1, pp. 497–515.

Bradley, Douglas E. 1997. *Life, Death, and Duality: A Handbook of the Rev. Edmund P. Joyce, C.S.C. Collection of Ritual Ballgame Sculpture*. Notre Dame: Snite Museum of Art, University of Notre Dame.

———. 2000. The Goddess in the Bodega: Sexing Preclassic Figurines. Paper presented at The International Colloquium on "Pre-Columbian and Ethnographic Collections of Latin America," Leiden.

Bradley, Douglas E., and Peter David Joralemon. 1993. *The Lords of Life: The Iconography of Power and Fertility in Preclassic Mesoamerica*. Notre Dame: Snite Museum of Art, University of Notre Dame.

Brambila, Rosa, Ana María Crespo, and Juan Carlos Saint-Charles. 1993. Juegos de Pelota en el Bajìo. *Cuadernos de Arquitectura Mesoamericana*, no. 25, pp. 89–95. Mexico City: Universidad Nacional Autónoma de México, Facultad de Arquitectura.

Braniff, Beatriz. 1988. A Propósito del Ulama en el Norte de México. *Arqueología* 3, pp. 47–94. Mexico City: Dirección de Monumentos Prehispánicos, INAH.

Brüggemann, Jürgen K. 1992. Los Juegos de Pelota de El Tajín. In *El Juego de Pelota en Mesoamérica: Raíces y Supervivencia*, ed. María Teresa Uriarte, pp. 91–95. Mexico City: Siglo Veintiuno Editores.

———. 1994. La Ciudad de Tajin. In *Arqueología Mexicana I*, no. 5, pp. 26–30. Mexico City: Editorial Raíces, INAH.

Cabrero, C. Maria Teresa. 1989. *Civilización en el Norte de México: Arqueología de la Cañada del Rio Bolaños (Zacatecas y Jalisco)*. Mexico: Universidad Nacional Autónoma de México.

Casas, Bartolomé de las. 1909. *Apologética Historia de Las Indias*. Nueva Biblioteca de Autores Españoles, vol. 13.

———. 1966. *Historia de las Indias*. Mexico City: Editorial Porrúa.

Caso, Alfonso. 1978. *El Pueblo del Sol*. Mexico: FCE.

Castro Leal, Marcia. 1986. *El Juego de Pelota, una Tradición Prehispánica Viva*. Mexico.

Chapel, E. 1892. *Le Caoutchouc et la Gutta-Percha*. Paris: Merchal et Billard.

Clark, John E. 1996. Early Complex Societies on the Pacific Coast of Chiapas, Mexico. In *The Prehistory of the Americas*, eds. Thomas R. Hester and Laura Laurencich Minelli, pp. 43–54. Forli: Abaco.

Clavijero, Francisco Javier. 1964. *Historia Antigua de México*. Mexico City: Editorial Porrúa.

Códice Mendocino. 1979. Mexico City: San Angel Editores.

Coe, Michael D. 1965. *The Jaguar's Children: Pre-Classic Central Mexico*. New York: Museum of Primitive Art.

———. 1972. Olmec Jaguars and Olmec Kings. In *The Cult of the Feline: A Conference in Pre-Columbian Iconography*, ed. Elizabeth P. Benson, pp. 1–12. Washington, D.C.: Dumbarton Oaks Research Library and Collections, Trustees for Harvard University.

Coe, Michael D., and Richard A. Diehl. 1980. *In the Land of the Olmec: The Archaeology of San Lorenzo Tenochtitlán*, vol. 1. Austin: University of Texas Press.

Coggins, Clemency, ed. 1992. *Artifacts from the Cenote of Sacrifice, Chichén Itzá, Yucatán*. Cambridge, Mass.: Peabody Museum of Archaeology and Ethnology, Harvard University.

Coggins, Clemency Chase, and John M. Ladd. 1992. In *Artifacts from the Cenote of Sacrifice, Chichén Itzá, Yucatán*, ed. Clemency Chase Coggins, pp. 345–57. Cambridge, Massachusetts: Harvard University Press.

Cohodas, Marvin. 1991. Ballgame Imagery of the Maya Lowlands: History and Iconography. In *The Mesoamerican Ballgame*, eds. V.L. Scarborough and D.R. Wilcox, pp. 251–88. Tucson: University of Arizona Press.

Compagnon, P. 1986. Le Caoutchouc Naturel. In *Techniques Agricoles et Productions Tropicales*. Paris: G.–P. Maisonneuve and Larose.

Conant, Roger, and Joseph T. Collins. 1991. *A Field Guide to Reptiles and Amphibians: Eastern and Central North America*. 3rd ed. Boston, Mass.: Houghton Mifflin Co.

Cook, Angel Garcia. 1994. Cantona. *Arqueología Mexicana VIII*, no. 10, pp. 60–65. Mexico City: Editorial Raíces, INAH.

Coran, Aubert Y. 1994. Vulcanization. In *Science and Technology of Rubber*, eds. James E. Mark, Burak Erman, and Frederik R. Eirich, pp. 339–85. New York & London: Academic Press.

Corona Núñez, José. 1992. Deportes Prehispánicos. In *Estudios de Antropología e Historia*, pp. 83–87. Mexico: Universidad Michoacana de san Nicolás de Hidalgo.

Cortés Ruiz, Efraín. 1992. El Juego de Pelota Mixteca. In *El Juego de Pelota en el México Precolombino y su Pervivencia en la Actualidad: Museu Etnòlogic*, pp. 169–74. Barcelona: Fundación Folch, Ajuntament de Barcelona.

Cuevas de Álvarez, Bertha. 1970 manuscript. Carrizal, un Sitio Pre-Clásico: Tesis para Obtener el Título de Maestro en Ciencias Antropológicos, Especializado en Arqueología. Xalapa: Universidad Veracruzana.

Cyphers, Ann. 1997. El Contexto Social de Monumentos en San Lorenzo. In *Poblacion, Subsistencia y Medio en S an Lorenzo Tenochtitlan*, ed. Ann Cyphers, pp. 163–94. Mexico: Universidad Nacional Autonóma de Mexico, Instituto de Investigaciones Antropológicas.

Cyphers Guillén, Ann, and Fernando Botas. 1994. An Olmec Feline Sculpture from El Azuzul, Southern Veracruz. *Proceedings of the American Philosophical Society*, 138, no. 2, pp. 273–83.

Daneels, Annick. 1990. Patrón de Asentamiento Prehispánico en la Cuenca de Veracruz. Consejo de Arqueología, *Boletìn*, pp. 79–82. Mexico: INAH.

———. 1991. Patrón de Asentamiento Prehispánico en la Cuenca de Veracruz. Consejo de Arqueología, *Boletìn*, pp. 71–72. Mexico: INAH.

Davies, Nigel. 1980. *The Toltec Heritage: From the Fall of Tula to the Rise of Tenochtitlán*. Norman: University of Oklahoma Press.

Day, Jane Stevenson. 1998. The West Mexican Ballgame. In *Ancient West Mexico, Art and Archaeology of the Unknown Past*, ed. Richard F. Townsend, pp. 151–67. Chicago: The Art Institute of Chicago; New York: Thames & Hudson.

Dern, William F. 1911. *El Hule; su Historia, Naturaleza, Cultivo; Química y Técnica*. Mexico City.

Diaz del Castillo, Bernal. 1956. *The Discovery and Conquest of Mexico*, trans. A.P. Maudslay. New York: Farrar, Strauss, and Cudhay.

Dobkin de Rios, Marlene. 1984. *Hallucinogens: Cross Cultural Perspective*. Albuquerque: University of New Mexico Press.

Drucker, Philip. 1943. Ceramic Stratigraphy at Cerro de las Mesas, Veracruz, Mexico. *Bureau of American Ethnology Bulletin 141*. Washington, D.C.: Government Printing Office.

————. 1959. La Venta, Tabasco: A Study of Olmec Ceramics and Art. *Bureau of American Ethnology Bulletin 153*. Washington, D.C.: Government Printing Office.

Durán, Fray Diego. 1967. *Historia de las Indias de la Nueva España e Islas de la Tierra Firme*. Mexico City: Editorial Porrúa.

————. 1971. *Book of the Gods and Rites and the Ancient Calendar*, trans. and eds. Fernando Horcasitas and Doris Heyden. Norman: University of Oklahoma Press.

Easby, Elizabeth K., and John F. Scott. 1970. *Before Cortés: Sculpture of Middle America*. New York: The Metropolitan Museum of Art.

Eaton, Jack D., and Barton Kunstler. 1980. Excavations at Operation 2009: A Maya Ball Court. In *The Colhá Project Second Season, 1980 Interim Report*, eds. T.R. Hester et al., pp. 121–32. San Antonio: University of Texas at San Antonio.

Ekholm, Gordon F. 1949. Palmate Stones and Thin Stone Heads: Suggestions on Their Possible Use. *American Antiquity* 15, no. 1, pp. 1–9.

————. 1973. The Eastern Gulf Coast. In *The Iconography of Middle American Sculpture*, pp. 40–51. New York: The Metropolitan Museum of Art.

Eliade, Mircea. 1958. *Birth and Rebirth*. New York: Harper and Row Publishers, Inc.

Fash, William L., and Sheree Lane. 1983. El Juego de Pelota. In *Introducción a la Arqueología de Copán, Honduras*, pp. 501–53. Tegucigalpa, D.C.: Proyecto Arqueológico Copán, Secretaria de Estado en el Despacho de Cultura y Turismo.

Fernández de Oviedo y Valdez, Gonzalo. 1944. *Historia General y Natural de las Indias, Islas y Tierra Firme del Mar Océano*. Asunción: Editorial Guaranía.

Fialko, Vilma. 1986. El Marcador de Juego de Pelota de Tikal: Nuevas Referencias Epigráficas para el Clásico Temprano. *Primer Simposio Mundial Sobre Epigrafía Maya*, pp. 61–79.

Filloy, Laura. 1993. Les Balles de Caoutchouc en Mésoamérique. Réflexions à Propos de leur Conservation, Fonction et Signification. Unpublished Master's thesis, Institut d'Art et d'Archéologie, Université de Paris-I, Panthéon-Sorbonne.

————. 1996. Rubber Balls as Ritual Offerings: Archaeology and Conservation. Paper presented at the VIII ABRACOR Congress, Minas Gerais, Brazil.

————. 2000. Rubber. In *The Oxford Encyclopedia of Mesoamerican Cultures*, ed. Davíd Carrasco. New York: Oxford University Press.

————. In preparation. Las Pelotas de Hule en Mesoamérica. Reflexiones Acerca de su Conservación, su Función y su Significado. Oxford: British Archeological Reports.

Filloy, Laura, and Miguel Ángel Canseco. 1996. Conservación y Deterioro de Objetos de Hule Prehispánico. Paper presented at the International Material Research Congress, Cancún, Mexico.

Filloy, Laura, José Luis Criales, Leonardo López Luján, Raúl Chávez Sánchez, and Ximena Chávez Balderas. 2000. The Use of Helical Computed Tomography (Helical CT) in the Identification of the Manufacturing Techniques of Pre-Columbian and Contemporary Rubber Balls. *Antropología y Técnica*, no. 6, pp. 5–10. Mexico City: Instituto de Investigaciones Antropológicas, Universidad Nacional Autonóma de México.

Fischer, Walther. 1981. *Mesoamerikanische Ballspiel*. Vienna: Graz.

Fox, John G. 1993. The Ball Court Markers of Tenam Rosario, Chiapas, Mexico. *Ancient Mesoamerica* vol. 4:1, pp. 55–64. Cambridge & New York: Cambridge University Press.

————. 1996. Playing with Power: Ballcourts and Political Ritual in Southern Mesoamerica. *Current Anthropology* 37:3, pp. 483–509.

Fox, John W. 1991, The Lords of Light Versus the Lords of Dark: The Postclassic Highland Maya Ballgame. In *The Mesoamerican Ballgame*, eds. Vernon L. Scarborough and David R. Wilcox, pp. 213–38. Tucson: University of Arizona Press.

Freidel, David, Linda Schele, and Joy Parker. 1993. *Maya Cosmos: Three Thousand Years on the Shaman's Path*. New York: William Morrow.

Furst, Peter T. 1974. Hallucinogens in Precolumbian Art. In *Art and Environment in North America*, Special Publication 7, pp. 11–101. Lubbock: Texas Tech Museum.

García Barrios, Ana. 1992. Estructura DZ 10 ó Juego de Pelota. In *Oxkintok 4*, pp. 93–106. Misión Arqueológica de España en México, Proyecto Oxkintok, 1990. Madrid: Ministerio de Cultura.

García Cook, Angel, and Beatriz Leonor Merino Carrión. 1998. Cantona: Urbe Prehispánica en el Altiplano Central de México. *Latin American Antiquity* 9:3, pp. 191–216.

García Moll, Roberto. 1977. Los Escalones Labrados del Edificio 33, Yaxchilan, Chiapas. *Revista Mexicana de Estudios Antropológicos* 23:5, pp. 395–423.

García Payón, José. 1947. Sinopsis de Algunas Problemas Arqueológicas del Totonacapan. *El México Antiguo* 6, pp. 301–32.

————. 1971. Archaeology of Central Veracruz. In *Handbook of Middle American Indians*, vol. 11, pp. 505–542. Austin: University of Texas Press.

Garibay, Ángel María. 1953. *Historia de la Literatura Náhuatl*, 2 Vol. México.

Génin, Auguste. 1928. Note Sur les Objets Précorteziens Nommés Indûment Yugos ou Jougs. In *Atti. XXII Congreso Internazionale Degli Americanisti*, 1, pp. 521–28. Rome: Istituto Cristoforo Colombo.

Gillespie, Susan D. 1991. Ballgames and Boundaries. In *The Mesoamerican Ballgame*, eds. Vernon L. Scarborough and

David R. Wilcox, pp. 317–46. Tucson: University of Arizona Press.

Gillmeister, Heiner. 1988. La Dissémination Géographique des Jeux Traditionnels. L'Unité et la Diversité des Jeux Traditionnels en Europe. In *Séminaire sur les Jeux Traditionnels. Comité pour le Développement du Sport*. Villa Réal.

Gómara, F. López de. 1826. *Historia de las Conquistas de Hernando Cortés*, ed. C.M. Bustamente. Mexico.

Graham, Ian. 1982. *Corpus of Maya Hieroglyphic Inscriptions 3(3), Yaxchilán*. Cambridge, Mass.: Peabody Museum of Archaeology and Ethnology, Harvard University.

Greene Robertson, Merle. 1991. The Ballgame at Chichén Itzá: An Integrating Device of the Polity in the Post-Classic. In *The Mesoamerican Ballgame*, eds. Gerard W. van Bussel, Paul L.F. van Dongen, and Ted J.J. Leyenaar, pp. 91–110. Leiden: Rijksmuseum voor Volkenkunde.

Grube, Nikolai. 1990. The Primary Standard Sequence on Chocholá Style Ceramics. In *The Maya Vase Book*, vol. 2, pp. 320–30. New York: Kerr Associates.

Guevara, Sara Landrón de. 2000. El Juego de Pelota en El Tajín. In *Arqueología Mexicana VIII*, no. 44, pp. 36–41.

Gussinyer, Jordi. 1970. Un Adoratorio Dedicado a Tláloc. *Boletín INAH*, no. 39, pp. 7–12. Mexico: INAH.

———. 1974. Una Ofrenda Dedicada al Juego de Pelota. XLI ICA, Mexico (unpublished).

Gutierrez, Mary Ellen. 1990. The Maya Ball-Game as a Metaphor for Warfare. *Mexicon*, vol. 12, 6, pp. 105–08.

Gyarmati, Janós. 1995. Investigaciones Arqueológicas en el Valle del Rio Necaxa, Vera Cruz. *Mexicon*, vol. 17, 4.

Hammond, Norman. 1994. Classic Maya Ball Courts at La Milpa, Belize. In *Ancient Mesoamerica*, vol. 5:1, pp. 45–53. Cambridge & New York: Cambridge University Press.

Haury, Emil W. 1937. A Pre-Spanish Rubber Ball from Arizona. *American Antiquity* 2, no. 4, pp. 282–88.

———. 1992. *Prehistory of the American Southwest*. Tucson & London: University of Arizona Press.

Healy, Paul F. 1992. The Ancient Maya Ballcourt at Pacbitún, Belize. In *Ancient Mesoamerica*, vol. 3:2, pp. 229–39. Cambridge & New York: Cambridge University Press.

Hellmuth, Nicholas. 1975. *Pre-Columbian Ball Game: Archaeology and Architecture*. vol. 1, no. 1. Guatemala and Los Angeles: Foundation for Latin American Anthropological Research Progress Reports.

———. 1987. *Human Sacrifice in Ball Game Scenes in Early Classic Cylindrical Tripods, 1*. Culver City: Foundation for Latin American Anthropological Research.

———. 1991. A Hunting God and the Maya Ballgame of Guatemala: An Iconography of Maya Ceremonial Headdresses. In *The Mesoamerican Ballgame*, eds. Gerard W. van Bussel, Paul L.F. van Dongen, and Ted J.J. Leyenaar, pp. 135–59. Leiden: Rijksmuseum voor Volkenkunde.

Hernández, Francisco. 1959. *Historia Natural de Nueva España I*. Mexico City: Universidad Nacional de México.

Hill, Warren D., Michael Blake, and John E. Clark. 1998.

Ball Court Design Dates Back 3400 Years. *Nature*, 392, pp. 878–79.

Hirth, Kenn. 1980. *Eastern Morelos and Teotihuacan: A Settlement Survey*. Vanderbilt University Publications in Anthropology, no. 25. Nashville, Tennessee: Vanderbilt University.

Historia Tolteca-Chichimeca. 1942. ed. Ernst Mengin. Copenhagen.

Hofmann, Werner. 1989. *Rubber Technology Handbook*. New York: Hanser Publishers.

Hosler, Dorothy, Sandra L. Burkett, and Michael J. Tarkanian. 1999. Prehistoric Polymers: Rubber Processing in Ancient Mesoamerica. *Science* 284, pp. 1988–91.

Houston, Stephen D. 1983. Ballgame Glyphs in Classic Maya Texts. In *Contributions to Maya Hieroglyphic Decipherment, I*, pp. 26–30. New Haven: Human Relations Area Files.

Ichon, Alain. 1991. Les Terrains de Jeu de Balle dans l'Est du Guatemala. In *Vingt Études Sur le Mexique et le Guatemala, Réunies à la Mémoire de Nicole Percheron*, eds. A. Breton, J.P. Berthe et S. Decoin, pp. 325–36. Toulouse: Coll. Hespérides, PUM.

Ixtlilxochitl, F. de Alva. 1975. *Obras Históricas*, vol. 1. Mexico.

Jimenez Lara, Pedro. 1992. Tajín y su Periferia. Paper presented at the Congreso Internacional de Antropología e Historia, Veracruz.

Johnstone, David. 1994. Excavations within the Ball-Court Plaza. In *Yaxuna Project Final Report 1993*. ed. David Freidel. Dallas: Southern Methodist University.

Joralemon, Peter David. 1974. Ritual Blood Sacrifice Among the Ancient Maya, Part 1. *In Primera Mesa Redonda de Palenque*, ed. Merle Greene Robertson, pp. 59–77. Pebble Beach, California: Robert Louis Stevenson School.

———. 1976. The Olmec Dragon: A Study in Pre-Columbian Iconography. In *Origins of Religious Art and Iconography in Preclassic Mesoamerica*. ed. H.B. Nicholson, pp. 27–71. UCLA Latin American Studies Series, ed. Johannes Wilbert, vol. 31. Los Angeles: UCLA Latin American Center Publications and Ethnic Arts Council of Los Angeles.

Kaminitz, Marian. 1988. Amazonian Ethnographic Rubber Artifacts. In *Modern Organic Materials*, pp. 143–50. Edinburgh: SSCR.

Kelley, Charles. 1991. The Known Archaeological Ballcourts of Durango and Zacatecas, Mexico. In *The Mesoamerican Ballgame*, eds. Vernon L. Scarborough and David R. Wilcox, pp. 87–100. Tucson: University of Arizona Press.

Kelley, Ellen A. 1976. Gualterio Abajo: Early Mesoamerican Settlement on the Northwestern Frontier. *XIV Mesa Redonda*, pp. 41–50. Mexico: Sociedad Mexicana de Antropología, Tegucigalpa.

Kirchhoff, Paul. 1943. Mesoamérica sus Límites Geográficas. In *Acta Americana I*, pp. 92–107.

Koontz, Rex Ashley. 1994. The Iconography of El Tajín, Veracruz, Mexico. Ph.D. diss., University of Texas, Austin.

Kowalski, Jeff Karl, 1992. Las Deidades Astrales y la Fertilidad Agrícola: Temas Fundamentales en el Simbolismo del Juego de Pelota Mesoamericano en Copán, Chichén Itzá y Tenochtitlán. In *El Juego de Pelota en Mesoamérica, Raíces y Supervivencia*, ed. Maria Teresa Uriarte. Mexico: Siglo Veintiuno Editores.

Kowalski, Jeff K., and William L. Fash. 1991. Symbolism of the Maya Ball-Game at Copán: Synthesis and New Aspects. *Sixth Palenque Round Table 1986*, eds. M. Greene Robertson and V. M. Fields. pp. 59–67. Norman: University of Oklahoma Press.

Krickeberg, Walter. 1966. El Juego de Pelota Mesoamericano y su Simbolismo Religioso. In *Traducciones Mesoamericanistas* trans. Juan Brom O., vol. 1, pp. 191–313. Mexico City: Sociedad Mexicana de Antropología.

Lahr, John. 1976. The Theater of Sports. In *Sport in the Sociocultural Process*, ed. Marie Hart, pp. 199–209. Dubuque, Iowa: Wm. C. Brown Co.

Le Bras, Jean. 1969. *Le Caoutchouc*. Paris: Presses Universitaires de France, *Que sais-je?*, no. 136.

Leyenaar, Ted J.J. 1978. *Ulama, The Perpetuation in Mexico of the Pre-Spanish Ball Game Ullamaliztli*. Leiden: Rijksmuseum voor Volkenkunde.

———. 1992. Los Tres Ulamas del Siglo XX. In *El Juego de Pelota en Mesoamérica, Raíces y Supervivencia*, ed. María Teresa Uriarte, pp. 357–89. Mexico: Siglo Veintiuno Editores.

———. 1997. *Ulama. Ballgame, from the Olmecs to the Aztecs*. Lausanne: Olympic Museum.

Leyenaar, Ted J.J., and Lee A. Parsons. 1988. *Ulama: The Ballgame of the Mayas and the Aztecs, 2000 B.C.–A.D. 2000*. Leiden: Spruyt, Van Mantgem & de Does.

Lincoln, Charles. 1987. Primera Temporada del Proyecto Arqueológico Chichén Itzá. *Boletìn*, no. 86, pp. 3–43.

Lloyd, Francis E. 1911. *Guayule (*Parthenium argentatum *Gray) a Rubber-Plant of the Chihuahuan Desert*. Washington, D.C.: Carnegie Institution of Washington.

López Arenas, Gabino. 2000. Unpublished thesis. Mexico.

López Luján, Leonardo. 1998. Anthropologie Religieuse du Templo Mayor, Mexico: La Maison des Aigles. Ph.D. diss., Université de Paris X-Nanterre, Paris.

López Luján, Leonardo, Robert H. Cobean T., and Alba Guadalupe Mastache F. 1995. *Xochicalco y Tula*. Milano: Jaca Books.

Lothrop, Samuel K. 1923. Stone Yokes from Mexico and Central America. *Man*, 23, pp. 97–98.

Lounsbury, Floyd G. 1973. On the Derivation and Reading of the 'Ben-Ich' Prefix. In *Mesoamerican Writing Systems*, ed. E.P. Benson, pp. 99–143. Washington, D.C.: Dumbarton Oaks Research Library and Collection.

Love, Michael. 1995. La Ceramica de El Ujuxte, Retalhuleu; un Estudio Preliminar. *VIII Simposio de Investigaciones Arqueológicas en Guatemala*, pp. 19–24. Guatemala: Museo Nacional de Arqueología y Etnografía, Ministerio de Cultura y Deportes, I.A.H.-Asociación Tikal.

Marion, Marie Odile. 1992. Le Pouvoir des Filles de Lune: La Dimension Symbolique des Formes d'Organisation Sociale des Lacandons du Fleuve Lacanjá (Mexique).

Ph.D. diss., École des Hautes Études en Sciences Sociales, Paris.

Mark, James E., Burak Erman, and Frederick R. Eirich, eds. 1994. *Science and Technology of Rubber*. New York & London: Academic Press.

Markman, Charles W. 1981. Prehispanic Settlement Dynamics in Central Oaxaca, Mexico. *Vanderbilt University Publications in Anthropology*, no. 26. Nashville, Tennessee: Vanderbilt University.

Marquina, Arq. Ignacio. 1960. *El Templo Mayor de México*. Mexico: INAH.

Martínez Cortés, Fernando, Carlos Viesca Treviño, José Sanfilippo B., Javier Valdés Gutiérrez, and Hilda Flores Olvera. 1986. *El Hule en México*. Mexico City: Ediciones Copilco.

Martinez, Maximino. 1994. *Catálogo de Nombres Vulgares y Científicos de Plantas Mexicanas*. Mexico City: Fondo de Cultura Económica.

Mártir de Anglería, Pedro [Martyr d'Anghiera]. 1944. *Décadas del Nuevo Mundo*. Buenos Aires: Editorial Bajel. Colección de Fuentes para la Historia de América.

Mártir de Anglería, Pedro [Martyr d'Anghiera]. 1964. *Décadas del Nuevo Mundo*. Dominican Republic: Soc. Dom. De Bibliofilos.

Matos Moctezuma, Eduardo. 1992. Arqueología Urbana en el Centro de la Ciudad de México. In *Estudios de Cultura Náhuatl*, no. 20, pp. 133–41. Mexico: UNAM.

Matos Moctezuma, Eduardo, Francisco Hinojosa, and J.Alvaro Barrera Rivera. 1998. Excavaciones Arqueológicas en la Catedral de México. *Arqueología Mexicana VI*, no. 31, pp. 12–19. Mexico City: Editorial Raíces, INAH.

Maynard, David F., and Frances Berdan. 2000. NMR and GC/MS Analysis of Rubber, Casa de las Águilas, Unpublished report, San Bernardino, California State University.

McNeill, William. 1995. *Keeping Together in Time*. Cambridge, Mass.: Harvard University Press.

Medellín Zenil, Alfonso. 1960. *Cerámicas de Totonacapan*. Xalapa: Universidad Veracruzana.

Michelet, Dominique. 1986. Gente del Golfo Tierra Adentro? Algunas Observaciones Acerca de la Región de Rio Verde, San Luis Potosí. *Cuadernos de Arquitectura Mesoamericana*, no. 8, pp. 80–83. Mexico: Universidad Nacional Autonóma de México, Facultad de Arquitectura.

Miller, Mary Ellen. 1975. *Jaina Figurines: A Study of Maya Iconography*. Princeton: Art Museum, Princeton University.

———. 1986. *The Murals of Bonampak*. Princeton: Princeton University Press.

———. 1989. The Ballgame. *Record of the Art Museum of Princeton University*, 48, no. 2, pp. 22–31.

———. 1991. Rethinking the Classic Sculptures of Cerro de las Mesas, Veracruz. In *Settlement Archaeology of Cerro de las Mesas, Veracruz, Mexico*, ed. Barbara L. Stark, monograph 34, pp. 26–38. Los Angeles: Institute of Archaeology, University of California.

Miller, Mary E., and Stephen D. Houston. 1987. Stairways and

Ballcourts Glyphs: New Perspectives on the Classic Maya Ballgame. *RES*, vol. 14, pp. 47–66.

Miller, Mary Ellen, and Karl Taube. 1993. *The Gods and Symbols of Ancient Mexico and the Maya. An Illustrated Dictionary of Mesoamerican Religion*. London & New York: Thames & Hudson.

Montmollin, Olivier de. 1997. A Regional Study of Classic Maya Ballcourts from the Upper Grijalva Basin, Chiapas, Mexico. *Ancient Mesoamerica*, vol. 8: 1, pp. 23–42. Cambridge& New York : Cambridge University Press.

Motolinía, Toribio de Benavente. 1903. *Memoriales de Fray Toribio Motolinía (Manuscrito de la Col. Icabaleeta)*. Mexico.

Museo Etnologic (Barcelona, Spain). 1992. *El Juego de Pelota en el México Precolombino y su Pervivencia en la Actualidad: Museu Etnòlogic*. Barcelona: Fundació Folch, Ajuntament de Barcelona.

Naylor, Thomas H. 1985. Casas Grandes Outlier Ball Courts in Northwestern Chihuahua. Preliminary Paper for the International Mesoamerican Ball Game Symposium. Tucson.

Nicholson, Henry B. 1985. A Tale of Two Ball-courts: Laguna de Moctezuma, Sierra de Tamaulipas (Tm2 304) and Ixtapaluca Viejo (Acozac), Basin of Mexico. Preliminary Paper for the International Mesoamerican Ball Game Symposium, Tucson.

Niederberger Betton, Christine. 1987. *Paléopaysages et Archéologie Pré-Urbaine du Bassin de Mexico*. Études Mesoamericaines, vol. 2. Mexico: Centre d'Études Mexicaines et Centraméricaines.

Nissley, Marla C. 1985. Ball Court Architecture in the Prehistoric New World. Ph.D. thesis, University of Michigan, Ann Arbor.

Ochoa Castillo, Patricia. 1992. La pelota prehispánica y el origen del juego de pelota en el altiplano central mexicano. In *El Juego de Pelota en el México Precolombino y su Pervivencia en la Actualidad, Museu Etnòlogic*, pp. 26–38. Barcelona: Fundación Folch, Ajuntament de Barcelona.

Oliveros, José Arturo. 1974. Nuevas exploraciones en El Opeño, Michoacán. In *The Archaeology of West Mexico*, ed. Betty Bell, pp. 182–201. Ajijic, Jalisco, Mexico: Sociedad de Estudios Avanzados del Occidente de México.

———.1992. Apuntes Sobre Orgenes y Desarrollo del Juego de Pelota. In *El Juego de Pelota en Mesoamerica: Raíces y Supervivencia*, ed. Maria Teresa Uriarte, pp. 39–54. Mexico City: Siglo Veintiuno Editores.

Oliver Vega, Beatriz. 1992. Reminiscencias Prehispánicas del Juego de Pelota. In *El Juego de Pelota en el México Precolombino y su Pervivencia en la Actualidad, Museu Etnòlogic*, pp. 149–55. Barcelona: Fundación Folch, Ajuntament de Barcelona.

Olsson-Seffer, Pehr. 1907. *Rubber Planting in Mexico and Central America*. Singapore: Kelly and Walsh Limited.

———. 1908. *Yearbook of the Rubber Planters Association*. Mexico City: Hulls Printing Est.

Ortíz, Ponciano, and María del Carmen Rodríguez. 1989. Proyecto Manatí 1989. *Arqueología* 1, segunda época, pp. 23–50.

———. 1994. Los espacios sagrados Olmecas; El Manatí, un caso especial. In *Los Olmecas en Mesoamérica*, ed. John E. Clark, pp. 69–92. Mexico City: Citibank, El Equilibrista, Turner Libros.

———. 2000. The Sacred Hill of El Manatí. A Preliminary Discussion of the Site's Ritual Paraphernalia. In *Olmec Art and Archaeology in Mesoamerica*, ed. John E. Clark and Mary E. Pye, pp. 75–93. Washington, D.C.: National Gallery.

Ortíz, Ponciano, María del Carmen Rodríguez, and Agustín Delgado. 1992. Las Ofrendas de El Manatí y su Posible Asociación con el Juego de Pelota: un Yugo a Destiempo. In *El Juego de Pelota en Mesoamérica: Raíces y Supervivencia*, ed. María Teresa Uriarte, pp. 55–67. Mexico City: Siglo Veintiuno Editores.

Ortíz, Ponciano, María del Carmen Rodríguez, and Paul Schmidt. 1988. El Proyecto Manatí, Temporada 1988. Informe preliminar. *Arqueología* 3, pp. 141–54.

Oviedo y Valdés, Gonzalo Fernández de. 1851–55. *Historia General y Natural de las Indias*, vol. 1. Madrid.

Parsons, Lee A. 1988. The Ballgame in the Peripheral Coastal Lowlands. In *Ulama: The Ballgame of the Mayas and Aztecs, 2000 B.C.–A.D. 2000, from Human Sacrifice to Sport*, eds. Ted J.J. Leyenaar and Lee A. Parsons, pp. 22–55. Leiden, Netherlands: Spruyt, Van Mantgem & de Does.

———. 1991 The Ballgame in the Southern Pacific Coast Cotzumalhuapa Region and its Impact on Kaminaljuyu during the Middle Classic. In *The Mesoamerican Ballgame*, eds. Vernon L. Scarborough and David R. Wilcox, pp. 195–212. Tucson: University of Arizona Press.

Pasztory, Esther. 1972. The Historical and Religious Significance of the Middle Classic Ball Game. In *Religion in Mesoamerica XII Mesa Redonda*, ed. Jaime Litvak King and Noemi Castillo Tejero, pp. 441–53. Mexico.

Patrois, Julie. 1999. *Les Sculptures Associées aux Terrains de Jeu de Balle, dans les Basses Terres Mayas*. Paris: Mémoire de Maîtrise, Université de Paris I.

Pickering, Robert B. 1997. Maggots, Graves, and Scholars. *Archaeology* 50:6, pp. 46–47.

Piña Chan, Román. 1955. *Las Culturas Preclásicas de la Cuenca de México*. México: Fondo de Cultura Económica.

Pincemin, Sophia. 1993. Remontando el Río. Reconocimiento Arqueológico del Río Candelaria, Campeche. *Colección Arqueologìa 2*. Campeche: Universidad Autonóma de Campeche.

Polhamus, Loren G. 1962. *Rubber: Botany, Production, and Utilization*. London: Leonard Hill Books Ltd.; New York: Interscience Publishers, Inc.

Pomar, Juan Bautista. 1941. Relación de Tetzcoco. In *Relaciones de Texcoco y de la Nueva España*, eds. Juan Bautista Pomar et al., pp. 1–64. Mexico City: Editorial Chávez Hayhoe.

Porter, Muriel Noé. 1953. *Tlatilco and the Pre-Classic Cultures of the New World*. New York: Viking Fund Publications in Anthropology 19.

Pozorski, Thomas, and Shelia Pozorski. 1995. An I-shaped Ball-Court Form at Pampa de Las Llamas-Moxeke, Peru.

Latin American Antiquity 6:3, pp. 274–80. Society for American Archaeology.

Proskouriakoff, Tatiana. 1954. Varieties of Classic Central Veracruz Sculpture. In *Contributions to American Anthropology and History*, vol. 12, no. 58:61–93. Washington D.C.: Carnegie Institution of Washington, Publication 606.

Quintana Samayoa, Oscar. 1995. El Programa de Rescate del Subproyecto Triángulo Yaxha-Nakum-Naranjo. *IX Simposio de Investigaciones Arqueológicas en Guatemala*, pp. 25–35. Guatemala: Museo Nacional de Arqueologìa y Etnografia, Ministerio de Cultura y Deportes, I.A.H.-Asociación Tikal.

Quirarte, Jacinto. 1977. The Ballcourt in Mesoamerica: Its Architectural Development. In *Pre-Columbian Art History*. eds. Alana Cordy-Collins and J. Stern, pp. 191–212. Palo Alto, California: Peek Publications.

Raesfeld, Lydia. 1990. New Discoveries at El Tajín, Veracruz. *Mexicon*, vol. 12: 5, pp. 92–95.

———. 1992. Die Ballspielplatze in El Tajin, Mexico. *Etnologische Studien,* no. 8. Münster-Hamburg: lil Verlag

Recinos, Adrián. 1950. *Popol Vuh: The Sacred Book of the Ancient Quiché Maya*, trans. Delia Goetz and Sylvanus G. Morley. Norman: University of Oklahoma Press.

Reents-Budet, Dorie. 1994. *Painting the Maya Universe: Royal Ceramics of the Classic Period.* Durham and London: Duke University Press.

Ringle, William H., and George Bey. 1992. The Center and Segmentary State Dynamics. Draft prepared for the Segmentary State Dynamics Symposium.

Rivera Dorado, Miguel. 1996. *Los Mayas de Oxkintok.* Madrid: Ministerio de Educación y Cultura, Instituto del Patrimonio Histórico.

Rodríguez, Ma. del Carmen and Ponciano Ortiz. 1994. *El Manatí, un Espacio Sagrado del los Olmeca.* Jalapa, Veracruz, Mexico: Universidad Veracruzana.

Roldán, Julio A. 1995a. Estudio Preliminar Sobre los Juegos de Pelota de Ixtontón: Función y Significado. *VIII Simposio de Investigaciones Arqueológicas en Guatemala*, pp. 665–78. Guatemala: Museo Nacional de Arqueología y Etnografía, Ministerio de Cultura y Deportes, I.A.H.-Asociación Tikal.

———. 1995b. Los Complejos del Juego de Pelota en el Noroeste de las Montañas Mayas. *Atlas Arqueológico de Guatemala*, no. 3, pp. 1–14. Guatemala: Ministerio de Cultura y Deportes, I.A.H.-KfW Kreditanstalt für Wiederaufbau.

Rollins, Reed C. 1950. *The Guayule Rubber Plant and Its Relatives.* Contributions from the Gray Herbarium, no. 172. Cambridge, Mass.: Harvard University.

Sahagún, Bernardino de. 1956. *Historia General de las Cosas de Nueva España.* Mexico: Editorial Porrúa.

———. 1961. *Florentine Codex, Book 10: The People.* Salt Lake City: School of American Research and University of Utah.

———. 1970. *The Florentine Codex*, trans. A.J.O. Anderson and C.E. Dibble. Santa Fe: School of American Research and University of Utah.

———. 1954–81. *Florentine Codex: General History of the Things of New Spain.* Book 2, *The Ceremonies.* Book 8, *Kings and Lords,* trans. Arthur J.O. Anderson and Charles E. Dibbble. Monographs of The School of American Research. Santa Fe, New Mexico: School of American Research; Salt Lake City: University of Utah.

———. 1989. *Historia General de las Cosas de Nueva España,* 2 vols. Mexico City: Consejo Nacional para la Cultura y las Artes/Alianza Editorial Mexicana.

Sarro, Patricia Joan. 1995. The Archaeological Meaning of Tajín Chico, The Acropolis at El Tajín, Mexico. Ph.D. diss., Columbia University, New York.

Satterthwaite, Linton Jr. 1933. *The South Group Ball Court, with a Preliminary note on the West Group Ballcourt.* Philadelphia: University Museum, University of Pennsylvania.

———. 1944. *Piedras Negras Archaeology: Architecture.* pt. 4, no. 1. Philadelphia: University Museum, University of Pennsylvania.

Scarborough, Vernon L. 1982. Two Late Preclassic Ballcourts at the Lowland Maya Center of Cerros, Northern Belize. *Journal of Field Archaeology*, vol. 9:1, pp. 21–34.

Scarborough, Vernon L., and David Wilcox eds. 1991. *The Mesoamerican Ballgame.* Tucson: University of Arizona Press.

Scarborough, Vernon, Beverley Mitchum, Sorraya Carr, and David Friedel. 1982. Two Late Preclassic Ballcourts at the Lowland Maya Center of Cerros, Northern Belize. *Journal of Field Archaeology* 9, pp. 21–34.

Schele, Linda, and David A. Freidel. 1990. *The Forest of Kings: The Untold Story of the Ancient Maya.* New York: William Morrow and Company, Inc.

———. 1991. The Courts of Creation: Ballcourts, Ballgames, and Portals to the Maya Otherworld. In *The Mesoamerican Ballgame*, eds. Vernon L. Scarborough and David Wilcox, pp. 289–315. Tucson: University of Arizona Press.

Schele, Linda, and Mary Ellen Miller. 1986. *The Blood of Kings: Dynasty and Ritual in Maya Art.* Fort Worth: Kimbell Art Museum; London: Thames & Hudson.

Schieber de Lavarreda, Christa. 1994. A Middle Preclassic Clay Ballcourt at Abaj Takalik, Guatemala. *Mexicon*, vol. 16: 4, pp. 77–84.

Schöndube B., Otto, and L. Javier Galván V. 1978. Salvage Archaeology at El Grillo-Tabachines, Zapopán, Jalisco, Mexico. In *Across the Chichimec Sea*, eds. C.L. Riley and B.C. Hendricks, pp. 144–64. Carbondale: Southern Illinois University Press.

Schultes, Richard Evan, and Albert Hoffman. 1979. *Plants of the Gods: Origins of Hallucinogenic Use.* Maidenhead, England: McGraw-Hill Book Company, Ltd.

Scott, John F. 1964. The Tepatlaxco Stela. Manuscript, Columbia University, Department of Art History and Archaeology, Douglas Fraser archive, New York.

———. 1976. Los Primeros 'Yugos' Veracruzanos. In *Anales del Instituto de Investigaciones Estéticas*, 13, no. 46, pp. 25–48. Mexico City: Universidad Nacional Autónoma de México.

———. 1979. Evolution in Shape of Mesoamerican Stone Yokes. In *Pre-Columbian Art in Southern Collections,* ed. Carolyn Wood, pp. 11–17. Huntsville, Alabama: Huntsville Museum of Art.

———. 1982. The Monuments of Los Ídolos, Veracruz. *Journal of New World Archaeology 5*, no. 1, pp. 10–23.

———. 1987. *Ancient Mesoamerica: Selections from the University Gallery Collection.* Gainesville: University Presses of Florida.

———. 1991. The Evolution of *Yugos* and *Hachas* in Central Veracruz. In *The Mesoamerican Ballgame*, eds. Gerard W. van Bussel, Paul L.F. van Dongen, and Ted J.J. Leyenaar, pp. 203–13. Leiden: Rijksmuseum voor Volkenkunde.

———. 1997. Die Entwicklung der Yugos und Hachas im Präkolumbischen Veracruz. In *Präkolumbischen Kulturen am Golf von Mexico*, ed. and translated by Judith Rickenbach, pp. 119–26. Zurich: Museum Rietberg.

Seler, Eduard. 1963. *Commentarios al Códice Borgia.* Mexico: Fondo de Cultura Económica.

———. 1980. *Códice Borgia.* translated by Mariana Frank. Mexico: Fondo de Cultura Económica.

Serier, Jean-Batiste. 1992. *Histoire du Caoutchouc.* Paris: Éditions Desjonquères.

Serra Puche, Mari Carmen, and Karina Rebeca Durand Velasco. 1992. El Juego de Pelota en Mesoamerica. In *El Juego de Pelota en el México Precolombino y su Pervivencia en la Actualidad: Museu Etnològic.* Barcelona: Funcació Folch, Ajuntament de Barcelona.

Shook, Edwin M., and Elayne Marquis. 1996. *Secrets in Stone: Yokes, Hachas and Palmas from Southern Mesoamerica.* Memoirs of the American Philosophical Society, vol. 217. Philadelphia: American Philosophical Society.

Slusher, Howard. 1976. Sport and the Religious. In *Sport in the Sociocultural Process*, ed. Marie Hart, pp.380–93. Dubuque Iowa: Wm. C. Brown Co. Publishers

Smith, A. Ledyard. 1961. Types of Ball Courts in the Highland of Guatemala. In *Essays in Pre-Columbian Art and Archaeology*, ed. S.K. Lothrop, pp. 100–25. Cambridge, Mass.: Harvard University Press.

———. 1972. *Excavations at Altar de Sacrificios: Architecture, Settlement, Burials, and Caches.* Papers of the Peabody Museum of Archaeology and Ethnology, Harvard University, vol. 62:2. Cambridge, Mass.: Peabody Museum.

Solís Olguín, Felipe. 1992. Evidencias Arqueologicas de la Practica de Juego de Pelota en La Antiqua Mexico-Tenochtitlan. In *El Juego de Pelota en Mesoamerica: Raíces y Supervivencia*, ed. Maria Teresa Uriarte, pp.143–55. Mexico City: Siglo Veinteuno Editores.

Solís Olguín, Felipe, and David Morales. 1991. *Rescate de un Rescate: Colección de Objetos Arqueológicos de El Volador.* Mexico City: Instituto Nacional de Antropología e Historia.

Soustelle, Jaques. 1984. *The Olmecs: The Oldest Civilization in Mexico*, trans. Helen R. Lane. Garden City, New York: Doubleday.

Standley, Paul C. 1920. *The Trees and Shrubs of Mexico.* Washington, D.C.: Government Printing Office.

———. 1942. On the Use of Rubber by the Ancient Mexicans. *The Masterkey* 15, no. 4, pp. 123–24.

Stern, Theodore. 1949. *The Rubber-Ball Games of the Americas.* Monographs of the American Ethnological Society, 17. New York: J.J. Augustin.

———. 1966. *The Rubber-Ball Games of the Americas.* Monographs of the American Ethnological Society, 17. Seattle: University of Washington Press.

Stirling, Matthew W. 1943. *Stone Monuments of Southern Mexico.* Bureau of American Ethnology, Bulletin 138. Washington, D.C.: Government Printing Office.

Stresser Péan, Guy. 1977. *San Antonio Nogalar.* Études Mésoaméricaines, vol. 3. Mexico: Mission Archéologique et Ethnologique Française au Mexique.

Stuart, David. 1987. *Ten Phonetic Syllables.* Research Reports on Ancient Maya Writing 14. Washington, D.C.: Center for Maya Research.

Taladoire, Eric. 1975. Les Bains de Vapeur et les Systèmes d'Eau, dans leur Rapport avec les Terrains de Jeu de Balle. *XLI Congrés International des Américanistes, Actes*, vol. 1, pp. 262–69.

———. 1979a. La Pelota Mixteca: Un Juego Contemporáneo con Origenes Complejos. *XV Mesa Redonda*, vol. 1, pp. 431–39. Mexico: Sociedad Mexicana de Antropología.

———. 1979b. Ballgame Scenes and Ballcourts in West Mexican Archaeology: A Problem in Chronology. *Indiana*, vol. 5, pp. 33–44.

———. 1979c. Orientation of Ballcourts in Mesoamerica. *Archaeoastronomy*, vol. 2, pp. 12–13. College Park, Md.: University of Maryland.

———. 1981. *Les Terrains de Jeu de Balle (Mésoamérique et Sud-Ouest des États-Unis).* Études Mésoaméricaines II:4. Mexico City: Mission Archéologique et Ethnologique Française au Mexique.

———. 1990. Les Terrains de Jeu de Balle du Projet Michoacan. *TRACE*, no. 16. Mexico City: Centre d'Études Mexicaines et Centraméricaines.

———. 1991. Le Codex de Jalapa, ou Mapa del Juego de Pelota. In *The Mesoamerican Ballgame*, eds. Gerard W. van Bussel, Paul L.F. van Dongen, and Ted J.J. Leyenaar, pp. 111–18. Leiden: Rijksmuseum voor Volkenkunde.

———. 1993. Los Juegos de Pelota en el Norte de Yucatan: Una Revisión de los Datos. In *Perspectivas Antropológicas en el Mundo Maya*. eds. Ma. Josefa Iglesias Ponce de Leon and Francesc Ligorred Perramon. pp. 163–80. Madrid: Sociedad Española de Estudios Mayas.

———. 1994. El Juego de Pelota Precolombino. *Arqueología Mexicana II*, no. 9, pp. 6–15. Mexico City: Editorial Raíces, INAH.

———. 1995. Les Jeux de Balle en Amérique Précolombienne. *La Recherche*, no. 272, pp. 18–24.

———. 1998. Los Juegos de Pelota en el Occidente de México. In *El Occidente de México: Arqueología, Historia y Medio Ambiente, Perspectivas Regionales.(Actas del IV Coloquio de Occidentalistas)*, eds. Ricardo Avila et al., pp 175–87. Guadalajara, Jalisco, Mexico: Universidad de Guadalajara; Paris: ORSTOM.

————. 2000. El Juego de Pelota Mesoamericano: Origen y Desarollo. *Arqueología Mexicana VIII*, no. 43, pp. 20–27. Mexico City: Editorial Raíces, INAH.

————. In press. Las Maquetas de Juego de Pelota: Bi and Tridimensional Representations of Ballcourts in Mesoamerica. In *Coloquio Internacional /International Colloquium RMV Leiden 2000*, eds. Edward K. de Bock, Dorus Kop Jansen, and Ted J.J. Leyenaar. Leiden: Rijksmuseum voor Volkenkunde.

Taladoire, Eric, and Benoit Colsenet. 1991. Bois Ton Sang, Beaumanoir: The Political and Conflictual Aspects of the Ballgame in the Northern Chiapas Area. In *The Mesoamerican Ballgame*, eds. Vernon L. Scarborough and David R. Wilcox, pp. 161–74. Tucson: The University of Arizona Press.

Tarkanian, Michael J., 2000. 3,500 Years before Goodyear: the Processing and Use of Rubber in Ancient Mesoamerica. B.S. Thesis. Cambridge, Mass.: Department of Materials Science and Engineering, MIT.

Tarkanian, Michael J., and Dorothy Hosler. 2000. Elaboración de Hule en Mesoamérica. *Arqueología Mexicana VIII*, no. 44, pp. 54–57. Mexico City: Editorial Raíces, INAH.

Taube, Karl. 1985. The Classic Maya Maize God: A Reappraisal. In *Fifth Palenque Round Table, 1983*, vol. 7, eds. Merle Greene Robertson and Virginia Fields, pp. 171–81. San Francisco: Pre-Columbian Art Research Institute.

————. 1988. A Study of Classic Maya Scaffold Sacrifice. In *Maya Iconography*, eds. Elizabeth P. Benson and Gillett G. Griffin, pp 331–51. Princeton, New Jersey: Princeton University Press.

————. 1993. *Aztec and Maya Myths*. Austin: University of Texas Press; London: British Museum Press.

Tedlock, Dennis. 1996. *Popol Vuh: The Definitive Edition of the Mayan Book of the Dawn of Life and the Glories of Gods and Kings*. New York: Touchstone Books.

Tezozomoc, Hernando Alvarado. 1878. *Crónica Mexicana*. Mexico.

Thompson, Edward H. 1992. The Sacred Well of the Itzaes. In *Artifacts from the Cenote of Sacrifice, Chichén Itzá, Yucatan*, ed. Clemency Coggins, pp. 1–8. Cambridge: Peabody Museum of Archaeology and Ethnology X, no. 3, Harvard University.

Torquemada, Fray Juan de. 1975–1977. *Monarquía Indiana*, vol. 8. Mexico City: Universidad Nacional Autónoma de México.

Tozzer, Alfred. 1957. *Chichén Itzá and its Cenote of Sacrifice: A Comparative Study of Contemporaneus Maya and Toltec*. Cambridge: Peabody Museum of Archaeology and Ethnology XI and XII, Harvard University.

Tuerenhout, Dirk van. 1991. The Socio-Cultural Context of the Ballcourt of Mohmul, Belize. In *The Mesoamerican Ballgame*, eds. Gerard W. van Bussel, Paul van Dongen and Ted J.J. Leyenaar, pp. 59–70. Leiden: Rijksmuseum voor Volkenkunde.

Turok, Marta. 2000. El juego de pelota en la actualidad. In *Arqueología Mexicana VIII*, no. 44, pp. 58–65.

Uriarte, María Teresa. 1992. El Juego de Pelota en los Murales de Tepantitla, en Teotihuacán. In *El Juego de Pelota en Mesoamérica: Raíces y Supervivencia*, ed. María Teresa Uriarte, pp. 112–41. Mexico City: Siglo Veintiuno Editores.

Valdés Gutiérrez, Javier, and Hilda Flores Olvera. 1986. El Arbol del Hule. In *El Hule en México*, Fernando Martínez Cortés, et al. Mexico City: Ediciones Copilco.

Van Bussel, Gerard W. 1991. Balls and Openings: The Maya Ballgame as an Intermediary. In *The Mesoamerican Ballgame*, eds. By Gerard W. van Bussel, Paul L.F. van Dongen and Ted J.J. Leyenaar. Leiden: Rijksmuseum voor Volkenkunde.

Van Bussel, Gerard W., Paul van Dongen, and Ted J.J. Leyenaar. 1991. *The Mesoamerican Ballgame*. Leiden: Rijksmuseum voor Volkenkunde.

Van Ooststroom, S.J. 1940. *Blumea*. Leiden: Rijksherbarium.

Velazquez, Juan Luis. 1992. Excavaciones en el Complejo 75 de Nakbé. In *V Simposio de Investigaciones Arqueológicas en Guatemala: Museo Nacional de Arqueología y Etnología*, pp. 97–102. Guatemala: Ministerio de Cultura y Deportes, Instituto de Antropología e Historia, Asociación Tikal.

Weiant, Clarence W. 1943. *An Introduction to the Ceramics of Tres Zapotes, Veracruz, Mexico*. Bureau of American Ethnology, Bulletin 139. Washington, D.C.: Government Printing Office.

Weigand, Phil C. 1993. *Evolución de una Civilización Prehispánica*. Zamora: El Colegio de Michoacán.

Wilkerson, S. Jeffrey K. 1970. Un Yugo 'en Situ' de la Región del Tajín. *Boletín del Instituto Nacional de Antropología e Historia*, 41, pp. 41–44.

————. 1984. In Search of the Mountain of Foam: Human Sacrifice in Eastern Mesoamerica. In *Ritual Human Sacrifice in Mesoamerica*, ed. Elizabeth H. Boone, pp. 101–32. Washington, D.C., Dumbarton Oaks Research Library and Collection.

————. 1990. El Tajín: Great Center of the Northeast. In *Mexico: Splendors of Thirty Centuries*, ed. Julie Jones, pp. 155–81. New York: Metropolitan Museum of Art.

————. 1991. And Then They Were Sacrificed: The Ritual Ballgame of Northeastern Mesoamerica. In *The Mesoamerican Ballgame*, eds. Vernon L. Scarborough and David Wilcox. Tucson: University of Arizona Press.

Wyshak, Lillian W., R. Berger, John A. Graham, and Robert F. Heizer. 1971. A Possible Ball Court at La Venta, Mexico. *Nature*, vol. 232, pp. 650–51.

Zeitlin, Judith F. 1993. The politics of Classic Period Ritual Interaction. *Ancient Mesoamerica*, vol. 4:1, pp. 121–40. Cambridge & New York: Cambridge University Press.

Zimbardo, P.G. 1969. *The Human Choice: Individuation, Reason, and Order versus Deindividuation, Impulse, and Chaos*, eds. W.J. Arnold and D. Levine. Lincoln: University of Nebraska Press.

Zyska, Bronislaw. 1981. Rubber. In *Microbial Deterioration*. Economic Microbiology, ed. Anthony H. Rose, vol. 6, pp. 223–385. London & New York: Academic Press.

ILLUSTRATION CREDITS

Half-title: photo Michael Zabé.
Frontispiece: courtesy of Germanisches National Museum, Nürmberg.
p. 5: *(left)* Los Angeles County Museum of Art; *(right)* Philadelphia Museum of Art.

All photographs from the Mint Museum of Art by David H. Ramsey.

INTRODUCTION, E. MICHAEL WHITTINGTON: Timeline: drawing by Emily Blanchard and Craig Harmon, Mint Museum of Art; 1–2: drawing by Craig Harmon, Mint Museum of Art.

1 RUBBER AND RUBBER BALLS IN MESOAMERICA, LAURA FILLOY NADAL: 3 Peabody Museum of Archaeology and Ethnology, Harvard University; 4, 5, 6, 7, 14, 19, 20: redrawn by Craig Harmon, Mint Museum of Art; 8: Craig Harmon, Mint Museum of Art. 9, 10: photos Juan Manuel Malpica (INIF/SAGAR); 11: photo Michel Zabé; 12: Peabody Museum of Archaeology and Ethnology, Harvard University; 13: Leonardo López Luján (INAH), 15: drawing by Molly Avery Lawrence; 16–18: José Luis Criales (CT-Scanner de México).

2 GENDER, POWER AND FERTILITY IN THE OLMEC RITUAL BALLGAME, DOUGLAS E. BRADLEY: 21–25, 28, 29: The Snite Museum of Art; University of Notre Dame; 27: drawing courtesy Snite Museum of Art, University Notre Dame, after Coe and Diehl, 1980, fig. 499; 26: Art Museum, Princeton University.

3 UNITY IN DUALITY: THE PRACTICE AND SYMBOLS OF THE MESOAMERICAN BALLGAME, MARÍA TERESA URIARTE: 30: drawing by Molly Avery Lawrence, after *Codex Borgia*; 31, 34: Instituto de Investagaciones Esthésticas, UNAM, México; 32, 36–40: photos María Teresa Uriarte; 33: photo Michel Zabé; 35: from *Codex Borgia*, color facsimile edition of Academische Druck u. Verlagsanstalt (1976). 41: drawing after Barbara Fash.

4 DRESSED TO KILL: STONE REGALIA OF THE MESOAMERICAN BALLGAME, JOHN F. SCOTT: 42: The Cleveland Museum of Art; 43, 44, 46, 49, 51, 54, 57, 59–61: photos John F. Scott; 53: photo John F. Scott, courtesy Archivo Fotográfico, Instituto de Arqueología, Xalapa; 45, 47: The Art Museum, Princeton University; 48: drawing by Molly Avery Lawrence; 50, 55: San Antonio Museum of Art; 52: Los Angeles County Museum of Art: 56, 58: Mint Museum of Art; 62: drawing by Michael E. Kampen; 63: photo Michel Zabé.

5 PERFORMING ON THE COURT, JANE STEVENSON DAY: 64: photo H.E. Day; 65: Instituto de Investagaciones Esthésticas, UNAM, México; 66, 78: The Art Museum, Princeton University; 67, 72, 73, 75: Denver Art Museum; 68: Los Angeles County Museum of Art; 69: Worcester Art Museum; 70: San Antonio Museum of Art; 71, 74: photos Jane S. Day; 76: photo Brigitte Maria Mayer, © Gemeide Oberammergau; 77: photo E. Michael Whittington; 79: © 2000 Denver Museum of Nature and Science/Rick Wicker; 80: photo Michel Zabé.

6 THE MAYA BALLGAME: REBIRTH IN THE COURT OF LIFE AND DEATH, MARY MILLER: 81; 87: photos © Justin Kerr; 82: Art Institute of Chicago; 83: drawings by Helen Trik and Michael Kampen; 84: drawing by Tatiana Proskouriakoff; 85: Mint Museum of Art; 86, 93: drawings by Linda Schele; 88: drawing by Ian Graham; 89: National Museum of the American Indian, Smithsonian Institution; 90: photo ©Sotheby's, Inc; 91: New Orleans Museum of Art, 92: North Carolina Museum of Art, 94: drawing by Molly Avery Lawrence; 95: Mint Museum of Art.

7 THE BALL COURT IN TENOCHTITLAN, EDUARDO MATOS MOCTEZUMA: 96, 101, 102, 104, 105: Museo del Templo Mayor; 97: Drawing courtesy Museo del Templo Mayor; 98: drawing courtesy Programa de Arqueología Urbana, México, D.F.; 99: photo by E. Michael Whittington; 100, 103: photos Michel Zabé.

8 THE ARCHITECTURAL BACKGROUND OF THE PRE-HISPANIC BALLGAME: AN EVOLUTIONARY PERSPECTIVE, ERIC TALADOIRE: 106: Drawing by Molly Avery Lawrence; 107, 112; 114, 117, 118, 122, 123, 125, 126, 129, 130: photos Eric Taladoire; 108: photo Ted J.J. Leyenaar; 109: map by Craig Harmon, Mint Museum of Art; 110, 111: photos E. Michael Whittington; 113, 115, 124: drawings by Eric Taladoire; 116, 128: photos Jean Pierre Courau; 119: photo A. Ichon; 120: drawing by Jean-Pierre Courau; 121: drawing by Eric Taladoire after Schieber de Lavarreda; 122: photo Phil Weigand; 127: drawing by David Morgan.

9 An Ancient Tradition Continued: Modern Rubber Processing in Mexico, Michael J. Tarkanian and Dorothy Hosler: 131: photo Michael E. Abrams; 132–39: photos by Michael J. Tarkanian; 140: photo by Dorothy Hosler.

10 The Modern Ballgames of Sinaloa: A Survival of the Aztec Ullamaliztli, Ted J.J. Leyenaar: 141–51: Ted J.J. Leyenaar; 152: Los Angeles County Museum of Art.

11 Everything Old is New Again: The Enduring Legacy of the Ancient Games, E. Michael Whittington: 153: Instituto de Investagaciones Esthésicas, UNAM, México; 154, 155: photos © Bettmann/CORBIS; 156, 160: photos © The Charlotte Observer; 157: Fine Arts Museums of San Francisco; 158: Philadelphia Museum of Art; 159: Bowers Museum of Cultural History, photo Stuart Weiner; 161: Snite Museum of Art; 162: photo © Henry Leutwyler.

Catalogue (by catalogue number): 1, 35–37, 73, 93, 94, 114, 117–121, 132, 133: photos Michael Zabé; 2–4, 38, 67, 71: Peabody Museum of Archaeology and Ethnology, Harvard University; 5, 25, 33, 34, 54–56, 59, 78, 91, 96, 99, 127, 128, 134: Denver Art Museum; 6: The Field Museum; 7–12, 16–21, 26, 41, 49, 50, 97, 131: Snite Museum of Art, University of Notre Dame; 13–15, 22–24, 27, 28, 32, 87, 95, 106, 123: The Art Museum, Princeton University; 29, 62, 63, 77, 100: Yale University Art Gallery; 30, 51, 58, 85, 122, 126: Los Angeles County Museum of Art; 31, 101, 107, 108, 123: photos © by Justin Kerr; 39: North Carolina Museum of Art; 40, 68, 92: © 2000 Denver Museum of Nature and Science/Rick Wicker; 42, 47, 74, 81, 98, 129: Saint Louis Art Museum; 43, 44, 46, 105: Hudson Museum, University of Maine; 45, 69, 102–104, 125, 135, 137: Mint Museum of Art; 48, 53, 82, 89: San Antonio Museum of Art; 52, 60, 61, 72, 80, 88: American Museum of Natural History; 57, 110, 124: New Orleans Museum of Art; 64, 70, 75, 115, 116: Philadelphia Museum of Art; 65, 83: Fine Arts Museums of San Francisco; 66: Worcester Art Museum; 76, 86, 111, 130: The Cleveland Museum of Art; 79, 84, 90: Metropolitan Museum of Art; 109: Bowers Museum of Cultural Art; 112: National Museum of the American Indian, Smithsonian Institution; 113: © Sotheby's, Inc.; 136: Art Institute of Chicago.

Glyph, pp. 136 and 265: Molly Avery Lawrence.
Line illustrations: p. 213, p. 259: Michael E. Kampen; p. 239: Linda Schele, reprinted with permission from the Kimbell Art Museum; p. 240: Marvin Cohodas.

Abbreviations:
INAH   Instituto Nacional de Antropología y Historia
UNAM Universidad Nacional Autonóma de México

Identification of illustrations on pp. 6–7, 10–11, and 14–15

pp. 6–7

cat. 59, p. 188	cat. 101, p. 228	cat. 52, p. 184	cat. 13, p. 147	cat. 21, p. 155	cat. 41, p. 174
cat. 8, p. 142	cat. 100, p. 227	cat. 53, p. 185	cat. 43, p. 176	cat. 54, p. 186	cat. 11, p. 145
cat. 23, p. 157	cat. 105, p. 232	cat. 24, p. 158	cat. 15, p. 149	cat. 12, p. 146	cat. 100, p. 227
cat. 127, p. 255	cat. 106, p. 233	cat. 9, p. 143	cat. 127, p. 255	cat. 59, p. 188	cat. 16, p. 150

pp. 10–11

| fig. 107, p. 99 | fig. 114, p. 103 |
| fig. 64, p. 64 | fig. 130, pp. 114–115 |

pp. 14–15

fig. 6, p. 22	cat. 108, p. 235	fig. 5, p. 22	cat. 128, p. 256	fig. 36, p. 45
fig. 38, p. 47	cat. 137, p. 264	cat. 123, p. 251	fig. 37, p. 46	cat. 95, p. 222
cat. 107, p. 234	fig. 87, p. 82	fig. 35, p. 44	cat. 34, p. 167	fig. 40, pp. 48–49
fig. 129, p. 113	cat. 109, p. 235	cat. 135, p. 262	fig. 74, p. 72	cat. 111, p. 237

INDEX

blackstone 56, *59*

blood 30, 36, 44, 49, 62, 67, 72, 138, 252, 256, 260

bloodletting/sacrifice 33, 36, *36*, 47, 61, 161, 252; *see also* perforators

body decoration 43, *44*, *133*, *184*

Bonampak *19*, 74, 86, 99

bowls *see* vessels

Braniff, Beatriz 106–07

Bufo marinus 47, *181*, 55, 181, 185

burials 42, 54, 55, 69, 70

butterflies/butterfly imagery 45, 46, *47*

Cacaxtla *19*

Calakmul *100*; ballcourt *110*

calendar 58, 87, 170, 196, 198, 262

Campeche *19*, 24, 58, 71, 74, 79, 81, 98, 99, 103, 110, 226, 227, 228, 229, 230, 233, 234, 235, 252

Cantona *19*, 75, 76, 98, *100*

Capulac Concepción *100*

Caribbean 65, 108

Carmen Rodríguez, María del 27

Carolina Panthers 133, 134, *134*

Casas Grandes *18*

Castilla elastica 23, 24, 25, 28, 31, 117, 118, *118*, 119, 120, 121

Castillo, Juan del 23

ceramics 27, *27*, 34, 55, 65, 66, 67, 68–69, 70, 74, 82, 112, 138, 196, 231, 256; Olmec 36; Teotihuacan 42

Cerro de las Mesas *19*, 190

Cerros *19*, *100*

Cervantes, Professor Vicente 23

Chac 82, 229

Chalcatzingo *100*, 154

Chan, Román Piña 27

Charles V *18*, 23, 118, 123

Chiapas *19*, 24, 29, 74, 79, 83, 86, 97, 98, 109, 110, 113, 117, 118, 170, 172

Chicago, Soldier's Field 131, *132*

Chichén Itzá *19*, 44, 45, 48, 49, 59, 61, 72, 74, 84, 91, *100*, 112, 114, 132, 139, 140, 167, 256; Great Ballcourt 44, 48, 81, 100, *101*; Sacred Cenote 27, 120, 121, 138; Temple of the Jaguars 44

Chihuahua 24

Chinantecs, the 24

Chinkultic *19*, *100*, 110, 170, 262; ballcourt *111*

Chinkultic Disc *170*

Chontals, the 24

Chupícuaro 69

cinnabar *225*, *251*

Cinteotl (young Maize God) 43

Classic Period 16, 27, 29, 36, 53, 56, 70, 71, 121, 123, 135; *see also* Early Classic Period, Middle Classic Period, Late Classic Period

Clavijero, Francisco Javier 23

Coahuila 24

Cobá *19*, *100*

Codex Borgia 22, 40, 42–43

Codex Dresden 29, *29*

Codex Magliabechiano 31

Codex Mendoza 28, 29, *31*

Codex Nuttall 96

Coe, Michael 34

Colha *19*, *100*, 110, 113

Colima *19*, 24, 69, 70, 73, 179, 180, 181

Colonial Period 25, 94, 99, 123

Columbus, Christopher 22

Conquest, Spanish 16, 18, 28, 33, 41, 51, 66, 71, 97, 99, 117, 123

consciousness, altered states of 41, 44, 47, 121; *see also* hallucinogens; psychotropic substances

copal 21, 27, 120, 138, *139*, *140*

Copán *19*, 48, 80, 83, 86, 97, *100*, 110, 113, 114, 115, 131, 133, 164, 251; ballcourt *104*, *130*, 131, 168; Hieroglyphic Stairway 131

corn 35, 36, 38, 95, 150, *150*, *143*, *160*; *see also* maize; symbolism

Cortés, Hernán 18, 23, 91, 123

Costa Rica 36

costumes *see* equipment, costume, and accessories

cotton 93, 94

Cotzumalhuapa *19*, 48, 225

coyotes/coyote imagery *50*, 62, 133, 199, *199*, 258, *258*, *259*

crocodiles/crocodile imagery 17, 45, 46, 133, *134*, 198, *198*, 209, *209*, 241; *see also* Zipacna

Cuba *18*

Culiacán 123

Cyphers, Ann 68

Dainzú *19*, *41*, 42, 54, 94, *100*; ballcourt *109*

datura *see* plants

Day, Jane 163

de las Casas, Fray Bartolomé 22

decapitation 42, 44, 48–49, 59, 60, 61, 62, *63*, 67, 72, *72*, 74, 75, 85, 86, *172*, 182, 190, 215, 250, 254, *256*, 260, *261*; *see also* trophy heads

deer/deer imagery 133, 134, *140*, 196, *196*, 220, 231, *232*, *259*

deindividuation 133

Diehl, Richard 34

diorite *211*

dismemberment 45, 51, 62

Displayed Deity 39

dolphins/dolphin imagery *200*

Dominican Republic *18*

drums *see teponaztli*

duality 35, 36, 46–49, 182, 249, 260

Durán, Fray Diego *22*, 23, 76, 94, 135

Durango 24

dwarves 229, 237

eagles/eagle imagery 61, 133, *133*, 192, *193*, 257

Early Classic Period 42, 55, 63, 70, 81, 109, 128, 182, 201, 221, 224

Early Formative Period 21, 53, 54, 67, 150, 141, 142, 143, 146, 152, 153, 160

Early Postclassic Period 58, 61, 62, 63, 75, 250

earspools 214, 215, *217*, 227, *231*

earth monster 42, *185*, 191, 211, *211*, 215, *215*

eclipse, solar 243

Ecuador 117

Edzná *19*, *100*; ballcourt *103*, 110

Ehecatl 207

Ek Balam 114

El Aparicio *19*, 62, 72, 256, 261

El Arenal 177

El Azuzul *19*, 68

El Baúl *19*, 44, 56

El Carrizal *19*, 42, 54, 55, 60

El Chilillo 126, 128

El Habal 127, 128

El Manatí *19*, 27, 41, 49, 53, 63, 120, 138

El Opeño *19*, 42, 51, 54, *66*, 67, 70, 71, 156

El Palmar *26*

El Pital *19*, *100*

El Resbalón 97, 99

El Salvador 17, *18*, *19*, 60, 62, *100*

El Tajín *19*, 44, 45, 48, 51, 58, 61, 63, 75, 76, 94, 98, *100*, 132, 193, 202, 207, 217, 221, 250, 259, 260; ballcourt *46*, 62, 75, *99*, 258, 259

El Tigre 103, 106

El Trapiche *19*, 57

El Ujuxte *100*

El Vergel *100*

El Viejón *19*, 56, *59*

El Zapotal *19*, 56, 57, *59*, 60, 61, 63

equipment, costume, and accessories 33, 34, *34*, 36, 38,
52, 56, 65, 66, 71, 73, 123, 128–29, 153, 231, *239*; ankle bands 35, 36, 38, 182; anklets 233, *251*; aprons *251*; arm bands 36, 66, 69, 71, 142, 188–89; arm guards/padding 61, 71, 142, 174; ball deflectors 52; capes 42, *42*; chaps 160; cloth uniforms 163; cords 52, 174; costumes 70, *75*, 84, 167; "derby hat" 236; ear plugs 220; elbow pads 35, 38, 66; *faja* (cotton tape) 124; *fajado* 126; feet protectors 260; genital protectors 162, 163; gloves 54, 66, 94, 103, *182*; goals 55; groin protector 160; hand protectors 54; headbands 162; headdresses 35, 37, 38, 51, 60, 68, 81, *81*, 82, *82*, 134, 143, 170, 171, 172, 196, 202, 203, 204, 211, 218, 220, 215, 231, 232, 233, 235, 239, 241, 251, 253; headgear 179, 180–81; hip protectors 52, 54, 126, *126*, 148; hipcloths 81; hipguards 123; "hunter's hat" 82; kilts *170*, 207, *228*, *235*, 236; knee bands 260; knee guards 61; knee guards/ padding/ protectors 35, 36, *37*, 38, 52, 54, 56, 66, 67, 70, 103, 124, 135, 146, 146–47, 154, 174, 186, 231; lassos 48; leg bands 36, *142*; leg guards/ padding 67, 69, 71, *184*, 186; loincloths *34*, 36, 37, *37*, 54, 68, 123, 152, 179, 232, 233, 252, 260; *mazo 129*; pectorals 37, 43, 83, *164*, *251*; paddles 69, 73; panels 37; pendant straps 37, 38, 39, 153; pendants 162, 184, 217, 220, 231, 246; protective 21, 38, 51, 65, 68, 73, 128, 152; rattles *141*; ritual significance of 233; ropes 48; sandals 103; sash *230*, *233*; shin protectors 54; skirts 42, *42*, 54, 71; sticks *43*, 66, 73, 94, 123; straps 54; torso protectors 54, 57; turbans 226, 227; waist padding/ protectors *33*, *34*, 35, 36, *58*, 144, *228*; wrist bands/ guards/ padding 35, 38, 71, *184*, 233, *228*; *see also* bats; belts; *hachas*; helmets; jewelry; *manoplas*; masks; mirrors; *yuguitos*

Fat God 201, *201*

feathers 22, 60, 62, 81, 95, *215*, *251*, 262